Discovery Travel Adventures™

PADDLE SP

Beth Geiger
Editor

John Gattuso
Series Editor

Discovery Communications, Inc.

Discovery Communications, Inc.
John S. Hendricks, *Founder, Chairman, and Chief Executive Officer*
Judith A. McHale, *President and Chief Operating Officer*
Judy L. Harris, *Senior Vice President and General Manager, Discovery Consumer Products*

Discovery Publishing
Natalie Chapman, *Vice President, Publishing*
Rita Thievon Mullin, *Editorial Director*
Michael Hentges, *Design Director*
Mary Kalamaras, *Senior Editor*
Maria Mihalik Higgins, *Editor*
Rick Ludwick, *Managing Editor*
Chris Alvarez, *Business Development*
Jill Gordon, *Marketing Specialist*

Discovery Channel Retail
Tracy Fortini, *Product Development*
Steve Manning, *Naturalist*

Insight Guides
Jeremy Westwood, *Managing Director*
Brian Bell, *Editorial Director*
John Gattuso, *Series Editor*
Siu-Li Low, *General Manager, Books*

Distribution
United States
Langenscheidt Publishers, Inc.
46–35 54th Road, Maspeth, NY 11378
Fax: 718-784-0640

Worldwide
APA Publications GmbH & Co.
Verlag KG Singapore Branch, Singapore
38 Joo Koon Road, Singapore 628990
Tel: 65-865-1600. Fax: 65-861-6438

Discovery Communications produces high-quality nonfiction television programming, interactive media, books, films, and consumer products. Discovery Networks, a division of Discovery Communications, Inc., operates and manages the Discovery Channel, TLC, Animal Planet, Travel Channel, and Discovery Health Channel. Visit Discovery Channel Online at www.discovery.com.

Although every effort is made to provide accurate information in this publication, we would appreciate readers calling our attention to any errors or outdated information by writing us at: Insight Guides, PO Box 7910, London SE1 1WE, England; fax: 44-20-7403-0290; e-mail: insight@apaguide.demon.co.uk

Printed by Insight Print Services (Pte) Ltd, 38 Joo Koon Road, Singapore 628990.

Library of Congress Cataloging-in-Publication Data
Paddle sports / Beth Geiger, editor.
    p. cm. – (Discovery travel adventures)
    Includes bibliographical references (p.) and index.
    ISBN 1-56331-930-6 (pbk.)
    1. Canoes and canoeing – United States – Guidebooks.
2. United States – Guidebooks. I. Geiger, Beth, 1958- II. Series.

GV776.A2 P33 2000
797.1'22'0973 – dc21
                                        00-024909

B+T 1995 1b/

*P*addle Sports combines the interest and enthusiasm of two of the world's best-known information providers: **Insight Guides**, whose titles have set the standard for visual travel guides since 1970, and **Discovery Communications**, the world's premier source of nonfiction entertainment. The editors of Insight Guides provide both practical advice and general understanding about a destination's history, culture, institutions, and people. Discovery Communications and its website, www.discovery.com, help millions of viewers explore their world from the comfort of their home and encourage them to explore it firsthand.

About This Book

This guidebook reflects the work of dedicated editors and writers who have extensive knowledge of the best paddling in North America. **John Gattuso**, of Stone Creek Publications in New Jersey, worked with Insight Guides and Discovery Communications to conceive and direct the series. Gattuso turned to Seattle-based writer and editor **Beth Geiger** to help manage the project. Geiger started canoeing when she was a teenager and bought her first canoe at 18 with money she saved from baby-sitting jobs. A trained geologist as well as an expert paddler, she serves as a contributing editor at *Canoe & Kayak* magazine and writes often about outdoor sports and Earth science for a variety of publications. "Whitewater is my first love," she says, explaining that it offers entry into the wilderness and "the challenge of reading a river accurately" and executing precise moves. "My friends say that when I run rapids I'm always smiling." In addition to her editorial duties, Geiger offers tips on whitewater paddling, canoe touring, and trip planning and covers some of her favorite whitewater destinations, including the Rogue River in Oregon and the Middle Fork of the Salmon River in Idaho.

The book's other contributors are similarly drawn to rivers, lakes, and coastal waters with paddles in hand. Attracted to the "tranquillity of the sport," Massachusetts writer **Stephen Jermanok** has paddled many of the finest waterways in the Northeast but returns almost every summer to his boyhood haunts in the Adirondack Mountains, which he covers here. **Wayne Curtis** finds the same sense of peace among the islands of the Maine coast, though he warns that the tides and currents are strong and tricky: "You have to know when and where to go relative to the tides or you quickly find yourself in serious trouble." Based in Eastport, Maine, he brings detailed knowledge of his home waters to his coverage of Mount Desert Island.

North Carolina's Nantahala River is anything but tranquil, says **T. Edward Nickens**, who describes this Appalachian stream as a "nonstop, fun, splashy run." He encourages paddlers to enjoy the mountain scenery but warns them to keep their minds on the river: "If you take your eye off the ball, you'll be breathing fish."

Few people are more qualified to write about America's rivers than **Tim Palmer**, who has paddled more than 300 and authored a dozen books about them. He calls Pennsylvania's Youghiogheny the "formative river" of his youth and emphasizes that whitewater paddling isn't merely a sport but an act of environmental awareness: "By getting to know our rivers better, we're bound to become better caretakers of them." Elsewhere in the East, **Janisse Ray** covered the Okefenokee Swamp near her home in south

Georgia. Not surprisingly, she reports feeling most at home "in places where land and water meet."

Illinois writer **Larry Rice**, who covers the Upper Missouri River and the Apostle Islands, has penned four books and more than 300 articles on his wilderness adventures. "Traveling to wild places is the easy part," he says. "Staring at a blank computer screen and trying to write about it is the real adventure." Rice recently completed a quest to paddle on all seven continents. Fellow Midwesterner **Michael Furtman** brings more than 40 years of experience to his chapter on the Boundary Waters Canoe Area Wilderness in Minnesota, which he considers his "second home." He lives in nearby Duluth.

Though he rafts or canoes the Snake River at least a couple of times a year, **Thomas Schmidt** never gets tired of it: "The river changes daily. It's different every time I go." Much of its unpredictability is due to wildlife encounters. "My favorite time is the autumn rut, when you not only see elk all around but hear them bugling. If you hike into the woods, you may find bulls squaring off." **Alan Kesselheim**, a Montana writer with six books to his credit, had a very different feeling about the Green River in Utah. Drifting between the ancient sandstone walls of Labyrinth and Stillwater Canyons, he was struck by how little the landscape has changed since celebrated explorer John Wesley Powell floated the river in 1869.

Powell is best-known for his pioneering journey through the Grand Canyon, a trip that Arizona writer **Rose Houk** has made a dozen times in the past 20 years. She confesses to being a "three-buckle, white-knuckle" passenger on a raft, and says it's not the thrills and chills of the rapids that keep bringing her back but "the sound of moving water, the play of light on silken waves, the pure peace of the canyon."

Having grown up in the Southwest, **Lawrence W. Cheek** hadn't heard of a sea kayak before moving to Seattle in 1996. A tour quickly converted him: "I love paddling because it transforms me into a kind of honorary sea mammal, participating fully in the life of the ocean." He leads readers through the San Juan Islands.

In California, **Michael Powers**, a member of a team of extreme sea kayakers known as the Tsunami Rangers, writes about paddling in Monterey Bay. He's also a first-rate photographer, and his stunning pictures are found throughout the book. **Blake Edgar**, a frequent contributor to this series and editor of *Discovery Travel Adventures: Dinosaur Digs*, covers the South Fork of the American River, birthplace of the 1849 gold rush and now mother lode of California whitewater.

In the far north, **Nick Jans** covers the Noatak River in the Alaskan Arctic, where he's lived for the past 20 years. Denver writer **John Murray**, author or editor of more than 20 books, including guides to Alaska, explores Glacier Bay National Park.

Thanks to the many national park and forest rangers who reviewed the text. Thanks also to members of Stone Creek Publications' editorial team – **Edward A. Jardim**, **Nicole Buchenholz**, and **Sallie Graziano**.

Sunlight gilds Desolation Canyon in Utah (above).

A kayaker (opposite) explores a plunge pool at the base of a waterfall.

The Statue of Liberty (below) welcomes a kayaker to New York Harbor.

Previous pages: Champion kayaker Chris Spelius slices through whitewater.

Following pages: It's smiles all around on West Virginia's New River.

Table of Contents

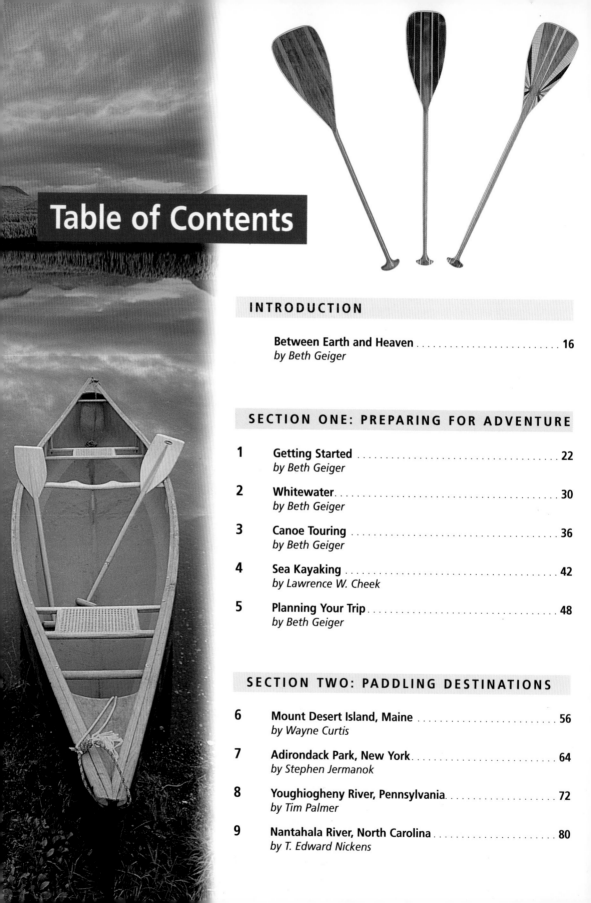

MAPS

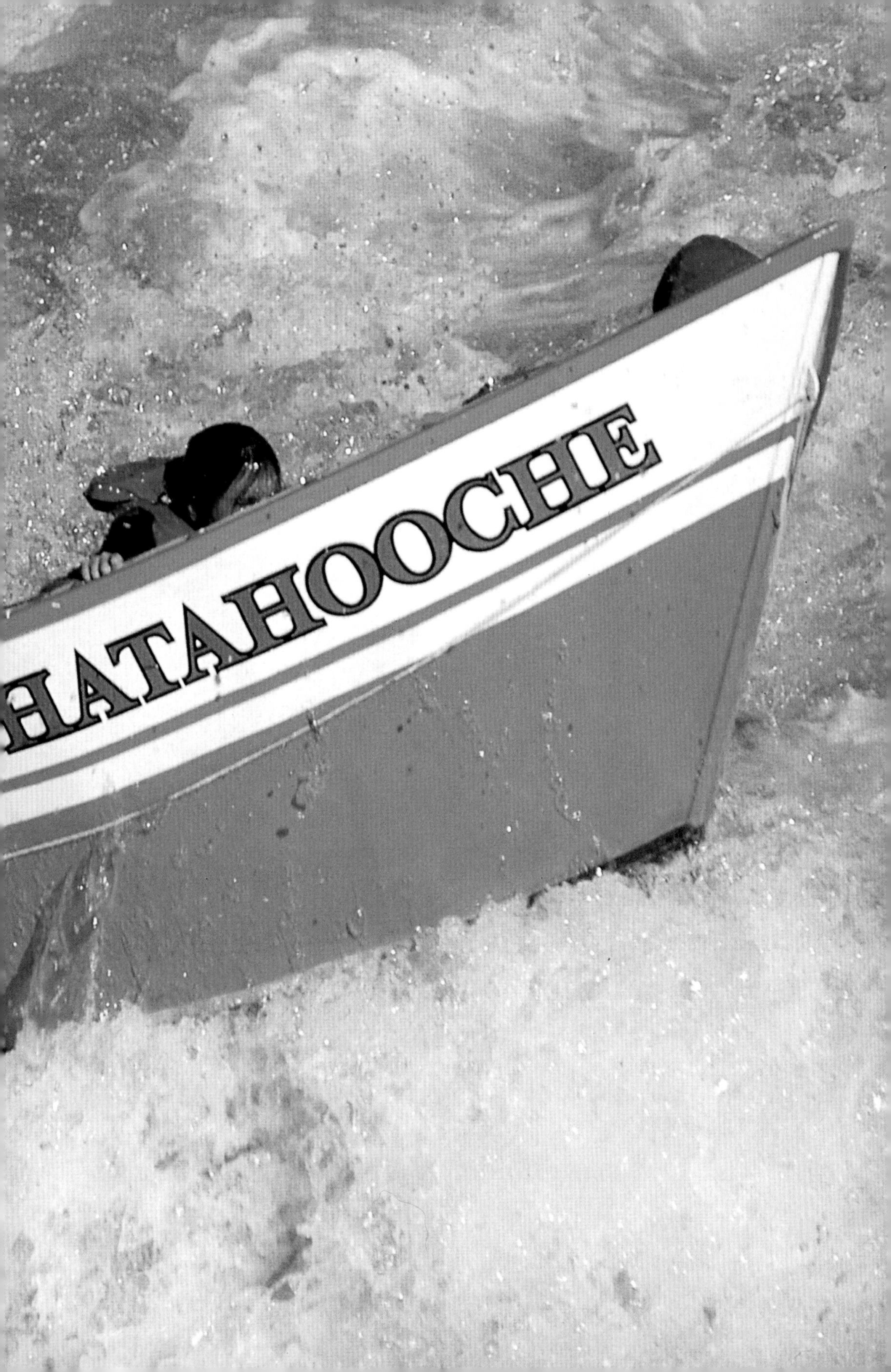
HATAHOOCHE

ater is the lifeblood we share with the planet. It makes up 71 percent of the Earth's surface and 65 percent of the human body, and like us it is always in motion – rushing down mountains, crashing against beaches, falling from the sky. So it comes as no surprise that nearly everyone who stands at the edge of a lake, river, or ocean instinctively wonders where it might take him.   ◆   There is perhaps no better way to find out than by paddling. Canoes, rafts, and kayaks give us the freedom to venture into coves too shallow and rivers too turbulent for larger boats. They open up places that are unreachable by road or trail and require us to move in harmony with winds, tides, and currents.   ◆   Nor is it surprising that when a paddle first stirs the mirrored surface of a lake or draws force from the urgency of a **Take up a paddle and launch** river, the connection we feel is more than **yourself into a watery world** physical. We are instantly united with **of challenge and wonder.** something greater than ourselves, a world that is strange and exciting and rich with mystery, yet compellingly familiar.   ◆   Of course, paddling has served a strictly practical function for as long as anyone can remember. Small boats have been used for millennia to move people and cargo from one place to another, and paddles or oars were used to move the boats. It wasn't until the last few centuries that people began paddling for fun, a pastime that reached a crest of enthusiasm in the early 20th century. Back then, a canoe was a means of transportation, a valuable tool, and a source of freedom (not to mention, in the days before rumble seats, a reasonably private if precarious place for romance).   ◆   The entire endeavor underwent a major transformation after World War II, when surplus

A kayak skims across the glassy surface of Lake Tahoe.

Preceding pages: Labyrinth Canyon, Green River, Utah; St. Mary's Lake, Glacier National Park, Montana; Lava Rapids, Grand Canyon of the Colorado River, Arizona.

A whitewater kayaker (left) scouts Washington's Snoqualmie River at the foot of Snoqualmie Falls.

A dory (right) slams through the boat-bashing waves of the Colorado River.

Handmade wood kayaks (below) give special satisfaction to those who build and paddle them.

rubber rafts became readily available. Pioneering rafters learned to negotiate previously impassable stretches of river, and running whitewater soon became the goal of paddling trips rather than something to avoid.

Interest in paddle sports has mushroomed since then, and never more explosively than in the past two decades. Some of the most popular destinations see as many as 50,000, even 100,000 people a year. The reasons are as varied as paddlers themselves. Some approach it as a way of escaping into the wilderness or encountering wildlife; others crave thrills and challenges or simply enjoy the exercise. But nearly all paddlers have one thing in common: a desire to explore the watery corners of the world the quiet way, under their own power.

With the growth of paddle sports has come an often bewildering proliferation of specialized gear. Canoes, rafts, and kayaks are now available in an amazing variety of designs and materials. Some boats are meant for rivers, others for oceans or lakes. Some models turn on a dime; others track like a javelin. There are boats that fold into your bags, and boats that your bags fold into. They come long or short, skinny or wide, and in a dazzling array of colors. On the electronic front, there are computerized tide charts, hand-held global positioning system receivers, and cell phones in case you get stranded in the wilderness. It's become so overwhelming that at times it seems as though the gear and gadgets are the ends rather than the means of the adventure.

For most of us, however, the simple act of pulling a paddle through the water and watching civilization and all its high-tech trappings fade from view is what keeps us coming back. It's a matter of finding a balance and pausing to remind ourselves of the inner needs that brought us to the water in the first place.

"These days in a canoe brought life in a new dimension," wrote William O. Douglas, the Supreme Court justice and outdoorsman, about a trip in Maine. "In calm waters we seemed to glide somewhere between earth and heaven, silently and gently."

Open your heart to adventure and attune your senses to the rhythms of oceans, lakes, and rivers. Your place between earth and heaven is only a few paddle strokes away.

Preparing For Adventure

A little planning goes a long way. Take stock of your interests, consult outfitters and instructors, hone your skills, and round up your equipment. The adventure begins at water's edge.

CHAPTER 1

All worthy endeavors start with a dream, and a paddling adventure is no different. So, for a moment, let your mind wander and your worries fall away, and try to picture this.   ◆   A circle of ripples spreads before the bow of your canoe as it slips through mist-shrouded waters. The morning air is so still you can almost feel the whispery beat of a heron's wings as it lifts itself into the air. You've already scouted a perfect lunch spot for later – a sun-soaked promontory with a fine view across the lake.   ◆   Or this: The river is loud, fast, and cold. A smooth "horizon line" heralds the beginning of another rapid. This time all you can see is an occasional leap of foam from somewhere over the brink. Your stomach tightens, resolve stiffens. The raft guide yells, "All forward!" and you slide down a glassy tongue **Let your goals and** into a maelstrom of whitewater.   ◆   Or this: **interests set a course for** Another sea otter pops its head out of the **waterborne adventure.** water, monitoring your progress with puppy-dog eyes and a quizzical look. You watch it for a minute, then kayak closer to the rocky shore. There, bright red and purple starfish glisten in the green water, and the rhythm of the surf seems to keep tempo with the easy cadence of your paddle stroke.   ◆   Paddling offers so many enticing possibilities that you may find yourself in the same fine dilemma as the proverbial kid in the candy store. Choosing the right setting and acquiring the necessary skills and gear may seem daunting at first, so try to narrow your search by thinking about why you want to get involved in paddling and what you hope to get out of it.

A canoeist noses her craft through a cluster of lily pads in Obabika Inlet, Lake Temagami, Ontario.

Preceding pages: An expert kayaker catches air at Auger Falls, Moose River, New York.

Your Paddling Persona

Begin by asking yourself a few basic questions. First, what's the appeal of a paddling vacation? A love of the outdoors and an appreciation for clean, self-propelled recreation are common starting points. But beyond these, your motivations may be rather specific. Do you crave solitude and the simplicity of a gentle paddle across a remote lake? Are you drawn to split-second decision-making and the rush of adrenaline that come with paddling a raging river? Or do you believe there's no water like salt water, with its dynamic tides and currents, rich marine life, and intricate shorelines? Perhaps you see paddling as a means of staying fit, or of reaching remote places. You may be looking for the perfect family activity

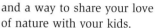

A life jacket (left) approved by the U.S. Coast Guard is essential equipment.

Icebergs (below) crowd the waters of Prince William Sound, Alaska.

and a way to share your love of nature with your kids.

How much tolerance do you have for risk? Capsized boats, foul weather, and seriously cold water are just a few of the hazards you may encounter. Traveling into remote locations where help is more than a telephone call away only compounds the danger. Tolerance for risk varies from person to person. Don't allow yourself to be talked into trying something that is clearly beyond your abilities or that simply doesn't feel right. Sometimes the bravest thing you can do is to say no.

What are the best paddling opportunities in your area? If you want to incorporate paddling into your lifestyle, consider what's readily available – rivers, lakes, a picturesque bay? Then, investigate local resources such as paddling clubs or schools and shops that specialize in outdoor gear. They offer a wealth of information and will put you in contact with people who have similar interests.

How fit are you? Arduous portages and relentless headwinds are just a few of the physical (and mental) challenges that paddlers are liable to face. You may relish the

idea. But if you don't, there are plenty of marvelous trips that require little more exertion than climbing in and out of a boat. Be realistic about what's right for you, and whether your goals include pushing your limits.

A Day or a Lifetime?

How you approach paddling also depends in part on your long-term expectations. Will paddling be an infrequent adventure, a once-in-a-lifetime trip to places like the Grand Canyon or the Boundary Waters? Or do you envision it as a lifelong commitment, from the patient acquisition of skills and gear to learning all the insider lingo?

If you fall into the first category or aren't yet sure where you fit in, you will probably want to go with a guide for your first time out. That inviting slogan, "no experience required," means that the adventure is ready and waiting. Hiring a reputable guide ensures that the trip will be safe and interesting, the food good, and the gear exactly what's needed. And a

Low-Impact Paddling

The essence of any backcountry trip is immersing yourself in the natural world. Preserving that world is satisfying, easy, and an ethical responsibility. Start with these basics and remember that "leave no trace" is as important for day-trips as it is for overnights.

● Pack it in, pack it out. Never leave garbage behind, even if you've buried it.

● Noise makes an impact, too. Leave radios, tape players, and your electric guitar behind.

● When it comes to campfires, small is beautiful. A petite fire is just as satisfying as a wood-munching, earth-scorching bonfire. Better yet, forgo all the smoke and hassle and bring a lightweight camping stove instead.

● Soap and water don't mix. Do all washing at least 100 feet from rivers, lakes or bays, even with biodegradable soap.

● When nature calls, answer with a trowel. Bury human waste at least six inches deep, and bury or carry out used paper.

● Forget the earth-moving projects. There's no need to trench around your tent for rain. Just pick a well-drained spot in the first place.

guided trip is the perfect try-before-you-buy approach if you're still deciding whether to jump into canoeing or kayaking on your own.

On the other hand, if you are ready to take on paddling as a long-term journey, start out with good instruction. From paddling a canoe in a

straight line to tackling hard-core whitewater, a class will minimize frustrating episodes and give you a chance to try out different boats before making a big purchase. Choose nearby courses, or head for one of the "total immersion" schools that make learning to canoe or kayak a real vacation, right down to gourmet meals and hot tubs. Back home, look for a good paddling club. You'll find group trips at various skill levels and instant camaraderie

Georgian Bay (top), a part of Lake Huron in Ontario, offers picturesque campsites.

An instructor (left) teaches bracing, rolling, and other basic paddling techniques.

Get the Picture?

Saffron sunsets or dolphins in arcing leaps? A kayak offers a fine platform for photographing either, but you'll have to decide on your prime objective before packing or buying equipment.

Professional kayaking photographers generally take the same equipment they use on land – several thousand dollars' worth of cameras and lenses, carried in a hard-shell, waterproof case prayerfully strapped to the deck. The camera, however, can be ready at hand only in calm water. If it gets dunked in salt water, it may as well continue on to the seafloor.

For watery action photography, a better choice is a weatherproof point-and-shoot camera. For some time the kayaker's standby has been the Pentax IQZoom105WR, a feature-packed midget that will survive amazing abuse. Its disadvantage is that its 38-105mm zoom lens is neither wide enough for many scenic shots nor long enough for a sea lion 100 yards away.

Learn to operate your camera with one hand, and if you're using a point-and-shoot, lean toward faster film (ISO 200 or 400). And remember that your pictures will be most rewarding when you concentrate on those shots possible only from a kayaker's-eye view. Capturing another kayak in a seascape's foreground tells a story in a way that a pristine nature shot cannot. – *Lawrence W. Cheek*

A **waterproof camera** (left) with automatic features is your best bet for waterborne photography.

Shifting body weight to the bow (opposite, top) can help a dory or raft "punch" through a hole.

Calm seas allow a kayaker to approach the eroded bluffs of Gabriola Island, British Columbia (opposite, bottom).

Sport sandals (below) are suitable for casual, warm-weather paddling.

addition to destination descriptions.

● Synthetic long underwear – whether polypropylene, Capilene, or fleece – has one crucial quality: it *isn't* cotton, which saps valuable heat from your body when it's wet. Buy a set for both your upper and lower body.

● Flatwater, salt water, or whitewater: they all reflect sunlight. Protect your eyes with a good pair of sunglasses. And never get into a boat without a glasses retainer or neck strap to keep them from flying off your face.

● A stampede of specialized water shoes is available these days. Neoprene booties are terrific for cold water and are the choice for most experienced whitewater paddlers. Make sure you get the type that has traction soles rather than the soft-bottom ones designed for scuba diving. Rubber boots fit inside most sea kayaks and

with other paddlers.

"Paddlefests" are a treasure trove of information, filled with everything from the oldest advice to the latest gear. At the annual Northwest Sea Kayak Symposium in Port Townsend, Washington, for example, hundreds of paddlers gather to try different boats, attend mini-courses and slide shows on interesting destinations, and swap used equipment. To learn about festivals or symposia near you, check calendar listings in paddle-sports magazines or call a paddle-sports retailer.

A Basic Starter Kit

Gear-heads unite! From state-of-the-art personal flotation devices (also known as PFDs or just old-fashioned life jackets) to self-bailing rafts with matching coolers, paddling can be as gear-intensive as you like. While you can depend on an outfitter or guide to provide you with a boat, paddle, and PFD, a few smaller items are certainly worth acquiring before you head out on any paddling trip:

● A paddling guidebook is an invaluable blend of information and inspiration. Many list regional clubs and relevant websites in

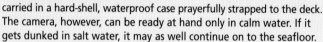

canoes and give the extra protection you'll want for sharp barnacles or rocks on shore. Sport sandals work fine for casual canoeing on a hot summer day (as long as they attach at the heel as well as the toe), but they don't offer much protection in the event of an accidental swim in whitewater or a rugged take-out. An old pair of sneakers may work, too, though they won't dry nearly as fast.

● A waterproof paddling jacket is a good investment. Many have sealing neoprene or rubber cuffs, which keep cold pools of water from accumulating at your elbows. Avoid metal zippers if you plan on paddling in salt water; they tend to corrode. Waterproof overpants may also be in order, depending on the destination.

● Designed just for paddlers and sealed with a special fold and clasp system, drybags are remarkably rugged and totally waterproof. Keep a small one handy on every trip for personal items like a camera, guidebook, and sunscreen. If you're stocking up for a self-guided adventure, buy drybags in a variety of sizes and colors, including transparent ones, to help with organization.

● A small first-aid kit is an essential item. And after a few hours of dipping your hands in water, you'll be grateful to have a ready supply of hand lotion. Travel-sized bottles slip into any pocket. Don't forget to add sunscreen and bug repellent, too.

Just Add Water

Canoeing, sea kayaking, or whitewater: within each there is endless room to tailor an adventure to your personal goals, skills, and interests. Canoe with the ducks at a nearby pond, explore a far-away wilderness, or train for the knife-sharp efficiency of a flatwater racer. Use a sea kayak to poke around protected bays and urban waterfronts, explore isolated islands, or test your skills in the open ocean.

Even whitewater doesn't have to be all brawn or expertise. It can be a delicate dance through a mellow rock garden, or a momentary test of precision and skill on a long wilderness trip.

Canoes, Kayaks, and Rafts

WHITEWATER KAYAKS

Recreational Kayaks

A good all-around river-running kayak has slightly rounded edges for predictable handling, allowing the paddler to focus on getting down the river instead of just staying upright. Volume is moderate to high so the boat can handle big water, and the substantial rocker (the banana-shaped curve of the hull) makes for quick turning.

Inflatable Kayaks

Bridging the gap between whitewater kayaks and rafts, inflatables are a forgiving, if less precise, version of their "hardshell" cousins. Many have a semirigid or inflatable floor; optional thigh straps and foot braces add control. The "open" design also helps make them safer since paddlers cannot be readily trapped inside. Inflatable kayaks come in one- or two-person models.

Play Boats

Play boats or rodeo kayaks are designed for getting the most of play spots like holes. With crisp edges and low end volume, they slice through the water for stunts like cartwheels but are tricky to handle and may be pinned under rocks more easily than an all-around kayak. Extreme rocker enhances spin speed, though the tradeoff is reduced tracking ability.

SEA KAYAKS

Decked Sea Kayaks

Decked sea kayaks, in fiberglass composites or molded plastic, are made for tracking and sea-worthiness. Longer and narrower means faster; for extra stability and cargo capacity, many paddlers prefer "beamier," or wider, kayaks. Sealed hatches keep gear dry; spray skirts make the cockpit watertight. Optional rudders help in tracking, and stretch-cord tie-downs on the deck are great for quick access to maps and rain gear.

Double Sea Kayaks

Double sea kayaks have the same features as singles but with two cockpits, and in some cases a third hatch or cockpit. Doubles tend to be more stable than singles and are popular on guided trips. Paddling double is also a perfect option when one partner is not as strong or experienced as the other.

Sit-on-Tops

Economical, easy-to-paddle, sit-on-top kayaks, single or double, are usually constructed of molded plastic. Some models are exceptionally stable and popular both as rentals and in warm climates. Many have hatches for keeping cargo dry and secure, and are molded for comfortable feet and hip positions.

CANOES

Recreational Canoes

The most versatile and popular canoes, these come in a range of designs and materials including Royalex, wood, aluminum, and fiberglass. Usually 15 to 18 feet long, they turn relatively easily, track fairly well, and are capable of handling lakes or easy rapids. The all-purpose design means they aren't generally high performers in any one area, such as speed.

Wilderness Trippers

Designed for optimum efficiency as well as cargo capacity, the best cruising canoes are often made of lightweight composites like Kevlar. Long (17 to 19 feet) and narrow for speed and efficient paddle strokes, they have minimal rocker so they track straight, and a low profile to minimize the effects of wind. Many have adjustable seats for balancing the paddlers' weight.

Whitewater Canoes

Specialized whitewater canoes are short (between nine and 13 feet for solos) with lots of rocker. This means spin-on-a-dime turning and a remarkable ability to handle both big and technical rivers: experts have even used them in the Grand Canyon. Paddlers equip their boats with "saddles" and thigh straps for a secure fit and air bags to displace water.

DORIES AND RAFTS

Paddle Rafts

River-worthy rafts are heavy-duty boats made of neoprene or other thick rubber and designed with as many as six or more separate air chambers for safety. Some are self-bailing with a "free-floating" floor to allow water to run out. They are usually paddled by a team of anywhere from four to 12, with a guide at the stern.

Oar Rafts

Rig an aluminum oar frame onto a paddle raft, and you have an oar raft. Rowed by one person, the long oars and rigid frame give the pilot exceptional leverage, power, and maneuverability. Though they can accommodate fewer passengers, oar rafts are well suited for carrying lots of gear, including rigid cargo such as large coolers.

Dories

Dories, also called drift boats, are an elegant breed of wood, aluminum, or fiberglass rowboat. Lots of rocker gives a dry ride through big water, and the boats can be maneuvered with amazing precision. The stability of dories is well suited to fly fishermen, who can stand up with little fear of capsizing the vessel.

The titles say it all: *Blazing Paddles, Southern Fried Creekin',
Paddle Mania.* These are just a few of the extreme whitewater videos that
are now de rigueur at any gathering of hard-core paddlers. They show kayakers
plunging over waterfalls and ripping through torrential narrows as if shot
from a fire hose. ◆ The videos are great fun to watch, but they miss
an important point: you don't have to be a daredevil to enjoy whitewater
paddling. There are many capable whitewater canoeists and kayakers who
are content to enjoy relatively calm Class II and III rivers, and many others
who learned to paddle in order to become well-rounded wilderness travelers.
Whether it's an exhilarating splash in a breathtaking canyon, a watery romp
through an intricate "rock garden," or a joyride on a green wave, the thrills
and chills of big "hydraulics" are only half **When it comes to**
the story of whitewater. ◆ Running rivers **whitewater, finesse**
is both safer and riskier than you may **and skill count for more**
think. It's safer partly because those big **than brawn alone.**
rollicking waves can be surprisingly innocuous, and because the expertise
to keep you out of trouble is readily available from guides and instructors.
It's trickier because the danger is often subtle and the action on a river
unfolds rapidly. A fallen tree, or snag, across even a benign stream can be
a death trap. Small mistakes, like trying to stand up in moving water, can
become perilous very quickly. Inexperience and poor judgment increase the
risk exponentially. The preponderance of paddling fatalities in the United
States involve unguided novices (often using inappropriate craft and no
personal flotation devices, or PFDs), alcohol abuse, or both.

A kayaker runs the Crystal River in
Colorado. Whitewater kayaking requires
subtle body movements and knowledge of
river dynamics as well as physical strength.

Rating Whitewater

All over the world, the common language of whitewater begins with the same six numbers: the International Scale of Whitewater Difficulty. Though river ratings are generally accurate, the degree of difficulty can change temporarily or permanently due to flooding, fallen trees or boulders, and other obstacles.

Class I: Easy. Fast-moving water with riffles and small waves. Few obstructions, all obvious and easily avoided with a little training.

Class II: Novice. Straightforward rapids with wide, clear channels that are evident without scouting. Rocks and medium-sized waves are easily negotiated by trained paddlers.

Class III: Intermediate. Rapids with moderate, irregular waves that may be difficult to avoid and that can swamp an open canoe. Complex maneuvers in fast currents and good boat control in tight passages are often required. Large waves may be present.

Class IV: Advanced. Intense, powerful rapids requiring precise boat handling in turbulent water. May feature large, unavoidable waves and holes or constricted passages demanding fast maneuvers. "Must-do" moves above dangerous hazards may be required. Risk to swimmers is moderate to high.

Class V: Expert. Extremely long, obstructed, or violent rapids that expose a paddler to added risk. Drops may contain large, unavoidable waves and holes or steep, congested chutes with complex, demanding routes. Swimming is dangerous, and rescue is often difficult even for experts.

Class VI: Extreme and exploratory. These are rarely attempted and exemplify the highest levels of difficulty, unpredictability, and danger. The consequences of error may be fatal.

Chaos reigns in Class V Gore Canyon on the upper Colorado River in Colorado (below).

To the River

The vast majority of people first experience whitewater on guided raft trips, which can range anywhere from three hours to three weeks and offer as many thrills as you're willing to handle. Once you get the brochures, you'll notice that outfitters use several types of boats. It's worth taking a minute to consider how different kinds of vessels will influence your journey.

Oar rafts are fitted with a rowing frame and powered by a single person who rows from the center facing forward. Though passengers don't row or steer, they may have to bail water, shift their weight as needed, and occasionally use the paddles they're given.

Paddle rafts are propelled by a team of paddlers (six is typical, but the number varies), usually captained by one person seated at the back of the boat. Depending on the river and guide, passengers may not need prior experience, but they should enjoy teamwork.

On a few rivers, particularly the Rogue in Oregon, the Colorado in the Grand Canyon, and the Middle Fork of the Salmon in Idaho, some outfitters offer trips by dory. These graceful, rigid boats look a bit like overgrown rowboats and are extremely river-worthy. Rowed by one person and generally carrying just one to three passengers, they are exceptionally maneuverable and, because the rigid design allows passengers to stand, they are popular for fly-fishing.

Increasingly, outfitters are also offering their clients a chance to paddle inflatable kayaks on quiet stretches of water. Inflatables give paddlers mobility and independence and are far more forgiving of beginners than their "hardshell" cousins. Having a few inflatables along provides variety and gives customers a taste of autonomy.

As you assemble at the

pinned between it and a rock. Avoid getting tangled in ropes. If you like getting wet, sit in front.

And then off you go, into a schizoid world of serenity and chaos, warm sun and cold water, glassy V-shaped tongues and turbulent curlers, fantastic scenery and blinding blurs of whitewater. By the time you get to the takeout point, you'll know the difference between eddies (the shadows downstream of rocks that provide stopping places) and holes (where the current recirculates with such force that, in extreme cases, it can fold a raft like a taco shell) – and whether or not whitewater is the sport for you.

Going Solo

Rafting down a river with an experienced guide is perfectly satisfying for some people, but for others it's merely the beginning. You may have noticed colorful little kayaks and canoes as you floated downstream. They dart around at will, surf every wave, perform amazing end-over-end acrobatics, and look like they're having a blast. It's

put-in of a guided raft trip, you and your fellow adventurers will look like an odd sort of invasion force, with matching paddles, PFDs, and possibly helmets and wet suits. The guide, usually distinguished by a glowing suntan and a PFD that looks suspiciously more stylish than yours, gives the customary

safety talk: If you fall out of the boat, keep your feet in front of you, and don't try to stand up. Stay upstream of the raft so you won't get

Boatmen (above) negotiate a relatively mellow section of whitewater in the Grand Canyon, much to the delight of their passengers.

Rafters (right) crash through a hole on the Ottawa River in Ontario.

Recreational kayaks (left), generally made of plastic, are designed to sustain collisions of considerable force. Helmets are mandatory for whitewater kayaking.

way to get there is to start with good instruction.

Picture this: your friends keep telling you to "just keep paddling," but so far you've had three traumatic swims and are feeling less confident by the minute. No one seems willing to wait while you work on basics. Another riot of breaking waves, holes, and rocks looms just ahead. Clenched with apprehension, you promise the river gods that if they let you through this one, you'll never bother them again. Sound like fun?

Now for Curtain Number Two: floating in a sunny eddy with three other students, you watch the instructor demonstrate a "peel out." He slices into the current, leans downstream, takes a few strokes and lands back in the eddy, explaining the whole move as he goes. The first student looks a little wobbly, but from the grin on her face you can tell something's clicked. Now it's your turn.

Simply put, whitewater paddling is not instinctive. You need instruction. Classes provide a supportive environment where you'll feel pushed just enough to stay on a learning curve and confident that your safety is a high priority. You'll learn essential skills more quickly than you would on your own, and most schools provide gear, so you

enough to make you jealous.

The good news is you don't have to be a brawny 20-something or an adrenaline junky in order to join them. In fact, when it comes to whitewater, finesse and common sense generally count for more than strength and bravado. What's more, there's never been a better time to take up the sport. "The qual-

ity of instruction has really skyrocketed in the last 10 years," says Kent Ford, a former U.S. world championship team member and one of the nation's most respected instructors. "What used to take people years to learn can sometimes take a weekend."

Your goal as a whitewater paddler should be to have fun and do it safely. The best won't have to invest your own money before you know what suits you.

School Days

Another option is to enroll in a whitewater school (see the Resource Directory for a list of regional schools). Set in scenic canyons, mountain towns, and on woodsy riverbanks, paddling schools offer fast-paced weekends or a full week of "total immersion." Take advantage of top-notch kayak or canoe instruction during the day, then return to a hotel, inn, or campground for a good meal, a soak in a hot tub, or a slide show and lecture. Most schools also offer private instruction, an option that provides flexibility and optimizes your own learning style.

As you shop for the right school, ask if the cost includes lodging, meals, and gear, and note if the instructors are certified by the American Canoe Association, which indicates that they have completed a rigorous instructor-training program.

No matter what whitewater experience you choose, always remember that the power of moving water is relentless. The best paddlers don't try to fight the current. They work with it, and their runs become a dance with one of the great forces of nature.

A river guide (above) muscles through rapids on the Fraser River in British Columbia.

Paddlers (below) talk strategy. Always scout unfamiliar rapids and ask experts for advice.

Fear and Judgment

Balancing fear and judgment is one of the great challenges of whitewater paddling. How can you tell if you're in over your head or just plain nervous? Are those butterflies in your stomach a real indication of danger, or do you merely have first-time jitters?

The first step in cultivating good judgment is to choose paddling partners or mentors who won't push you into situations that you're not prepared to handle and who are ready to help in case you get into trouble. Even well-intentioned companions may be more interested in their own agenda than your learning curve. Next, select runs that will build your skills and confidence gradually and without intimidation. Do your own research; you'll feel more in control if you know what to expect and stay involved in the planning. If possible, choose sunny days. Good weather adds an upbeat flavor to any experience. And remember, nobody's an instant expert. Be patient with yourself, and make sure you have realistic expectations.

Once you're on the river, spend lots of time warming up on the easy stretches. Making moves successfully is a great attitude booster. If a drop makes you uncomfortable, get out and look at it. What maneuvers will you need to run it successfully? Can you make them? If you miss, what will happen? Ask more experienced paddlers for their advice. And if you've been staring at the same rapid for an hour trying to decide, listen to your instincts and portage it. There will always be another time.

The dual heritage of paddling and wilderness tugs at North American heartstrings like the sweet notes of a bluegrass tune. From the very beginning, North Americans haven't marched through history so much as paddled across it. First were American Indians, ingeniously crafting their boats from birch bark and hollowed-out logs; then came French traders, the bold voyageurs of the 17th and 18th centuries who paddled the canoe routes of the Great Lakes region; and then came explorers and naturalists like Lewis and Clark and Sigurd Olson, who probed the continent's wild places by canoe. ◆ Today, canoe touring has evolved into a sort of Platonic ideal as much as a sport. Adventurers search for the perfect canoe moment – gently drifting, paddle in hand, through a serene wilderness far, far away from the workaday world of office meetings and e-mail. ◆ But wait. Exactly *which* perfect moment are we talking about? The one in which a canoe beaches gently at the meeting of an age-old portage trail and an isolated lake? The moment a toddler, secure at his parent's feet, spots his first trout through crystal-clear water? The burst of adrenaline as a canoe, running through a set of standing waves, seems to fly past rocky banks at lightning speed? Or the flash of exhilaration and doubt as a floatplane fades into the distance, leaving you and a pile of gear alone at the headwaters of an arctic river? ◆ Canoeing is all of these, offering versatility unmatched in other paddle sports. A canoe has more room for gear (not to mention children and dogs) than a kayak, and the relatively high paddling position gives better visibility. With thwarts for easy carrying, canoes are

From the simple pleasures of a day on a lake to the challenges of a wilderness trip, a canoe is the key to your escape.

A lone canoeist crosses the sapphire waters of Moraine Lake, nestled at the foot of glacier-carved peaks in Alberta's Banff National Park.

well suited for long portages. They allow quick access to cameras or fishing tackle, and many can be paddled by either one or two people.

Canoeing also has remarkable depth. Consider, for example, the forward stroke, the building block of all paddling. It seems so easy, until the canoe's natural tendency to veer into a stubborn zigzag defeats a lone paddler's efforts to go straight. On the other hand, watch a pair of flatwater canoe racers: elegant, fast, as synchronized as the wings of a bird, and definitely traveling in a straight line. Properly executed (top hand on the grip, not the shaft, with short strokes and a clean recovery), the forward stroke is a masterpiece of form and efficiency, and it can take years to achieve.

Paddling straight is one thing, maybe even *the* thing for novices, but most people want more from their canoe adventures. Fortunately, it doesn't take long to discover that canoeing opens up a lifetime of possibilities.

The ingredients for the simplest canoe trip are a sunny afternoon and a nearby canoe rental dock. For a few dollars and the temporary surrender of a driver's license, a miniature adventure awaits, complete with wildlife (most likely ducks), a little exercise, and perhaps a picnic on the shore. The gear may not be high performance, but it's perfectly adequate and ready to go. With some common sense, this little outing can be enjoyed with minimal skill and planning.

The next level is a weekend outing, based at a lodge or campground. Now, an hour of paddling a slow, leaky canoe with poor technique is one thing, but two or three solid days is another. Weekenders will want to refine their skills and investigate their gear a bit more closely. A longer, narrower canoe may track more efficiently but will be less stable. A light, stiff paddle makes things easier, especially for those who take the time to improve their technique with instruction. Then there's getting the boat to water, which involves car racks and a safe tie-down system, and planning where to go. Add some other skills, such as paddling in wind, waves, and current, and basic rescue techniques in case things go awry. If this list sounds daunting, consider signing on with a guide for your first couple of outings or seek professional instruction. The rewards for your efforts are solitude, adventure, and the pleasures of wilderness – in short, more of everything canoe touring has to offer.

Lining (left), a paddling term for maneuvering a boat with ropes, is sometimes the only way to travel upstream.

Canoes (opposite, top) have plenty of room for children and are ideal for family trips. Kids should be fitted with a life vest of the proper size, not one that's intended for an adult.

A portage trail (opposite, below) leads over Ontario's Mississagi River at Aubrey Falls.

Sunrise breaks over the St. Croix River in Maine (below). Early morning is an excellent time to observe wildlife.

surveyor, camper, and all-around beast of burden," wrote James West Davidson and John Rugge in their classic reference *The Complete Wilderness Paddler*. Independent canoeists may want to add a few other qualities to the list: chief cook and bottle washer, boat packer, first-aid and safety expert, navigator, personnel director, weather forecaster, environmentalist, storyteller, repairman. Impressive qualifications, but most are easily acquired or readily available in the person of a guide.

So where does all this fuss get the wilderness paddler?

Jack-of-All-Trades

The next big leap is overnight canoe touring – a journey beyond the reach of roads and civilization. Now the adventure includes not only paddling but camping and other outdoor skills. Many consider canoe camping to be the quintessential paddling experience, and it requires a versatile canoe. The craft must be narrow enough to track well but roomy enough for gear, sufficiently durable to survive an encounter with a rock but light enough for long portages. It also requires an accomplished canoeist, a renaissance paddler who is a wilderness jack-of-all-trades. "At odd moments the canoeist is a walker, backpacker, scaler of cliffs,

pleasures like a tailwind are a priceless blessing.

What really crystallizes the experience is time. One day won't do it. A long weekend gives a tantalizing view. Two weeks are optimal, allowing the subtle rhythms of wilderness paddling to come into focus: the slow march of stars across the night sky, the calls of birds and other wildlife, the nuances of a wild landscape.

The Right Canoe

Such fine moments await every canoeist, and modern gear has made arriving at them even simpler. Just ask Lewis and Clark, who certainly would have appreciated high-tech, lightweight boats when they portaged the Great Falls of the Missouri River during their epic journey. Unfortunately, it's

Away. Into places like the Alaskan Arctic (where caribou outnumber people), majestic red-rock country like Labyrinth Canyon on Utah's Green River, or the pristine network of streams, forests, and lakes of the Boundary Waters in Minnesota. These are places where the phone never rings and the food always tastes great, even if it's burned macaroni and cheese, and where simple

Every canoeist develops his or her own packing system (right).

Canoeists (opposite, top) make camp at the edge of Rock Lake in Algonquin Park, Ontario.

Nylon spray decks (opposite, bottom), like the one covering this canoe on the Nahanni River in the Northwest Territories, help keep gear secure and dry – and aren't a bad place for a nap.

Dawn reddens the sky over Robe Lake in the Chugach Mountains of Alaska (below).

Packing a Canoe

A poorly loaded canoe can cause a backache, poor handling, or worse. Follow these tips for a system that's efficient and safe.

● Balance the load with most of the weight in the bottom and center of the boat. Too much weight at the ends will make the canoe difficult to turn, and a top-heavy vessel is extremely unstable. If the load is uneven from side to side, you'll tend to compensate by twisting in your seat and will pay for it with a sore back.

● Tie down everything. Secure your gear with buckle-end straps that can be easily adjusted. Crisscross straps over and through the load and around the thwarts. Properly secured gear will stay in place during a capsize and won't entangle passengers.

● Keep supplies waterproof. Buy drybags in various colors and sizes for easy organization. Some have shoulder straps, but for long portages consider using an internal-frame backpack lined with a heavy plastic trash bag.

● Don't pack anything around your feet. It can easily get in your way and become a hazard.

● Use water jugs to fine-tune the balance. The canoe's trim (the way it sits in the water) should be even or slightly to stern. And don't forget to take into account differences in passengers' weights.

easy for beginners to be overwhelmed by the often confusing array of options.

The right canoe for the occasion depends on size, stability, cargo capacity, durability, and a host of other factors, including cost and even looks. No canoe does everything well: high performance in one area – say speed – tends to compromise another, like turning ability. In general, multipurpose touring canoes range from 15 to 18 feet long and 30 to 35 inches wide from gunwale (pronounced "GUNnul") to gunwale. Weight varies considerably, from a feathery 40 pounds to a beefy 80 pounds or more. One long portage with the old family canoe and it's easy to understand why so many paddlers spend extra money for "light" boats made of Kevlar or other composite materials. Keels for tracking have generally been replaced by updated hull designs. And no canoeist can get up a creek without a paddle: they come

in "T-grip" for precision in whitewater, "palm grip" for long-range comfort, and "bent shaft" for those who seek maximum stroke efficiency in flatwater. Wood is warm to the touch, but composites like graphite are lighter.

As naturalist Loren Eiseley observed, there's magic in water, and canoeing is generally a splendid way to discover it. But there's more to it than meets the eye. Training with guides or instructors, and having respect for both the power and the beauty of lakes and rivers, will ensure that the magic lasts a lifetime.

Sea Kayaking

t's a perfect morning on Admiralty Inlet in Washington, where twice each day the Pacific Ocean gathers itself to pour into Puget Sound. At the moment, the current is idle, so the sea is blue satin, and seals are nosing the warm autumn sunshine as if to absorb their fill before the winter gloom. On shore, 20 itchy kayakers are sitting in a classroom, where instructor Lena Conlan is urging them to list all the things – the bad things – that can happen on a kayak expedition.   ◆   "Icebergs," someone offers. "Right," she agrees. "When they calve – when a big piece falls off – a *mile* can be too close."   ◆   Conlan writes everything on a poster tablet, and the list soon sprawls across three pages. Fog, thunderstorms, tide rips, rogue waves, sunstroke, hypothermia, bumptious sea lions, even lost glasses. Anyone wandering in, maybe just thinking about trying sea kayaking, would blanch in fright. But these veterans can't wait to get out on the water. They understand the hazards of venturing on the sea in a 17-foot fiberglass banana and are spending time in Conlan's "Risk Management" class for a booster shot of preparedness. The rewards of sea kayaking are worth it.   ◆   Sea kayaking is altogether different than whitewater paddling. A sea kayak, to begin with, is a distinct creature – 15 to 18 feet long rather than eight, designed for straight tracking and sustained speed rather than maneuverability. It's surprisingly hard to convince a sea kayak to change direction, but surprisingly easy to cover long distances without pain. Anyone in decent physical condition can cruise at three knots. Twenty miles is a decent day's paddle. A modern sea kayak is as ideally designed for its environment as a letter opener is for its

Climb into a sea kayak and surrender to the cadence of the paddle, the rhythm of the tides.

A sea kayaker cruises across Lake Tahoe; long, sleek, and efficient, the vessels are ideal for lakes and gentle rivers as well as the sea.

A shallow draft enables sea kayaks to venture into waters that are inaccessible to other boats (left).

A shaft of light (opposite, top) streams through a sea arch on the Oregon coast; paddlers in heavy surf should always wear a helmet.

Warm, clear water and an enchanting desert landscape draw sea kayakers to the Sea of Cortez in Baja California (opposite, bottom).

work; no other watercraft obeys so perfectly Louis Sullivan's command that form should follow function.

No other watercraft has such a ridiculously puny powerplant, either, so the wise kayaker plots an excursion in detail, riding the currents wherever possible and factoring in the best available guesses on what the wind will do. There are few more intimate ways to experience the ocean, to become one with it.

Ocean Zen

Properly instructed and fitted into the boat, "a human paddler morphs into a kind of aquatic creature," as Chris Wood wrote in *Maclean's* magazine. The act of paddling "sometimes feels like a religious chant, a prayer offered to the sea," explained Tim Cahill in *Outside*. Novelist and travel writer Paul Theroux called paddling "something that clears the head and quiets the soul." Everyone who writes about sea kayaking eventually offers some variation on this theme of oceanic Zen. It has a lot to do with fitting into the rhythms of nature without disturbing her, of becoming a part of something much more powerful than yourself. Sea

kayakers become more aware of their environment than other seafarers because it can affect them so profoundly. A slight turn in the current, a brow of cirrus clouds on the far horizon, a dark ripple in the water ahead, all mean something – probably something important.

A sea kayak has a draft of about three inches, so it can poke into secluded coves and inlets where no other craft would dream of going. It makes virtually no noise, so it is an ideal platform for viewing aquatic life, from herons to orcas (although U.S. marine law forbids approaching aquatic mammals closer than 100 yards). It can swallow a week's worth of supplies for camping on uninhabited islands. And a sea kayak is hardly restricted to the sea. Lakes, leisurely rivers, and estuaries are equally suitable. Even urban waterways such as ship canals become entirely new experiences from a kayak's perspective.

Occasionally one hears of epic open-water crossings, such as a recent 20-day, 700-mile paddle across the Gulf of Mexico from the Yucatan

Peninsula to Louisiana. This is impressive in terms of physical endurance and chutzpah, but it violates common sense and the kayak's intrinsic nature. The kayak belongs in coastal waters, preferably those sheltered from the open sea, with land usually in sight – and at least one other paddler around to help if trouble arises.

Gearing Up

As with most participatory sports in the last couple of decades, sea-kayaking gear has exploded in sophistication and specialization and, of course, cost. The beginner faces bewildering choices in boats. A basic molded polyethylene boat can cost less than $1,000, an ultralight Kevlar kayak $3,000. There are sit-on-tops for casual paddling close to shore, and aluminum and fabric boats that collapse into duffel bags for flights to such faraway places as the fjords of Alaska.

Rudders are a furiously debated option; purists scorn them, but most practical kayakers appreciate them. There are singles and doubles, accommodating one paddler or two. Often a kayaker first ventures onto the water in a double (they're reassuringly stable) and eventually buys a single

(they're much more fun).

Every model has distinctive handling characteristics. One seems as nervous as a whippet, another so imperturbable a paddler could sleep in it. Big bodies generally require big kayaks and vice versa. With all these choices – and with serious money and safety at stake – the

only shopping strategy that makes sense is to spend a month or two renting or borrowing various models to find the best match. Some helpful advisers recommend trying boats in "challenging conditions," such as a heavy chop, but beginners should beware. Challenges are for experts looking for the ultimate kayak.

Along with the boat must come a closetful of safety and comfort equipment, typically another $1,000 to $2,000. Essentials include a PFD, spray skirt (forms a watertight seal around the paddler's waist and cockpit), and *two* paddles (a spare, lashed to the deck with shock cords, might be important just once in a paddler's career – and then it is surpassingly important). A wheeled portage cart might seem like a silly accoutrement, but every kayaker who's had to lug a 50-pound boat half a mile from parking lot to beach and then make a second trip back for gear will cheerfully buy one the next day. Waterproof weather radios are a good idea for extended trips, and GPS (global positioning system) receivers can definitely help with navigation.

Getting Started

Any normal human needs help with all these complexities, more help than this or any other book can provide. A professionally taught sea-kayaking course, or a series of courses, is an excellent idea. Proper paddling technique saves the shoulder muscles and prevents tendinitis; being able to roll reliably, or crawl back into a capsized boat if you can't, prevents tragedies. Kayak shops in coastal cities offer instruction, as do outdoor sports clubs. For a carefully supervised introduction to the wonders of sea kayaking, private outfitters scattered from Alaska to Florida put together guided expeditions in achingly scenic settings such as Alaska's Glacier Bay and Maine's Deer Isle Archipelago. Still another way to check out the sport is to sign up for one of the several annual sea kayaking symposia on the East or West

Coast, which pack dozens of lectures and classes into a waterside weekend, along with plenty of on-the-water opportunities to try boats and equipment.

Some natural athletes may take to sea kayaking like, well, fish to water, and deviate to high-adrenaline variations on the sport such as kayak surfing, racing, or touring remote regions and extreme climates (paddlers have explored the islands of Antarctica and, incredibly, the Arctic passage north of mainland Canada to Hudson Bay). But for most paddlers, the thrills remain in the almost spiritual quiet and simplicity of the undertaking.

"The slowness of paddling gives you time to see things happening," said Joel Rogers, the noted kayak-based photographer and author of *Watertrail*. "You can see geology happening from a kayak."

Still, as Emerson said, "Nature is no sentimentalist," and the sea is the least forgiving environment on Earth – at least for warm-blooded, poorly insulated creatures who have an odd need to stay upright and bobbing on the water's surface. Our very presence out there constitutes an unnatural act, and the only proper way to go is with plenty of intelligence and preparation – and even more humility.

A windswept campsite (above) is home for a night. Sea kayaks have ample room for outdoor gear.

Weather radios (opposite, top) are essential for marine trip planning.

A rock pillar (opposite, bottom) towers over a sea kayaker at Flowerpot Island, Lake Huron.

Marine charts and tide tables (below) provide information on reefs, currents, and dangerous tidal rips.

Tides and Currents

"We must take the current when it serves, or lose our ventures," wrote Shakespeare in *Julius Caesar*. It's the perfect admonition for kayakers four centuries later. Tidal currents are usually present around coastlines and can be swift and complicated within straits and archipelagos. They may be friends or adversaries, but they can't be ignored.

Smart kayakers plot the currents with a regional current atlas or one of the excellent software programs such as *Tides & Currents for Windows*. If the day's tides happen to be in sync with your schedule, you can ride the current to a destination, enjoy a leisurely lunch and beach nap, then get a free boost on the return current. Paddling across a current affects navigation; you have to adjust course "upstream" to compensate for the sideways push. Paddling against a current is never fun, but you can often hug the shoreline and catch a backcurrent or eddy.

Currents also affect safety. When wind and current move in the same direction, the sea is usually smooth. When one shifts to oppose the other, rolling waves can suddenly become toppling breakers. Tide rips occur when a current accelerates over a shoal or two currents converge; they sometimes look like ridges of whitewater. Mild ones are no cause for alarm, but some rips are so severe they roar like river rapids. An excellent credo: "Never paddle into a current you can hear."

Tides are of interest mainly when you park your boat on a beach. If the tide is coming in, your boat may go out – by itself.

There's that daydream again. It drifts through your mind during those long office meetings like a fresh breeze, fragrant with pine trees and clear water. It tantalizes – even taunts – as you commute to work. Soon you're checking a calendar for open dates and doing a little exploratory web surfing during lunch hour. Before you know it, road atlases, guidebooks, and brochures are spread across the dining-room table.   ◆   Getting there is half the fun, they say, and there's some truth to it. The planning phase of an adventure is a scenic journey of its own, shimmering with the promise of a dream becoming reality. Start yours by thinking about the type of trip that matches your ideal. Will paddling be just one part of a longer trip? How far do you want to travel to get there, and how many days can you devote to it?   ◆   And when? The adventure **Consider your limits, consult** of a lifetime and that dreaded "trip from hell" **with experts, and make** may be just weeks apart when it comes to **your dream trip a reality.** weather. Summer offers the broadest range of benign possibilities, and in many places, such as Glacier Bay, you will certainly want all the warm weather you can get. But don't discount other seasons. Locals near Stillwater Canyon in Utah, for example, prefer autumn when low water exposes sandbars perfect for camping. Fall also brings greater solitude, fewer mosquitoes, and in many places, a blaze of foliage. Winter and spring are the best times to visit Southern destinations like the Okefenokee Swamp, which offers lush respite from the cold but by summer seethes with heat and insects. Late spring and early summer are optimal months for rivers such as the Middle Fork of the Salmon in Idaho or the Youghiogheny in Pennsylvania, where water flow depends on snowmelt and spring rains.

Rafters prepare to enter Mariscal
Canyon on the Rio Grande, Big Bend
National Park, Texas. Wilderness
trips require thorough planning.

Bring the Kids

Kids love water, and paddling is a great way for them to enjoy its delights. Plan paddling adventures that will maximize both their safety and their fun. A canoe can accommodate passengers or extra paddlers of any age, with quick access to snacks and the space for little ones to nap while parents keep paddling. Start with short excursions centered on an interesting destination such as an island, beach, or waterfall. You can try a multiday trip once you and the kids are accustomed to being together in the canoe. Save sea kayaking for children who are old enough to share in the paddling and sit for a long time without fidgeting. With proper instruction, paddlers as young as 10 can learn the fundamentals of whitewater; look around for

A young paddler (left) takes a dip in the Jefferson River, Montana.

A kayaker camps on the Jemez River, New Mexico (below).

programs tailored especially for them. Many whitewater raft companies have minimum age requirements, so check before you bring children along on these types of trips.

There are stacks of books devoted to sharing outdoor adventures with children. These will advise you on everything from how to keep everyone entertained as you paddle to setting up a "kid-safe" camp. Look in the

Resource Directory for some suggested reading.

Where and when you go and if you're bringing kids are crucial planning points. *How* you go – guided, independent, or something in between – is another.

Guides can take you places otherwise inaccessible because of the necessary expertise, logistics, equipment, or permits. They will make your trip safe, fun, and maybe even a gourmet extravaganza; some of these folks are sensational cooks. Your experience will be enriched by tidbits of natural and cultural history, hard-to-find treasures like petroglyphs, and tall tales around the campfire. A guided trip

Sea kayakers head for an Alaskan adventure (left). A high-quality roof rack and secure tie-down system are essentials.

A whitewater trip begins near remote Wolf Creek in Colorado (below).

may include other guests, with the diversity of a larger group and the camaraderie of new friends. Many outfitters even offer specialized trips, with emphasis ranging from fishing to geology or even classical music.

When shopping for a trip, find out how long the outfitter has been in business and what the guide-to-client ratio is. Word of mouth is one of the most reliable ways to find a good outfitter, so don't hesitate to ask for references.

If guided trips are beyond your budget or you want more independence and solitude, consider other styles of paddling. Several options bridge the gap between a guided outing and a completely independent adventure: paddling schools (especially popular for whitewater and sea kayaking), "base camp" vacations, and outfitted but self-guided trips.

Paddling school is a terrific choice if you are serious about learning to canoe or kayak. Many schools provide gear, lodging, and meals and offer options for individual or group instruction. And some *are* a guided trip, focusing on instruction with adventure travel tossed in as a bonus. As

you research different schools, remember that an award-winning paddler doesn't necessarily make a good teacher. While some schools emphasize the achievements of their staff members in competition, you should make sure that the teachers also have an instructor certification from the American Canoe Association. The Resource Directory lists schools throughout North America.

"Base-camping" at a waterside lodge or campground allows flexibility and variety. One day invest in a paddling clinic. The next, explore an island with a guide or on your own. Your home base might be an inn equipped with sea kayaks in the San Juan Islands or a bustling resort in the Boundary Waters complete with rustic cabins and a staff of instructors.

Partial or full outfitting will give you the best of both worlds, providing an economical alternative if you have an independent spirit but can't bring your own equipment or are short on local knowledge. Many outfitters will furnish everything you need, including gear, shuttles, custom

itineraries, and food. Ask about starting your adventure with a half or full day of instruction and/or orientation.

Living by the List

If you are ready to strike out on your own, heed some advice from Davidson and Rugge's classic trip planning guide, *The Complete Wilderness Paddler*. "It all begins with a list," they write. "This list is your philosophy of the good life, and unlike the philosophers, you are going to have to live by it."

What Davidson and Rugge mean is, "write it all down." Make lists of what you hope to achieve and what it will take to succeed at going solo. Greater flexibility, privacy, and a sense of accomplishment would seem to be important goals, while extra judgment, fitness, and skill will be critical once you're in the

Re-evaluate your skills in light of the description. What's the best time of year to go? If your window of opportunity doesn't overlap with the suggested time frame, choose a different trip. Going to the right place at the wrong time could mean finding a river either in flood or too low to paddle, or being stuck on snowy access roads before you even start paddling. How many days should you allow? A reasonable planning distance for lake canoeing or sea kayaking – not factoring in wind or portages – is anywhere from six to 12 miles per day. River mileage can vary from three to 30 miles depending on current and how much rapid running, scouting, or portaging is involved. Do you need a permit? Does the guidebook give phone numbers, addresses, or websites for checking water levels, arranging shuttles, and getting up-to-date infor-

field. Ask yourself whether you have the time and inclination to spend hours or days researching and arranging logistics and gear. Do you look forward to discovery and experience more than you dread possible logistics snafus? The list is especially important when it comes to the details of gear and food. Once you're on the water, you won't be able to drop in at the corner store to pick up a forgotten item.

Make sure you choose a destination and itinerary appropriate for your skills. It's crucial to be conservative when you're on your own. Getting in over your head escalates risk dramatically and can stress morale to the breaking point. Pad your schedule with an extra day so

you won't feel pushed to get back if the winds or weather turn sour, especially on sea-kayaking trips. And before you go, brush up on your technique with a short shake-down trip and perhaps some instruction to help you develop a realistic idea of your technical ability and endurance.

Next, find a detailed guidebook for your destination and read it carefully.

Kayak cuisine (above) needn't be boring. A camp cook prepares seafood sauté in Washington's San Juan Islands.

Clear skies (right) are a rare treat on Prince William Sound, Alaska.

Paddling Clubs

You're new to paddling or perhaps an experienced paddler in a new town, a little short on partners and local knowledge. Join a club and instantly a whole world of trips, instruction, and companions is yours.

Paddling clubs are priceless resources. Different clubs specialize in every type of paddling and generally welcome members at all levels of skill. Hard-core paddlers depend on them for clinics, trips, updated information, and a united voice on important issues. For the occasional paddler, clubs are a steadfast presence, always there when you want to dust off the canoe and enjoy a safe, interesting trip without having to dredge up partners. Those inclined can volunteer to do everything from designing a web page to spearheading conservation actions or baking cookies. And the friendships formed last long after your gear is put away. To find a club near you, check the Resource Directory at the back of this book.

Club members (above) scout a rapid on the Cossatot River in Arkansas. Paddling clubs are a great source of advice and camaraderie.

Packing for a wilderness trip (below) is a balancing act; try to keep it light without skimping on essentials.

mation? If so, use them.

As you assemble your gear, do some backyard test runs on equipment like tents and camp stoves, lest you find yourself calling your canoe paddles into service to substitute for forgotten tent poles or struggling with an unfamiliar stove when you're famished and hampered by wind or darkness. Start with equipment lists provided in guidebooks, and remember that in the wilderness you have to bring everything you need. The difference between an unpleasant – or even unsafe – experience and what Davidson and Rugge call "the good life" can come down to a small item or two: good first-aid and repair kits, bug repellent, or enough chocolate bars.

Secrets of Success

Whatever type of paddling adventure you plan, these tried and true tips will help make it live up to your dreams.

Never underestimate the importance of food: bring enough and make it varied, nutritious, and simple to prepare. You'll need more than you think, especially snacks.

When paddling tandem in a canoe or kayak, try not to play "captain" from the stern. Trading positions and paddling partners once in a while will help keep team spirit and confidence on an even keel.

Little extras can go a long way. Treat yourself to one or two lightweight luxury items, like a flannel pillowcase or a little crème de menthe for your evening hot chocolate.

Don't be too ambitious. Plan to mix long days of paddling with relaxing ones. Layovers are essential on longer trips. They add variety to the experience and give you an opportunity to rest.

Finally, keep in mind the advice of adventure travel gurus: "There's no such thing as the wrong weather, only the wrong clothing." In other words, your trip can be rewarding no matter what you encounter, as long as you are mentally and physically prepared. By definition, "adventure" means a few surprises – some pleasant and some challenging. And remember that the challenging ones often make the best stories when you get home.

Paddling Destinations

*Guide a raft through foaming rapids, paddle
a kayak into hidden sea caves, glide in a
canoe across waterways rich with wildlife.
Paddle in hand, you can chart a course
through breathtaking American landscapes.*

Mount Desert Island
Maine

rom a distance, Maine's Mount Desert Island appears stern and forbidding, its grayish granite cliffs capped with somber spruce and lashed by pounding surf. But angle your sea kayak shoreward and ease into one of the quiet coves that ring the island. Where the sound of the surf fades into distant thunder, you'll find a delightful world of peace and beauty. The delicate pink flowers of the rugosa rose bloom improbably amid beach cobbles. Mountain ash berries add a touch of fire-engine red to the tangled forest. Amber starfish undulate across dark rock beneath the crystalline waters. Even the chartreuse lobster buoys tumbled up on shore seem part of a welcoming, pleasantly mannered landscape. ◆ About a five hours' drive northeast of Boston, this largest of Maine's islands is 12 miles wide by 15 miles long and is con-nected to the mainland by a causeway.

Granite headlands, peaceful coves, and the only fjord in the eastern United States lure sea kayakers to Maine's largest island.

As far back as 6,000 years ago, the island was a seasonal home for migratory Indians; the occasional shell middens along the shores attest to their presence. Among the first Europeans to probe the rocky coast was French explorer Samuel de Champlain, who wrote in 1604: "The mountain summits are all bare and rocky. I name it Isles des Monts Desert." The name (and the French pronunciation) stuck, and to this day it's called Mount *de-SERT*. Noted landscape painter Thomas Cole found his way to the island in the 1840s, and exhibits of his work caught the eye of the wealthy: Rockefellers, Fords, Vanderbilts, and Pulitzers soon arrived to "rusticate" in elaborate manses of shingle and stone along the ocean's edge. A number of their

The Otter Cliffs are typical of the dramatic scenery that attracts sea kayakers to Acadia National Park.

Preceding pages: A dory passes through a placid section of the Grand Canyon of the Colorado River.

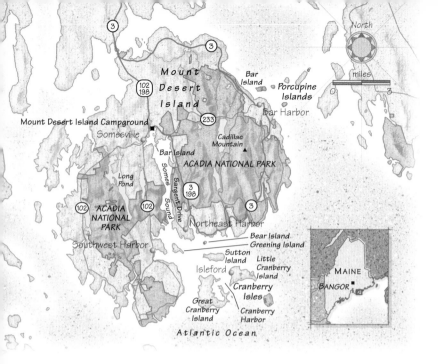

mid-50s and making an offshore capsize even in midsummer a race with hypothermia.

First-timers would do well to go out with an experienced paddler. Several kayak outfitters are based along Cottage Street in **Bar Harbor**, the island's commercial center. Trips typically run half a day, although full-day and multiday tours are also available. These guided expeditions depart from locations around the island, with wind and weather dictating the put-in spots. When booking, be sure to ask how many kayakers will be on your trip, and look for an outfitter that limits participants to a dozen or so. A convoy of six two-person kayaks is far more manageable and relaxed than the unwieldy flotillas favored by some companies.

Bar Harbor is also a good starting point for intermediate-level paddlers with their own boats. A gravel-and-mud spit extends out to **Bar Island** at mid- to low tide and serves as a popular put-in. Start by paddling southeastward along the shore. You'll track past downtown Bar Harbor and a handful of the island's grand mansions, several of which have been converted to inns.

Slanting offshore will bring you to the **Porcupine Islands**, a cluster of four islets that looks remarkably like a family of porkies ambling along. Keep an eye out for bald eagles, harbor seals, porpoises, and the occasional whale. From this group

heirs still enjoy the delightful summers.

Today, nearly half the island is encompassed by **Acadia National Park**, one of the most popular in the national park system. With more than two million visitors annually, the park can be crowded during the peak summer season. It is especially famed for its miles of elegant carriage roads, and it sometimes seems as if every other visitor travels by mountain bike, an ideal mode of transportation for exploring the stone-edged lanes through the lush forests of the interior. Sea kayaks are still relatively rare but are a perfect way to avoid the hordes and admire island panoramas as our forefathers did: from the ocean looking inland.

Seductive Sea

On a placid July day, with azure skies and warm zephyrs, the ocean seems about as threatening as a millpond. Yet beware. Novice paddlers must resist being seduced offshore, since conditions can change rapidly. Powerful winds often kick up with little warning, turning a leisurely half-hour paddle out to an island into a grueling and hazardous three-hour ordeal on the return. Disorienting fogs can creep in with disconcerting suddenness, putting one's navigational skills to the test. And the waters are icy, peaking only in the

A sea kayaker (right) takes advantage of a clear day. The area is notorious for fog, which can disorient even an experienced paddler.

The Beehive (below) rises behind Sand Beach. Sandy beaches are unusual on the rocky Maine coast.

of islands, the views back toward the gentle mountains on the main island are superb. The most commanding hill – 1,530-foot **Cadillac Mountain** – happens to be the highest point on the Atlantic Coast north of Rio de Janeiro.

Splendid Solitude

A quick glance at a map of the island will show that it's nearly cleaved in half by a narrow inlet. That's **Somes Sound**, the only true fjord – which is to say, a valley carved by a glacier and later filled by rising ocean water – on the East Coast of the United States. There's inviting and relatively protected paddling here; the hills gradually rise about 1,000 feet on either side, and you're never too far from shore if fog rolls in.

Put in along scenic **Sargent Drive**, north of **Northeast Harbor**, and paddle northward to the head of the sound. You'll see more bald eagles on yet another **Bar Island**, along with a variety of other birds: ospreys, cormorants, and great blue herons. If you're properly equipped, **Mount Desert Island Campground** – one of the best private campgrounds on the island – is at the tip of the sound and offers an excellent base for easy excursions.

The small ponds and lakes carved out by glaciers are worth visiting on days when wind or fog keeps you off the ocean. The most alluring is **Long Pond**, southwest of **Somesville**, where much of the western shoreline remains as wild as it was a century

ago. But when one of those perfect paddling days beckons – flat waters lapping languidly at the rocks, no forecast for fog or winds – you'll want to head south in your sea kayak from either **Northeast** or **Southwest Harbors**. A compact archipelago of handsome islands lies offshore, and you'll discover solitude here like few other places in the region. Those less sure of their paddling skills should restrict their explorations to the main shore and the inner islands – **Bear** and **Greening**. Both are privately owned and paddlers aren't allowed to come ashore, but a half-day excursion around them will bring you past rocky headlands where you can scan for eagles, ospreys, and loons, and a splendid lighthouse that has been serving mariners since 1838.

Farther out lie the **Cranberry Isles**, home to plucky settlers since the 18th century. You'll first paddle past **Sutton Island**, then come to **Little** and **Great Cranberry Islands**. Circumnavigating the islands borders on the spectacular, although it can be tricky owing to currents and winds; be prepared for a long and tiring day of paddling.

Between the two islands is **Cranberry Harbor**, which is reasonably well protected from the elements and uncommonly scenic. You can land at the village of **Isleford** on Little Cranberry, have a bite to eat at the dockside restaurant, stretch your legs strolling the island, and visit a history museum run by the National Park Service in a stout brick building near the waterfront.

Paddling back toward Northeast Harbor, take time to admire the turn-of-the-century homes that line the cliffs and points. These shingled, lichen-encrusted mansions seem to have grown from the very ledges and stands of spruce as if they were part of the natural scheme of things. And therein, of course, lies much of the island's charm.

Island Hopping

A sea kayak isn't really a small boat. It's a large backpack you can paddle. Day excursions are a treat all along the Maine coast, but for real adventure you may want to set out on a multiday camping trip. And for that, you'll want to follow a trail.

The **Maine Island Trail** is one of the nation's first and best water trails. It's actually a connect-the-dots adventure, weaving up the coast for 325 miles from **Portland** to **Machias**. Along the way are some 80 islands – large and small, private and public – most of which are open to overnight camping. With enough food, gear, and a modicum of experience, it's possible to paddle the whole length in three weeks or so.

The nonprofit Maine Island Trail Association was founded in 1988 to oversee the trail. Association members help monitor and maintain the islands and in return are granted access from island owners. Because of the trail's growing popularity, some islands now require advance reservations. An annual handbook outlines low-impact camping techniques and includes an up-to-date directory of private islands open to association members. Annual dues are $40. For more information, write the association at P.O. Box C, Rockland, ME 04841, or call 207-596-6456.

A quiet cove (above) is a good place for launching and landing. Beach kayaks above the high-water mark, lest they depart with the tide.

Daybreak illuminates a campsite on the Maine Island Trail (below). The route is renowned for nesting birds and marine mammals.

Coastal waters (right) are clear but cold, rarely exceeding 55°F.

DETAILS

When to Go

Sea kayaking is best from summer through early fall. Summer daytime temperatures vary widely, from 45° to 90°F, and nights can be in the 40s or below. Autumn highs are in the low 70s; nights dip below freezing. Anticipate rain, fog, and strong winds. Black flies may aggravate visitors in spring and early summer. Winter is prohibitively cold, with daytime temperatures in the mid-30s and nights often below zero. Beware of tidal exchanges from nine to 14 feet.

How to Get There

Mount Desert Island is about 45 miles west of Bangor International Airport. Colgan Airlines serves a small airport in Trenton, about 20 minutes from Bar Harbor. Vermont Transit, 207-288-3366, operates bus service between Bangor and Bar Harbor in summer. Car rentals are available at the airport. There is no public transportation within Acadia National Park.

Permits

A $10 permit, available at entrance stations, is required for access to Acadia National Park.

INFORMATION

Acadia National Park

P.O. Box 177, Bar Harbor, ME 04609; tel: 207-288-3338.

Bar Harbor Chamber of Commerce

Bar Harbor, ME 04609; tel: 800-288-5103 or 207-288-5103.

Maine Island Trail Association

P.O. Box C, Rockland, ME 04841; tel: 207-596-6456.

Southwest Harbor–Tremont Chamber of Commerce

P.O. Box 1143, Southwest Harbor, ME 04679; tel: 800-423-9264 or 207-244-9264.

CAMPING

Backcountry camping is not permitted in Acadia National Park. The park has two automobile-accessed campgrounds, Blackwoods and Seawall. Blackwoods is on the busy eastern side of Mount Desert Island. Open year-round, the campground has 306 sites, with separate RV and tent areas. Reservations are accepted from June 15 to September 15; call 800-365-2267, or write to NPRS, P.O. Box 1600, Cumberland, MD 21502. Seawall, located on the quiet southeast side of Mount Desert Island, has 200 wooded sites, available on a first-come, first-served basis from late May to September. Isle au Haut has five lean-to shelters, which may be reserved after April by calling 207-288-3338; a permit is required for camping on the isle.

LODGING

PRICE GUIDE – double occupancy

$ = up to $49 $$ = $50–$99

$$$ = $100–$149 $$$$ = $150+

Black Friar Inn

10 Summer Street, Bar Harbor, ME 04609; tel: 207-288-5091.

This 1910 house has wood-paneled common areas and seven guest rooms with private baths and antique furnishings. Some rooms have fireplaces. A full breakfast and afternoon tea are included. The inn conducts several "Sea Kayak Development Weekends," which include

instruction and gear, a guided day trip, and two-night stays. $$–$$$

Harbor View Motel and Cottages

P.O. Box 701, Southwest Harbor, ME 04679; tel: 800-538-6463 or 207-244-5031.

The motel has 28 units, most with decks overlooking the harbor. Three of the units have a bedroom, living area, and full kitchen. Seven one- and two-bedroom cottages, rented on a weekly basis, have full kitchens. $–$$$

Inn at Bay Ledge

1385 Sand Point Road, Bar Harbor, ME 04609; tel: 207-288-4204.

Perched above a private beach on Frenchman Bay, the venerable cottage offers 10 rooms with four-poster beds, quilts, and antiques. Three additional cottages offer accommodations amid a grove of pine trees. Amenities include a sauna, swimming pool, and fireplaces. $$–$$$$

Inn at Canoe Point

Eden Street, Route 3, P.O. Box 216, Bar Harbor, ME 04609; tel: 207-288-9511.

The inn, built in 1889, occupies two secluded acres on a cove on Frenchman Bay, a few minutes from Bar Harbor. A common room with a granite fireplace overlooks the sea. Most of the inn's five guest rooms have ocean views; all rooms are furnished with antiques. Breakfast and afternoon tea are included. $$–$$$$

Mira Monte Inn

69 Mount Desert Street, Bar Harbor, ME 04609; tel: 800-553-5109 or 207-288-4263.

One of the original Bar Harbor summer cottages, this elegant 1860s inn is surrounded by formal gardens. Mira Monte's 16 guest rooms have private baths, period furnishings, and air conditioning. Thirteen of the rooms are housed in the main building; three multiroom suites are in a separate structure. Rates include a full buffet breakfast and evening reception. Open in summer only. $$$–$$$$

TOURS AND OUTFITTERS

Acadia Outfitters

106 Cottage Street, Bar Harbor, ME 04609; tel: 207-288-8118.

Acadia Outfitters offers kayak rentals and half- to full-day guided tours.

Coastal Kayaking Tours

48 Cottage Street, Bar Harbor, ME 04609; tel: 800-526-8615 or 207-288-9605.

Adventures include sunset tours of the park, inn-to-inn paddling, and scenic island camping. Registered guides also lead private and group tours.

H2Outfitters

P.O. Box 72, Orr's Island, ME 04066; tel: 207-833-5257.

This paddling school and guide service offers instruction and guided overnight trips to Penobscot Bay and other areas.

Maine Island Kayak Company

70 Luther Street, Peaks Island, ME 04108; tel: 800-796-2373 or 207-766-2372.

The company specializes in guided adventure and natural-history trips along the New England coast. Sea-kayaking instruction programs are available, as are navigation and rescue clinics.

Excursions

Penobscot Bay

Maine Island Trail Association, P.O. Box C, Rockland, ME 04841; tel: 207-596-6456.

Considered one of the nation's premier sea-kayaking destinations, Penobscot Bay looks like a big dent in the southern Maine coast. The area teems with picturesque fishing villages, pink granite beaches, and spruce-covered islands. Lobster boats, seals, and whales pass through the bay's mist. Superb opportunities are available for inn-to-inn paddling, complete with lobster dinners and perhaps a cozy room in an island lighthouse.

Saco River

Saco Bound Outfitters, P.O. Box 119, Center Conway, NH 03813; tel: 1-800-677-7238.

On its eastward run from the White Mountains of New Hampshire to the coast of Maine, the Saco River offers paddlers a little bit of everything. The 40-mile section from Center Conway, New Hampshire, to Hiram, Maine, is the most popular, renowned for its clean water, smooth paddling, views of the White Mountains, and pristine sand beaches. The three-day trip is perfect for exploration by canoe or touring kayak.

St. John River

North Maine Woods, P.O. Box 425, Ashland, ME 04732; tel: 207-435-6213.

The tea-colored St. John River flows north through remote Maine woods, joining the Allagash River along the Canadian border. There are no lakes or dams on this spectacular 85-mile stretch of free-flowing river, which passes the remains of once-rowdy logging camps and tumbles over challenging Class II and III drops. Moose, deer, and many types of wildfowl are commonly seen along the route. A five-day trip starts at Baker Lake, reached by a three-hour drive on private dirt roads or by floatplane from Ashland.

Adirondack Park
New York

CHAPTER **7**

The water's stillness is interrupted only by the rhythm of your stroke as you slowly paddle to a lone campsite on a pine-covered island. At either side, verdant mountains slope to the water's edge. White-throated sparrows whistle from balsam thickets, loons yodel in the distance, and, at dusk, coyotes and owls join the chorus. Many regions in the country claim to be wild, but here in New York State's **Adirondack Park**, you can truly find a restorative solitude that is nowadays something to cherish – all the more so because the park is situated in the most heavily urbanized corner of the United States. ◆ Size is one great benefit. Adirondack is immense, the largest park of any kind in the lower 48 states, greater in extent than Yellowstone, Yosemite, Grand Canyon, and Olympic National Parks combined. Its six million acres hold more than 2,800 ponds **A sprawling mountain** and lakes, 1,500 miles of rivers, and 30,000 miles of **wilderness in upstate** brooks and streams, including the source of **New York is laced with** the Hudson River and tributaries of the St. Lawrence. **thousands of ponds,** Moreover, 90 percent of all plants and animals that exist **lakes, and streams.** north of the Mason-Dixon line and east of the Mississippi River can be found somewhere in the Adirondacks. So for anybody who wants to do some exploring, there are plenty of places to go and things to see. ◆ Another major factor is the park's relative obscurity. Northeasterners are in on its secret, but tourists from the Midwest and West are more likely to focus on the big cities. The millions of people who swamp Yellowstone and Yosemite every summer just don't go to the Adirondacks. Besides, getting around in the park can be difficult. Few major roads have been built outside the well-known towns of **Lake Placid** and **Saranac Lake**. Thus, to savor the

Follensby Pond is one link in a "pond-hopping" loop through the Adirondacks' St. Regis Wilderness Canoe Area.

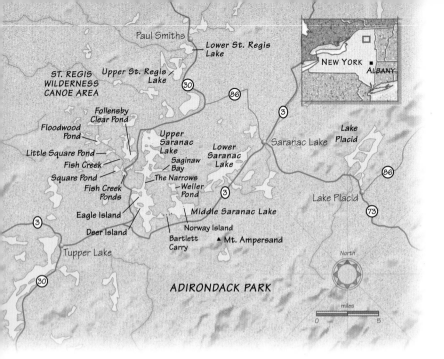

endless combination of canoeing options. So pack lightly, get ready to throw your canoe onto your shoulders, and venture to these pristine waters for a journey lasting anywhere from one day to three weeks.

One of the finest jaunts is a four-day, figure-eight loop in the Adirondacks' **St. Regis Wilderness Canoe Area** that includes eight ponds and the **Upper** and **Middle Saranac Lakes**. In most cases, navigable creeks connect the usually placid ponds. However, the 2,500-foot mountains surrounding the Saranacs often create a wind-tunnel effect that can be challenging to paddle against. Nevertheless, this route is a good choice for the novice to intermediate paddler.

From the put-in at the northernmost point of **Floodwood Pond**, gradually make your way southeast to **Fish Creek**, where

wilderness, you either hit more than 2,000 miles of hiking trails or embark on canoe trips that traverse up to 120 continuous miles of waterways.

Portages and Wind Tunnels

Starting from the southwest corner of the park, at **Old Forge**, paddlers can follow a sinuous blue line all the way north to the **Saranac Lakes**. However, the word *portage* (or carry, as New Yorkers say) had better be in your vocabulary. The countless rivers, lakes, and ponds are connected by short trails, resulting in a seemingly

Autumn brings brilliant colors (right) and thinner crowds, but expect frosty mornings and lower river flows.

Saranac Lake (opposite), seen here from Mount Pisgah, has dozens of island campsites.

you'll immediately notice the presence of the ubiquitous beaver. If you don't see this furry fellow swimming on his back with large twigs sticking out of his mouth, then you will certainly recognize the fruits of his labor. Two stacks of wood will inevitably stand side by side, connected by a shallow network of branches. If you're fortunate, a flowing stream may pass through the mesh of branches. If not, it's up to you to bypass the dams.

Fish Creek continues through **Little Square Pond** and **Square Pond**, finally emptying into **Fish Creek Pond**. Here, you'll canoe through an inlet lined with private houses and docks into Upper Saranac Lake. Gliding easily with the current, you'll cross the widest part of Upper Saranac, arriving at state-owned **Saginaw Bay**, a secluded paradise of towering spruces, pines, and birches.

Climbing Mount Ampersand

This is the setting for your first and longest portage, a grueling mile-and-a-half carry through the mosquitoes to majestic **Weller Pond**. A tiny tributary connects the southeastern point of Weller Pond with Middle Saranac Lake, your first night's stop. The lone camping facility on **Norway Island**

The Adirondack Tradition

The **Adirondack Museum** is one of the best regional museums in the East. Enter the grounds on the hillside overlooking Blue Mountain Lake and you can still see part of a log hotel built here in 1876. In the Boats Building, birch-bark canoes and beamier guideboats dating back to the 1840s are on display alongside numerous other small craft. The guideboats are indigenous to the Adirondacks. Light, fast, and maneuverable, with oars rather than paddles, they were designed for an environment of small ponds and narrow, winding creeks.

One of the highlights of the museum's antique boat display is J. Henry Rushton's Nessmuk model Wee Lassie canoe. Rushton was the foremost builder of lightweight canoes and guideboats in the 1880s. His rugged, finely crafted products saw service on expeditions to the headwaters of the Mississippi as well as in such faraway lands as France, Egypt, the Philippines, and Australia. In the Adirondacks, his 20-pound Nessmuk canoes became popular when writer George Washington Sears wrote articles about his canoeing adventures in *Forest and Stream*. Rushton's lightweight designs, which builders still copy, cost approximately $30 per boat at the time – and perhaps 100 times that today as collectibles.

Dams and Lodges

Paddlers won't get far in the Adirondacks without encountering signs of beavers. Though the animals are rarely seen during the day, their handiwork is unmistakable. Beavers are master architects, building dams of branches and mud that turn free-flowing streams into private ponds. They do this to maintain sufficient depth for their lodges, which they enter from below the surface. They also use the ponds to store food, sticking branches into the mud at the bottom and eating the bark in winter when the surface freezes over.

The largest rodents in North America, beavers are a marvel of natural selection. Their massive incisors, which can fell small trees in only a few minutes, grow as they are worn away and are kept sharp by constant gnawing; scent glands in their rear ends produce musk oil which waterproofs the fur and is used to mark territory and attract mates (indeed, the rather unpleasant odor of beaver musk indicates that a lodge is active); webbed hind feet aid in swimming; and enlarged lung capacity enables the animals to stay submerged for up to 15 minutes. Contrary to popular belief, their broad, scaly tails aren't used to scoop up mud and slap it on the lodges but serve as rudders when swimming or as props when standing on hind legs. Smacking the tail against the water is a warning to others of potential danger.

It's yet another adaptation, the dense coat, that nearly proved the beaver's undoing. Beaver-felt hats were all the rage in Europe for much of the 18th and 19th centuries, and trappers had nearly exterminated the creatures by the late 1800s. Beavers have made a strong recovery since then, but had styles not changed, their numbers wouldn't be as robust as they are today.

Beavers (above) can be elusive. You're more likely to hear a tail slap than actually see one, but their handiwork is obvious.

The Oswegatchie River (right) in the western Adirondacks is known for loons and virgin white pines.

A canoeist pulls his boat up the Raquette River (below). Traveling upstream is sometimes necessary during a loop trip.

offers many soft, flat spots to pitch your tent for one or two nights. The length of your stay depends on whether you decide to climb 2,800-foot **Mount Ampersand** the following day or continue on the canoe loop. With such a wealth of mountains, one of the great advantages of the Adirondacks is that you can give your arms a break and put your legs to work.

To climb Ampersand, paddle five minutes to a small beach at the southeastern point of the lake, and take the three-mile trail behind the picnic area. The gradual ascent grows steeper in the last quarter of the climb as you hike through copses of spruces, firs, sugar maples, and birches. Work your way around the large boulders to the peak and you'll get a sense of the vast wilderness that defines the region. The round-trip climb will take approximately four hours.

This leaves your afternoon open to relax on Norway Island or take a highly recommended side-trip on the **Saranac River** to the locks. The river winds past a huge marsh

shadowed by Mount Ampersand; you'll find herons and egrets in the marsh, and with luck you may spot white-tailed deer, moose, even black bears along the route.

The Philosopher's Camp

Day three is usually the most strenuous. You paddle to the western point of Middle Saranac Lake and through the lower half of Upper Saranac Lake against a strong easterly current. **Bartlett Carry**, a portage of about half a mile, connects the lakes. The wind tends to pick up between **Deer** and **Eagle Islands** as you traverse Upper Saranac; even a short break will cost you precious distance. Three or four hours from Norway Island, you'll reach a region called the **Narrows** where the breeze subsides and the water is tranquil for the remainder of the trip. Make your way back to Fish Creek Pond and proceed north to **Follensby Pond** where a number of island campsites are available. Ralph Waldo Emerson spent the month of August 1858 at Follensby with fellow poet James Russell Lowell and famed naturalist Louis Agassiz. Emerson later dubbed this idyllic

setting "The Philosopher's Camp." After a restful night, you'll understand why he found it so hard to leave.

The northern half of the pond loop awaits you on the final day. It's the perfect antidote to the winds and currents encountered the previous day: five placid ponds and five relatively short portages ending back at Floodwood Pond. Before you leave, take a few moments to savor the serenity. As Emerson's friend, Henry David Thoreau, said of another pond, "the smooth water, full of light and reflections, becomes a lower heaven itself, so much the more important."

Naptime (below) is easy in a canoe. Short portages help make the St. Regis area ideal for family trips.

TRAVEL TIPS

DETAILS

When to Go

The weather in the Adirondacks is best in summer, but be prepared for black flies, mosquitoes, and some company. Daytime temperatures from June through August range from 60° to 90°F. Nights are in the low 40s or 50s. Locals also recommend the last week of September and first week of October, when autumn foliage is at its peak and the buzz of insects has receded. Temperatures drop below freezing beginning in mid-October. Cold weather can keep waterways frozen from November through April.

How to Get There

The town of Paul Smiths is a three- to four-hour drive north of Albany, New York, and about a half-hour north of Lake Placid. The Saranac Lake–Adirondack Airport is just 10 miles from Floodwood Pond and is served by USAir (800-428-4322).

Permits

Advance permits are required only for groups of 10 or more, or any group camping in the same location for four or more nights. Maximum group size in the St. Regis Canoe Area is 12. Permits can be obtained from the appropriate State Forest Ranger for the area: for St. Regis, contact Joseph Rupp, RR1, Box 210, Vermontville, NY; tel: 518-891-0255.

INFORMATION

Adirondack Mountain Club Information Center

Adirondack Loj Road, P.O. Box 67, Lake Placid, NY 12946; tel: 518-523-3441.

Adirondack Regional Tourism Council

P.O. Box 2149, Plattsburgh, NY 12901; tel: 518-846-8016; or P.O. Box 51, West Chazy, NY 12992; tel: 800-487-6867.

The council will provide the *Adirondack Waterways* booklet, a guide to paddling in the area.

Franklin County Tourism

63 West Main Street, Malone, NY 12953; tel: 518-483-2900 or 800-709-4895.

Public Lands Information Services

New York State Department of Environmental Conservation, P.O. Box 296, Route 86, Ray Brook, NY 12977; tel: 518-897-1200.

CAMPING

Fish Creek Pond State Campground

Star Route, Box 75, Saranac Lake, NY 12983; tel: 518-891-4560 or 800-456-2267 (reservations).

This large, developed campground has showers, bike trails, interpretive programs, and canoe rentals on several ponds. Many sites are set on the shore of Fish Creek Pond, nearby Square Pond, or along streams.

Rollins Pond State Campground

Star Route, Box 75, Saranac Lake, NY 12983; tel: 518-891-3239 or 800-456-2267 (reservations).

This 257-site campground offers showers, a boat ramp, interpretive programs, and canoe rentals for Rollins Pond.

Saranac Lake Islands State Campground

Ampersand Bay Road, Box 24, Saranac Lake, NY 12983; tel: 518-891-3170 or 800-456-2267 (reservations).

Several islands in Saranac Lake have boat-in camping with dozens of sites. Campsites are primitive, with pit toilets and no potable water. Reservations are accepted on a site-by-site basis.

LODGING

Adirondack Loj

P.O. Box 867, Lake Placid, NY 12946; tel: 518-523-3441.

The Adirondack Mountain Club owns this classic, rustic 1920s lodge situated a few miles outside of Lake Placid on scenic Heart Lake in the High Peaks region. The lodge features a huge stone fireplace and simple bunk-style accommodations in private rooms or dorms. It also operates a campground. Breakfast is included; lunch and dinner, served family style, are also available. $–$$

Hotel Saranac

101 Main Street, Saranac Lake, NY 12983; tel: 518-891-2200 or 800-937-0211.

For that one-night stop before or after a St. Regis trip, this historic 92-room hotel offers in-town convenience and professional service, thanks in part to hospitality-management students from nearby Paul Smith's College. It features a wood-beamed lobby with a grand piano, a full dining room, and a pleasant lounge. $$

Lodge at Lake Clear

Box 46, Lake Clear, NY 12945; tel: 518-891-1489.

This popular bed-and-breakfast and restaurant is famous for its German cuisine and hospitality. It boasts 20 woodsy lakeside acres. Guests are welcome to use the lodge's rowboats and canoes. The lodge has four rooms with private baths. There are also fully equipped chalets with fireplaces, and a one-bedroom summer chalet. $$–$$$

Sunday Pond Bed-and-Breakfast

Star Route 150, Saranac Lake, NY 12983; tel: 518-891-1531.

You can paddle right into the St.

Regis Canoe Area from this family-owned inn. There are four rooms, two with private baths. $$

TOURS AND OUTFITTERS

Adirondack Lakes and Trails Outfitters

168 Lake Flower Avenue, Saranac Lake, NY 12983; tel: 518-891-7450 or 800-491-0414.

Services include half- to two-day instruction, including a three-hour "Quickstart Your Canoeing" course. Outfitting and guided trips are available, including a fall foliage trip in the St. Regis area.

McDonnell's Adirondack Challenge

Route 30, Rural Route 1, Box 262, Lake Clear, NY 12945; tel: 518-891-1176.

Shuttle services, canoe rentals, and a variety of guided trips are provided by this outfitter near the St. Regis Canoe Area. The owners also offer guide service for clients with physical challenges.

St. Regis Canoe Outfitters

Floodwood Road at Long Pond Portage, P.O. Box 318, Lake Clear, NY 12945; tel: 518-891-1838.

Just 100 yards from Floodwood Pond, this is the most convenient canoe outfitter in the St. Regis area. The owners provide full or partial outfitting, instruction, route suggestions and maps, shuttles, and guide service.

Excursions

Delaware River

Delaware National Scenic River, c/o Delaware Water Gap National Recreation Area, Bushkill, PA 18324; tel: 717-588-2451.

The Delaware flows through hardwood forests along the Pennsylvania, New York, and New Jersey borders. Nearly a hundred miles of this free-flowing river are navigable by canoe, with trips ranging from a few hours to a week and novice to intermediate in difficulty. A tapestry of public and private lands along the river provides options for camping and visiting an occasional village or bed-and-breakfast.

Pine Barrens

Wharton State Forest, 4110 Nesco Road, Hammonton, NJ 08037; tel: 609-561-0024.

One of the East's biggest aquifers lies beneath this 2,000-square-mile won-derland of quiet rivers, forests, and bogs in South Jersey. Sandy soil protected the Pine Barrens from early agricultural development, and state

protection assures that the area will remain largely free of suburban sprawl. Deer, foxes, badgers, and a variety of waterfowl are common. The sense of peace and isolation is so encompassing that it can be hard to believe the area is so close to millions of people. Canoeists usually plan trips of one to three days.

Raquette River and Long Lake

Adirondack Park, New York Department of Environmental Conservation, Region 5 Headquarters, Route 8, Box 296, Ray Brook, NY 12977; tel: 518-897-1200.

A short drive south of the St. Regis area, another Adirondack gem awaits canoeists. Nestled in the shadow of the Adirondacks' highest peaks, 14-mile-long Long Lake features 20 scenic waterside shelters. The lake can be combined with the gentle Raquette River to make a multiday run of 30 miles to Tupper Lake (including a 1.3-mile portage around Raquette Falls) or 45 miles to Upper Saranac Lake.

Youghiogheny River

Pennsylvania

CHAPTER 8

f there were a Hall of Fame for whitewater rivers, Pennsylvania's **Youghiogheny** (Yock-a-GEN-ee) would be on just about everybody's list. Rich in history – George Washington negotiated some of the gentler sections while seeking a western water route – the river found its modern incarnation in the 1950s when the first rafters and canoeists pioneered their way through a profusion of obstacles. ◆ This whitewater showcase lies at the tiny mountain hamlet of **Ohiopyle**, a onetime mining town reborn as a recreational paradise 90 minutes from Pittsburgh and four hours from Washington, D.C. Nine miles of rock-studded, champagne-foaming rapids twist through a geologically corrugated landscape. The classic day-trip embarks at the base of 18-foot-high **Ohiopyle Falls**, churns through a dozen major rapids, calms in deep pools, and transports paddlers on a rare tour of the Appalachians at their finest. ◆ If you're game but have never rafted before, a guided trip on the "Yock"

Rafters, canoeists, and kayakers get a white-knuckle ride on a feisty Appalachian River.

can be ideal, offering the whitewater rush with a time-tested safety net. Just make a reservation with one of the outfitters in Ohiopyle. The clients, usually four to a 12-foot raft, are responsible for the paddling while good-humored guides carry lunch and coach them through the drops. Other guides dart about in kayaks and serve as "safety boaters," skillfully pulling in paddlers who occasionally get catapulted from their craft. For people with experience, rental rafts are available. Then you pick your own way through the stony slaloms and tend to your own rescues.

A canoeist plows through a hole in Entrance Rapid on the Youghiogheny, where generations of Mid-Atlantic paddlers have cut their teeth.

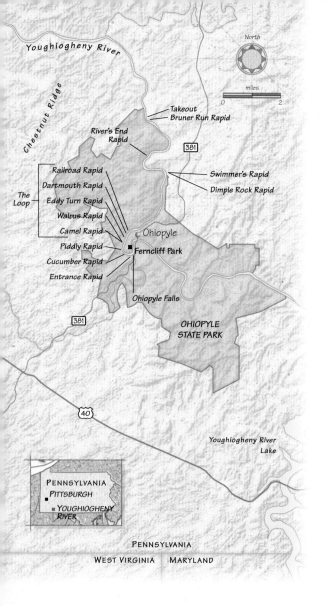

Youghiogheny River

Chestnut Ridge

North

miles
0   2

Takeout
Bruner Run Rapid

River's End
Rapid

381

Railroad Rapid
Dartmouth Rapid
Eddy Turn Rapid
Walrus Rapid
Camel Rapid
Piddly Rapid
Cucumber Rapid
Entrance Rapid

The
Loop

Swimmer's Rapid
Dimple Rock Rapid

Ohiopyle
Ferncliff Park

Ohiopyle Falls

381

OHIOPYLE
STATE PARK

Youghiogheny River
Lake

40

PENNSYLVANIA
PITTSBURGH

YOUGHIOGHENY
RIVER

PENNSYLVANIA

WEST VIRGINIA   MARYLAND

A Busy River

For the intermediate or advanced kayaker and advanced canoeist, the Youghiogheny is supreme. The number and intricacy of Class II, III, and occasionally IV rapids invite hours and hours of whitewater play. There may be no better place in America to hone swift-water skills and enjoy the demands of technical rapids replete with multiple channels, surfing holes, finely scribed eddy lines, and exquisite paths of rock-dodging turbulence.

One warning beyond the usual precautions about foot entrapment and undercut rocks: this is a busy river. More than 100,000 people annually float the most popular reach below Ohiopyle. The daily crowd on a Saturday or Sunday in summer can top 2,000. State park personnel ration out the bathing-suited boaters at 15-minute intervals throughout the summer months. Intensive management, efficiently executed, is all that saves the Youghiogheny from becoming impossibly congested.

More Rocks Than Water

At Ohiopyle, simply swimming in the Jacuzzi-like pour-overs and strolling for a close-up view of the falls is a treat. But the real adventure begins just below the falls. **Entrance Rapid** starts you out with a bang, an explosive drop that right away tells you what's in store.

At the top of Entrance, wings of sandstone dip down from the shorelines and plane into the river, funneling everything inexorably toward the center. Deep streaks of river look like mint jelly where the water begins to slip over ledges. Next, the smooth green turns white at diminutive pour-overs. Then the whole river bursts into full-fledged rapids. Rocks stud the center of the channel and seem to have a magnetic quality. Even more rocks are under the surface, causing the Youghiogheny to mound up as though some dragon were blowing bubbles from below. In an instant, the ledges, rocks, waves, constricted chutes, and boiling "Maytags" all seem to come at once, as the paddler digs and pulls away from the hazards and leans to avoid flipping in a kayak or canoe. Rafters who collide with bedrock quickly "high-side," deliberately throwing their weight to the side of the raft that's being pushed up against the rock by the force of the current. You mop the water from your face, paddle double-time

Paddlers in specialized kayaks like this "squirt boat" (left) practice advanced moves for hours on the Loop.

A squadron of rafters (right) listens to a safety talk before beginning the trip.

The "ledgy" character of the Youghiogheny's rapids (below) is typical of Appalachian rivers.

to evade the next sharp ledge, then finally swirl out into calmer water at the end.

While many popular western rivers demand that you set up your boat in the correct place and then drop through big waves with some minor maneuvering, the Youghiogheny is the archetypal Appalachian stream – more rocks than water. To paddle here you have to read the intricacies of the flow, evade the toothy obstructions, and catch eddies for breathers. Known as a "pool-drop" river, the Youghiogheny has rapids in all but the highest flows that spill into short interludes of flatwater where boaters can sigh, laugh, bail, and regroup.

The Upper Youghiogheny

For those who seek one of the ultimate thrills in difficult, intricate whitewater, the upper Youghiogheny leaves you craving nothing more. South of Ohiopyle in Maryland, this one-day trip from **Sang Run** to **Friendsville** is only for expert paddlers or seasoned clients in guided rafts. Rapids plunge below a horizon line where you see the tops of trees down below. Sieving into rock gardens at drops called **Meat Cleaver** and **Snaggle Tooth**, the river pushes you toward multiple chutes, virtually unreadable from a boat. In some sections the river falls an impressive 120 feet per mile.

Five Class V rapids and long sections of continuous Class IV rapids present challenges with startling speed and regularity. Yet the danger of the place is matched by its beauty. Necklaces of boulders line the shores, and the dense Appalachian forest shades narrow channels under thick canopies of dozens of tree species.

The upper "Yock" (above), known for steep, technical rapids, is a proving ground for expert paddlers.

Trips are possible only when water flows from **Deep Creek Dam**, a few miles upstream, where the Pennsylvania Electric Company releases a boatable volume on summer afternoons, Monday through Friday. Even expert boaters are advised to run this stretch first with paddlers who know the river. Experienced rafters seeking the most difficult water can find outfitters in Ohiopyle and West Virginia that are licensed for this demanding run.

Cucumber and the Loop

Right after Entrance comes **Cucumber Rapid**, named for a small tributary stream with a spectacular waterfall only a few hundred yards upstream from its confluence with the Youghiogheny. A look at the waterfall is worth the short walk if you don't mind stopping so early in the trip. Cucumber begins wide and fast but soon narrows and accelerates as if shooting down the neck of a funnel. The constriction of giant boulders at the bottom creates some nasty holes, and then you're pummeled through the spout of the funnel and into the pool below.

In quick succession the river rips over rapids called **Piddly**, **Camel**, and **Walrus**, **Eddy Turn**, **Dartmouth**, and then the formidable maze of **Railroad Rapid**, lying just upstream of a high trestle where a hiking and biking trail crosses the river at a dizzying height.

This completes the famous **Loop**, a 1.7-mile route that drops 60 feet in Class III rapids (Class IV in high water). An extraordinary feature in America's geography of rivers, the Youghiogheny arcs in a horseshoe bend that nearly joins itself, the closest thing nature offers to the paddler's fantasy of a whitewater river that goes around in a circle. Many kayakers and canoeists come to the Youghiogheny simply for the Loop, which they paddle over and over again. On sultry summer evenings, it's an experience that even seasoned paddlers will remember

the rest of their lives. From the Loop's takeout at the old railroad bridge, you simply carry your boat a quarter mile back to the road.

Memorable Challenge

Below Railroad Rapid, there's more terrific whitewater. Long sections of riffling current monopolize some stretches, until **Dimple Rock** forces paddlers to do some tight maneuvering. At **Swimmer's Rapid**, a wide hydraulic is like a steep-sided ocean wave that can trap the unwary. At **River's End** – perhaps the most memorable challenge – the waterway twists abruptly and is churned by rocks the size of buses.

Everybody disembarks at the **Bruner Run** takeout. The guided boaters catch the bus back to Ohiopyle, and the independent boaters load their gear onto a boat trailer and ride to the top of the hill to a parking lot where vehicles have been shuttled.

For those who want easier water – a Class II run just right for the intermediate canoeist or beginning kayaker – the middle Youghiogheny is the ticket. Lying immediately above Ohiopyle, this section offers 12 miles of gentler rapids interspersed with flatwater paddling starting at the town of **Confluence** and ending at the Ohiopyle bridge only a quarter mile above the death trap of Ohiopyle Falls. **Riversport**, a renowned paddling school, occupies an idyllic site just below the town of Confluence and offers one-day to week-long classes in kayaking and canoeing.

Both the middle and lower Youghiogheny are surrounded by **Ohiopyle State Park**, a gem of protected land set aside by the Western Pennsylvania Conservancy in the 1960s. Embracing the river and mountain landscape, the park turned the tide of an exploitative century. Without the park, strip mining and land development would have turned this Appalachian enclave into a sorry remnant of what we see today. While much remains to be done to safeguard the upper river and its tributaries, the park demonstrates that there is a better way.

Ohiopyle State Park offers many other diversions such as hiking, mountain biking, and splashing around in the water (left).

Meadow Run (right), a tributary of the Youghiogheny, spills over a rocky ledge.

TRAVEL TIPS

DETAILS

When to Go

Spring and summer are the best times to paddle the Youghiogheny; water levels drop considerably by fall. Daytime temperatures range from 42° to 66°F in April, and from 75° to 98°F in July.

How to Get There

The lower Youghiogheny flows through Ohiopyle State Park about 15 miles from the West Virginia and Maryland borders. Pittsburgh International Airport is about 70 miles northwest. Car rentals are available at the airport. The nearest large town is Uniontown, Pennsylvania, about 18 miles west.

Permits

The state park requires a $2.50 fee for rafting or paddling on the Youghiogheny River.

INFORMATION

Laurel Highlands Visitors Bureau

Town Hall, 120 East Main Street, Ligonier, PA 15658; tel: 724-238-5661 or 800-925-7669.

Ohiopyle State Park

Pennsylvania Department of Conservation and Natural Resources, P.O. Box 105, Ohiopyle, PA 15470; tel: 724-329-8591.

Pennsylvania Travel

Room 453, Forum Building, Harrisburg, PA 17120; tel: 717-787-5453 or 800-847-4872.

CAMPING

Laurel Hill State Park

Pennsylvania Department of Conservation and Natural Resources, 1454 Laurel Hill Park Road, Somerset, PA 15501; tel: 814-445-7725 or 888-727-2757 (reservations).

A few miles north of Ohiopyle, Laurel Hill has about 4,000 acres of wooded, mountainous terrain and a 63-acre lake. The park's campground has hot showers and 264 sites.

Ohiopyle State Park

Pennsylvania Department of Conservation and Natural Resources, P.O. Box 105, Ohiopyle, PA 15470; tel: 724-329-8591 or 888-727-2757 (reservations).

The park campground is a few miles from the launch area at Ohiopyle Falls. The wooded location has 237 sites, hot showers, several play areas for children, and wall tents on wooden platforms.

Tall Oaks Campground

544 Camp Riamo Road, Farmington, PA 15437; tel: 724-329-4777.

The privately owned campground, about 20 minutes from Ohiopyle, has more than 100 wooded sites. Amenities include a swimming pool and store. Cabins are available for rent.

LODGING

Historic Summit Inn

101 Skyline Drive, Farmington, PA 15437; tel: 724-438-8594.

Built in 1907, this large mountain resort occupies 1,200 acres. A large deck offers an expansive view; a stone fireplace warms guests in the lobby. Amenities include indoor and outdoor swimming pools, golf, and tennis. $$–$$$

Laurel Highlands River Tours/Guest Houses

P.O. Box 107, Ohiopyle, PA 15470; tel: 800-472-3246 or 724-329-8531.

Laurel Highlands operates three guest houses with three or four bedrooms in each. $$–$$$

Nemocolin Woodlands Resort and Spa

1001 Lafayette Drive, Farmington, PA 15437; tel: 800-422-2736 or 724-329-8555.

The luxury resort offers a golf course, horseback riding, a children's program, mountain-bike rentals, and swimming pools. The resort's new 125-room, French-style chateau has a jeweler, cigar bar, and French restaurant. A 4,000-foot airstrip is on the grounds. $$$$

Ohiopyle Log House Rental

Route 381, Ohiopyle, PA 15470; tel: 724-329-5935.

About 10 minutes from Ohiopyle, these four restored log cabins sleep five to eight people each. The rustic units have handmade furniture, kitchens, and fireplaces.

River's Edge Café Bed-and-Breakfast

203 Yough Street, Confluence, PA 15424; tel: 814-395-5059.

This 1890 inn/restaurant on the banks of the Youghiogheny River has six guest rooms with double beds and shared baths. $$

TOURS AND OUTFITTERS

Laurel Highlands Outdoor Center

P.O. Box 107, Ohiopyle, PA 15470; tel: 800-472-3846.

The center runs both self-bailing

and traditional flat-floor rafts on the lower Youghiogheny and Cheat Rivers; it also operates a kayak school. Guided trips are available for all skill levels, and qualified paddlers can take self-guided trips.

Riversport School of Paddling

P.O. Box 95, Confluence, PA 15424; tel: 800-216-6991.

Set on the banks of the Youghiogheny River, Riversport teaches whitewater kayaking and canoeing using its campground and paddle-sports shop as a base.

Whitewater Adventurers

P.O. Box 31, Ohiopyle, PA 15470; tel: 800-992-7238.

Guides lead trips of three to five hours on the lower, middle, and upper Youghiogheny and Cheat Rivers. Self-guided trips are available. Rentals include canoes, inflatable kayaks, and four- to six-person rafts.

Wilderness Voyageurs

P.O. Box 97, Ohiopyle, PA 15470; tel: 800-272-4141.

The company guides peaceful floats on the middle Youghiogheny and thrilling trips on the lower Youghiogheny. Kayak clinics and rentals are available. Mountain-biking/rafting packages include meals, tents, and activities. Self-guided excursions are available on the Cheat and upper Youghiogheny Rivers.

Excursions

Chesapeake Bay

Chesapeake Paddlers Association, P.O. Box 341, Greenbelt, MD 20768.

Chesapeake Bay has hundreds of miles of shoreline and scores of tidewater inlets, known locally as creeks. Its size also favors those who enjoy challenging open-water paddling. The bay is home to a rich ecosystem, with wild-rice marshes and stands of bald cypress. Thousands of migrating waterfowl arrive in autumn. Prime Hook and Blackwater National Wildlife Refuges are prime paddling destinations.

New River

New River Gorge National Recreation Area, P.O. Box 246, Glen Jean, WV 25846; tel: 304-574-2115.

This river, one of the continent's oldest, runs through southern West Virginia, just east of Beckley. The recreation area protects 53 miles of the waterway and operates four visitor centers. West Virginia is known for big, brawny rapids, and, according to the park, the "lower New River Gorge has some of the biggest of the big." The scenery, for those who have time to look up, is also spectacular: a deep forested gorge.

Potomac River

Atlantic Canoe and Kayak Company, 1201 North Royal Street, Alexandria, VA 22314; tel: 800-297-0066.

Visitors to the nation's capital often overlook the beautiful tidal river that passes between Washington, D.C., and Virginia. Many of the city's grand monuments and buildings, such as the Jefferson Memorial, Roosevelt Island, and the Kennedy Center, are situated directly off the Potomac. Sea kayaking affords unique views of these landmarks and the colonial-era waterfronts of Georgetown and Old Town Alexandria. The Potomac also has a thriving riparian ecosystem, with waterfowl, marshes, and quiet coves. The Great Falls of the Potomac, about nine miles upstream, have some of the most extreme whitewater in the East; only experts need apply.

Nantahala River
North Carolina

CHAPTER 9

hen botanist and explorer William Bartram crested the **Great Smokies** of North Carolina in 1776, he stood dumbstruck at the vision stretching before him, "a sublimely awful scene of power and magnificence, a world of mountains piled upon mountains." And far, far below, deep in a thousand-foot gorge, Bartram saw the mirrorlike glint of the Nantahala River, homeland of the Cherokee Indians and a stream destined for whitewater paddling glory matched by few other rivers in North America. ◆ The river's frothy, frantic rush through a cleft in Bartram's world of "power and magnificence" is arguably the most popular stretch of whitewater on the planet. It is host to Olympic athletes and family vacationers, to paddlers in rafts, canoes, kayaks, and various inflatables. Fringed with sycamore and white pine, dropping 265 feet in its descent to **Fontana Lake**, the river offers a virtually nonstop whitewater ride across rocky ledges, over standing waves,

Thrilling rapids, a first-class paddling school, and more than a dozen outfitters are just a few reasons why this Smoky Mountain river is a whitewater mecca.

and through exhilarating chutes filled with foam. Each year nearly a quarter million thrill seekers shriek and splash down the Nantahala, some of them showboating for the crowds that gather streamside to applaud their antics, others white-knuckled as rafts buck wildly through boulder-strewn rapids. ◆ First-timers and whitewater junkies alike can depend on the river's water levels, because the Nantahala is a dam-controlled stream. The waters are impounded in fjordlike **Nantahala Lake**, then pumped through an enormous pipe for six miles beneath the mountains before being released on a scheduled basis just upstream from the river put-in. That water, clear

A paddler in a C-1, or decked canoe, pops an "ender" at Nantahala Falls. The Nantahala is a hub of high-performance paddling.

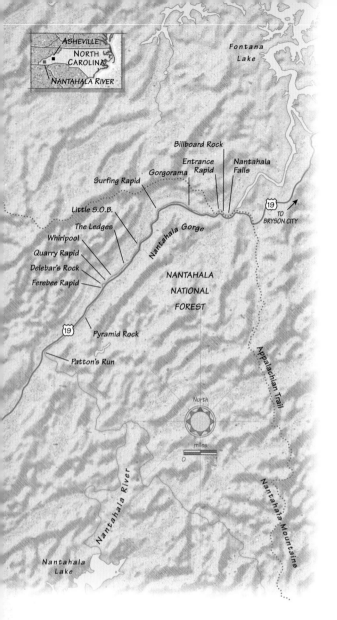

Home Water

The river's popularity is due in large part to the **Nantahala Outdoor Center** (NOC), where "river rats" come to see and be seen. Started by three whitewater enthusiasts in 1972, and run initially with college students and Explorer Scouts as guides, the NOC has grown into a sprawling complex with two dozen buildings scattered along a wide bend in the river. Along the way it's turned the Nantahala into a sort of Euphrates of whitewater paddling in the eastern United States, the home water of many of the sport's early legends. Half of the 1996 U.S. Olympic whitewater team as well as 1992 Olympic gold medalists Joe Jacobi and Scott Strausbaugh cut their teeth – or lost them – in rapids such as **Patton's Run**, **Little S.O.B.**, and **Crapchute**. Many whitewater legends return to teach at the NOC's acclaimed paddling school. Now, the NOC has been joined by 14 other outfitters holding rafting permits from the U.S. Forest Service, and on Saturdays in summer the gorge is like a carnival, jammed with hundreds of rafts. Converted school buses lumber up and down the riverside road, shuttling paddlers back and forth. On pockets of private land along the river, streamside vendors hawk barbecue, boiled peanuts, and hot coffee.

The result is a river that appeals to a wide range of paddlers. In a raft, the Nantahala run is a roiling, splashy gauntlet through gorgeous forests, safe enough for families but with thrills enough for a few weeks of raucous dinner conversation. Many outfitters offer a full range of guide options. Beginners can sign up for fully guided trips, in which a guide is stationed in every boat. On "guide assisted" trips, groups of rafts form a small convoy, with guides aboard the lead boat,

as gin and cold as a trout's gaze, never climbs above 53°F. And when it meets the hot summer air, a thick fog blankets the river for miles, an odd phenomenon that lends the river an almost mystical allure.

Playing is hard work (left). Most serious paddlers train in the weight room, too.

the last or "sweeper" raft, and every second or third craft in between. More intrepid travelers can rent a raft on their own or try a canoe or kayak if they're feeling extra adventurous.

Into the Gorge

It all starts at an outfitter's headquarters, where rafters board buses piled high with bright orange rafts. As they ride to the well-maintained U.S. Forest Service put-in, the palisades of the chasm soar straight overhead, leaving blue sky as a stripe in the heavens. It's easy to understand what the Cherokee meant when they called the river *nundayeli*, which means "midday sun," for the gorge is so steep that only a few hours of sunlight bathe the river.

But paddlers have little time to consider the heavens, for mere moments after pushing off into the quicksilver flow of the river, a rapid called **Patton's Run** serves as a wet welcome to the Nantahala's special brand of speed bump. Here the **Snowbird Mountains** butt into the **Nantahalas**, forcing the river into a hard right turn into the maw of **Nantahala Gorge**. Long, frothy shoals bump rafts and hard boats alike as they

ferry across to the right side of the river, thread the eye of a narrow ledge, and edge out of reach of rhododendrons whose evergreen fingers snatch at paddlers who cut too close to shore. That's when the first of the Nantahala's signature wave-trains smashes the boats, sending plumes of cold water over the bows. Peals of laughter echo off the rocks. Pull out the bailer, and keep it handy! Two rapids, **Tumble Dry** and the **Isle of Dumping**, await just downstream. In the first mile of water, boaters navigate four named rapids and innumerable shoals, wave-trains, and eddies. And the party has only started.

Spin Cycle

When Bartram crossed the river near here he described the gorge as being "almost encircled by distant ridges of lofty hills," and by chance bumped into the great Cherokee chief Atakullakulla. Both men would no doubt scratch their heads in wonder at the

The V-shaped wave (left) on river left is a "cleaner" route than the big hole this kayaker is approaching.

A tandem decked canoe (right), called a C-2, competes in one of the NOC's many slalom races.

sight and sound of the pristine Nantahala now flecked with rafts, canoes, and kayaks in wild colors.

From its upper reaches, the river pours into a long middle section introduced by **Pyramid Rock**, rising from the swirling flow like the back of a breaching whale. The river's swift waters tumble over moss-covered boulders into pools so clear that the bottom seems within reach but deep enough to send most anyone over his or her head. The river twists and turns, making paddlers maneuver from left bank to right in order to line up for safe passage across and around **Ferebee Rapid**, **Delebar's Rock**, and **Quarry Rapid**. At **Whirlpool** the more playful guides will nudge a corner of their rafts into a power-fully circulating eddy to jump-start the boats into 360-degree spins downriver.

A student (left) gets help adjusting a kayak's hip and foot braces. A snug fit allows better control of the boat.

Nantahala Falls (below) is the run's grand finale and is guaranteed to get paddlers wet.

Hot Dog!

It's just the sort of maneu-ver that gives family floaters a taste of the kind of play boating for which the Nantahala is famous. Downstream of Whirlpool, beyond Little S.O.B. and the Ledges, rafters get a good look at **Surfing Rapid**, the tail end of a river-splitting island that spews up a long train of foamy waves. It's a great place to watch experienced kayakers "hot dog" as they gather at Surfing Rapid to paddle sharply upstream into the trough between two waves, where the competing currents

moving upstream and down hold them steady as if they were balancing on a pair of buckboards. More and more paddlers are performing their stunts in the hot new rodeo kayaks, often described as a "beach ball with pointy ends" for their high-volume cockpits and lancelike profiles.

Below Surfing Rapid the river relaxes for a while, lapping placidly along the **Gorgorama** stretch. Here, you may catch a glimpse of the brightly colored, steam-powered excursion train that threads the narrow gorge on a regular schedule. But the break doesn't last long, for just below Gorgorama the Nantahala packs a one-two-three punch of rapids culminating in **Nantahala Falls**. Although the river float is mostly a Class II fun run, a whole new level of excitement awaits at the falls. There, at the tail end of the gorge, the river takes a right-hand turn at **Entrance Rapids**, piling up water around a large undercut boulder known as **Billboard Rock**, then rushes in breaking waves to the mazelike falls – two ledges that open to a hole framed by submerged rocks and violent breakers.

Twenty years ago, the falls were rated a Class V rapid. Since then, they have been downgraded to Class III, not because of any change in the water, but because paddling techniques and equipment have evolved so highly. Even so, it's a fitting exclamation point to a float through more than 20 named rapids in an eight-and-a-half-mile stretch. The falls are so spectacular that bleacher seats have been erected streamside, guaranteeing shouts and applause for boaters who run the rocky gauntlet with grace – or at least a grin.

It's a fast, furious two and a half hours afloat. And one of the best things about this Great Smokies joyride is that when you're finished, there's usually enough daylight to do it again.

Most recreational kayaks (above) are less than 10 feet long in contrast to the 13 feet required for slalom boats.

A great play hole makes Nantahala Falls (left) a popular showcase for rodeo paddlers. Spectators watch from riverside bleachers.

TRAVEL TIPS

DETAILS

When to Go

Some local enthusiasts paddle the river year-round, but most outfitters and instructors operate March through October. Summer is humid and frequently rainy, with temperatures ranging from the high 80s to the low 50s. Temperatures in late spring and early fall are in the 70s, dropping into the 40s at night.

How to Get There

Bryson City, on the southeast edge of Great Smoky Mountains National Park, is about 60 miles west of Asheville, North Carolina. Asheville is served by several regional airlines, including Delta. Rental cars are available at the airport.

Permits

The Forest Service requires user-registration permits, available on a seasonal or daily basis. Season passes cost $5, daily passes $1. They are available at put-ins at Ferebee Park and near Patton's Run, or at the Nantahala Outdoor Center.

INFORMATION

Bryson City Chamber of Commerce

P.O. Box 509, Bryson City, NC 28713; tel: 800-867-9246 or 828-488-3681.

Nantahala National Forest

100 Otis Street, Box 2750, Federal Courthouse, Asheville, NC 28801; tel: 828-257-4200.

Nantahala Outdoor Center

13077 Highway 19 West, Bryson City, NC 28713; tel: 888-662-1662.

CAMPING

Brookside Campground and Rafting

Highway 18, P.O. Box 93, Topton, NC 28781; tel: 828-321-5209.

One mile from the Nantahala put-in, this campground has 42 sites, some on a creek and others backed by forest. A swimming pool, showers, and a laundry facility are on the premises. Raft rentals are available.

Lost Mine Campground

1000 Silvermine Road, Bryson City, NC 28713; tel: 828-488-6445.

The campground offers a quiet atmosphere a mile from the Nantahala Outdoor Center. Its 100 wooded acres include a stream and waterfall. Showers and RV hookups are on the grounds.

Tsali Campground

Nantahala National Forest, Cheoah Ranger District, Route 1, Box 16A, Robbinsville, NC 28771; tel: 704-479-6431.

This wooded campground, about 10 minutes from the river, occupies a peninsula on 30-mile-long Fontana Lake. Flush toilets, showers, and 41 sites are available.

LODGING

PRICE GUIDE – double occupancy

$ = up to $49 $$ = $50–$99
$$$ = $100–$149 $$$$ = $150+

Euchella Sport Lodge

Box 177, Almond, NC 28702; tel: 800-446-1603 or 828-488-8835.

Five minutes from the river, this lodge offers a variety of options, including secluded mountain cabins and cottages with kitchens and living areas. Mountain bikes, canoes, and kayaks are available for rent. $$–$$$$

Falling Waters Adventure Resort

Nantahala River Gorge, NC 28713; tel: 800-451-9972.

This 22-acre resort a few miles west of Bryson City has frame tents with knotty pine floors, four-poster queen-sized beds, private decks, and stereos. The resort's Group Barn has a recreation hall, dining area, and meeting room, and sleeps up to 40 people in eight-person bunk rooms. $–$$

Folkestone Inn

101 Folkestone Road, Bryson City, NC 28713; tel: 888-812-3385 or 828-488-2730.

Less than a mile from Great Smoky Mountains National Park, this 1920s mountain farmhouse offers 10 guest rooms, each with a private bath, some with a private balcony and mountain vista. One room, Boats and Paddles, features prints and photographs of whitewater paddling. The house has flag-stone floors, pressed-tin ceilings, and antiques. $$–$$$

Hemlock Inn

P.O. Drawer EE, Bryson City, NC 28713; tel: 828-488-2885.

This inn occupies a converted farmhouse. Private baths are available in each of the Hemlock's 23 rooms and three cabins. $$$–$$$$

Nantahala Outdoor Center

13077 Highway 19 West, Bryson City, NC 28713; tel: 888-662-1662 or 828-488-2175.

The river's preeminent paddling school and outfitter has a variety of accommodations, ranging from dorms and motel units to expensive guest rooms. $–$$$$

TOURS AND OUTFITTERS

Adventurous Fast Rivers

14690 Route 19 West, Bryson City, NC 28713; tel: 800-438-7238.

Set on the banks of the Nantahala River, the outfitter

operates guided raft trips and rents rafts, sit-on-top kayaks, and whitewater canoes.

Carolina Outfitters Whitewater Rafting

12121 Highway 19 West, Bryson City, NC 28713; tel: 800-468-7238 or 828-488-6345.

Both guided and unguided raft trips are available on the Nantahala River.

Endless River Adventures

P.O. Box 246, Bryson City, NC 28713; tel: 828-488-6199.

The company runs rafting trips and offers instruction in whitewater kayaking.

Nantahala Outdoor Center

13077 Highway 19 West, Bryson City, NC 28713; tel: 888-662-1662 (instruction) or 888-232-7238 (rafting).

One of the nation's top whitewater schools, the center conducts a wide variety of courses, from beginning kayaking and canoeing to advanced slalom and play boating. The center also offers daily raft trips.

Rolling Thunder River Company

P.O. Box 88, Almond, NC 28702; tel: 800-408-7238 or 828-488-2030.

Rolling Thunder leads guided raft trips, offers a shuttle service for private boaters, and rents canoes, kayaks, and rafts.

Wildwater Ltd.

P.O. Box 309, Long Creek, SC 29658; tel: 800-451-9972 or 864-647-9587.

This outfitter runs trips on a variety of rivers, including the Chattooga and Nantahala.

Excursions

Outer Banks

Cape Hatteras National Seashore, Route 1, Box 675, Manteo, NC 27954; tel: 919-995-4474.

North Carolina's Barrier Islands are ideal for sea kayakers. On the islands' ocean side are miles of sandy beach, dynamic surf, rugged currents, and a great view of the celebrated lighthouse on grassy, windswept Hatteras Island, whose pristine dunes are a must-see. When seaward conditions are rough, paddlers retreat into Pamlico Sound, a quiet environment teeming with birds and rich marshes. Beware of potentially dangerous ocean currents.

Chattooga River

Sumter National Forest, Andrew Pickens Ranger District, 112 Andrew Pickens Circle, Mountain Rest, SC 29664; tel: 864-638-9568.

Made famous by the 1972 film *Deliverance*, the Chattooga River, one of the Southeast's few remaining free-flowing streams, rolls through dense hardwood forest along the South Carolina–Georgia border. The river has four sections, each taking about a day to paddle: Section I, a gentle float; Section II, a relatively calm stretch with one Class III rapid; Section III, an advanced-to-expert run full of sharp Class III-IV drops; and Section IV, a challenging whitewater run with a series of steep, complex Class IV drops.

Ocoee River

Cherokee National Forest, Ocoee Whitewater Center, Route 1, Box 285, Highway 64 West, Copperhill, TN 37317; tel: 423-496-5197.

The 1996 Olympic whitewater slalom course, also the site of a popular whitewater rodeo, is a 4.5-mile stretch of the dam-controlled Ocoee River. About an hour east of Chattanooga, this run between the Tennessee Valley Authority's diversion dam No. 2 and its No. 2 powerhouse offers warm water, a long season, and almost continuous Class III-IV whitewater. The Ocoee Whitewater Center, developed upstream for the Olympics, provides visitors with information about the river and local outfitters.

Okefenokee Swamp
Georgia

At the southern extremity of Georgia lies the largest swamp in North America, where a world of fascinations awaits those who enter upon its dark, life-rich waters. It is a moody paradise approximately 700 miles square, whose name, **Okefenokee**, means "land of trembling earth," so called for the floating islands of peat, slowly colonized by grasses, shrubs, and trees, that quiver when a person walks on them. ◆ The best way to see the Okefenokee is to travel by canoe. A good plan is to cross the swamp from east to west – a trip that takes three days – sleeping on wooden platforms erected at intervals along the way. Put in at **Kingfisher Landing**, a remote dock at the end of a dirt road between **Waycross** and **Folkston**, Georgia. Here a finger of flowing water reaches out to draw you into the hummocks of loblolly bay, swamp titi, and red maple. There is usually no one about. Wisps of morning fog hang over the dark-brown, tannic water and mingle with the Spanish moss that drips from trees. ◆ Suddenly birdsong fills the

Otters, alligators, and other swamp creatures accompany canoeists on a passage through the "Land of Trembling Earth."

air and a small warbler, so brightly golden that it takes your breath away, flashes across the waterway into a tall cypress. It is a prothonotary, the "flame-bird" of the southeastern wetlands. Long-billed and plump, singing *sweet, sweet, sweet*, prothonotary warblers will accompany you across the swamp, flitting along the trails as you follow the signs from one watery intersection to another. ◆ Paddles dip in, sweep against the water and rise, over and over. The eyes and nostrils of an alligator break the water's surface. As the canoe approaches, it waits unmoving, then slowly sinks deeper into the swamp. As the day heats up, animals emerge into

The amiable gaze of a red-eared pond slider turtle reminds visitors that they are never alone on the Okefenokee's life-rich waters.

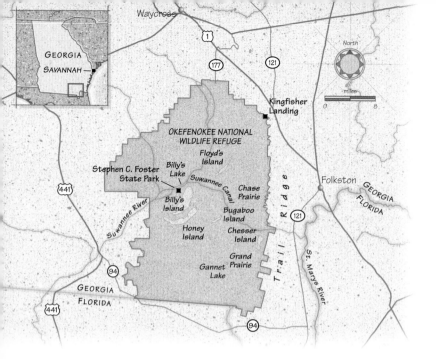

About one-fifth of the swamp is boggy prairie, predominantly on the eastern side. In these flooded marshes, where water levels rise and fall as much as two feet depending on seasonal rains, blankets of wildflowers celebrate life by making more of it – floating hearts, and yellow and white water lilies blooming by the thousands. Rooted on the bottom, lavender-spiked pickerel weed, yellow-eyed grass, and golden club, with its tender spadix of yellow flowers, emerge between the floating plants.

On these prairies, sandhill cranes dance their courtship rituals among sedges and sphagnum moss. The round-tailed water rat lives here; a relative of the muskrat, this rodent builds a platform of grass as a resting place above the water and roofs it as a protection from predators. White ibis use their long, curved bills to probe the mud for insects and crayfish. Prehistoric-looking wood storks roost in nearby snags.

Two of the larger prairies are **Grand**, which is five miles by three miles, and **Chase**, named for hunters who chased bears and deer across its open spaces. The fishing is excellent in the deep-water lakes that dot the swamp. The largest is **Billy's Lake**, stretching for three miles near **Stephen C. Foster State Park** on the western

the subtropical sunshine: A Florida cooter, drab save for the yellow stripes on its head, suns itself on a fallen log but soon plops into the water. A 10-foot alligator, its scutes shining gray in the sun, lies ponderously at water's edge, its languor belying the animal's speed and agility.

Geologically, the swamp is young, having been formed in the early Pleistocene, when the coastline lay about 75 miles farther inland. A saucer-shaped depression was separated from the receding ocean by an ancient barrier dune, now called **Trail Ridge**, and once the water changed from salty to fresh, plants began to take hold.

An alligator (above) munches on a luckless bullfrog.

Color-coded signs (right) guide paddlers on the six canoe trails that wind through the swamp.

A cypress (right) is draped with Spanish moss, the only member of the pineapple family native to the United States.

side of the swamp.

Although spring and fall are the best seasons for canoeing, mild winter days can be wonderfully rewarding. Without their needles, the cypress draw beautiful lines against the sky, and the swamp is a monochrome of taupe, so that you have to look closely for brilliance: a vividly plumaged male wood duck in a backwater pond, a hooded merganser spiffy in his black-and-white tuxedo garb, bright little eyes glittering like golden marbles. In winter, other waterfowl collect on the prairies and lakes: mallards, black ducks, coots, green-winged teal, and ring-necked ducks. Alligators are less active in cold weather, which emboldens the swamp's population of otters and will give you an opportunity to see families ducking and playing.

Summer brings newborn fawns and young herons, egrets and ibis leaving their rookeries. Nighthawks and chuck-will's-widows snatch moths from the air. Dragonflies zip over the water. Summer also brings hot, humid weather, and thunderstorms often tear open the afternoon sky with a quiver of lightning bolts.

Swamp Ghosts

Until about 1850, the Okefenokee was inhabited by Creek Indians, described in 1791 by explorer William Bartram as a race of tall, ferocious men and exceptionally beautiful women called "Daughters of the Sun." Their burial mounds, built to "raise the spirits," exist on almost every island of habitable size. Bartram described the Okefenokee as "the most blissful spot on earth."

After the Indians were driven out, the place was inhabited by white settlers who hunted deer and bears for subsistence and poled their bateaus through the lily-clogged waterways. They loved music and gave voice to "hollerin'," a type of yodeling that

connected individuals or parties across several miles, the cadences bouncing off the still water. Hollerers sang for sheer pleasure, or to announce their arrival home with a bounty of meat.

In 1891, a timber company attempted to drain the area, and the **Suwannee Canal**, a long, straight ditch that crosses the swamp, is evidence of its failure. Nevertheless, the Okefenokee was heavily logged for about 35 years, leaving vast expanses of stumps and a number of logging camps, now ghost towns.

Much credit for preserving the great swamp goes to Francis Harper, a naturalist who made his first visit in 1912, at the age of 25, with a team of biologists

from Cornell University. Harper explored the Okefenokee for nearly three decades, collecting specimens and folklore. Finally, in 1937, his efforts and those of other environmentalists convinced President Franklin D. Roosevelt to create the 438,000-acre **Okefenokee National Wildlife Refuge**, of which 90 percent is now designated as a wilderness area. The trees have been growing for six decades, and except for a rusting rail here and there, the logging scars have faded. In many places, too, where the logging cables could not reach, the ancient cypress still stand. Indeed, cypress forests make up about a quarter of the swamp.

Hundreds of small streams feed into the Okefenokee, giving birth to two substantial rivers: the coffee-colored **Suwannee** (made

Swamp Creatures

The Okefenokee Swamp is blessed with a greater diversity of wildlife than anywhere in the southeastern United States, including more than 200 species of birds, 50 species of mammals, 39 of fish, and 100 of reptiles and amphibians. The king of this domain is the alligator. While gators are normally shy creatures, their jaws and muscular tails are fearsome weapons. Never approach a female guarding young, and never attempt to feed them; gators can become extremely aggressive.

Four of the Okefenokee's 36 species of snakes are venomous – three rattlers and the coral snake – but keep an eye out for other reptiles that are both harmless and beautiful, particularly the indigo and the iridescent black ribbon snake, with red stripes running the length of its body. More than 20 species of frogs and toads will entertain you with calls unique to their kind. You're virtually certain to spot deer and beaver, and might glimpse a mink or an elusive bobcat. But the largest and most impressive creature is one that found sanctuary in the swamp after being driven out of the surrounding coastal plain. The Okefenokee is the last stronghold of the black bear in the Southeast. About 500 live here. If you miss seeing *Ursus americanus* in person, you'll come across their trails and notice shredded tree bark where they have sharpened their claws.

Water lilies (above), sweetbay flowers, and other blooming plants brighten the Okefenokee in spring.

The least bittern (far left) is an elusive, small heron skilled at wending through dense marsh vegetation. Paddlers may hear its soft clucking during breeding season.

The green anole (left) can change color to blend in with its surroundings.

Frogs (below) make quite a racket on spring evenings.

famous by the Stephen Foster song) which flows southward to the Gulf of Mexico; and the **St. Marys**, which forms part of the Florida–Georgia border and winds 175 miles east to the Atlantic. In addition, more than 200 miles of canoe trails beckon to explorers.

Camping platforms (left) keep canoeists dry and away from alligators. Only seven groups can stay in the swamp each night.

American alligators (below) number about 10,000 in the Okefenokee. They can grow to nearly 20 feet long but average about five feet.

Night Magic

By the end of a day, a paddler in the land of trembling earth is dog tired. A night on one of the wooden platforms (complete with chemical toilets) may not be totally restful, but offers its own magic. In spring as many as a dozen frog species fill the darkness with their chorus; barred owls boom their *Who cooks for you? Who cooks for you-all?*; and mating alligators may be heard bellowing territorial warnings. With the dawn, the paddler eagerly continues, and begins noticing an amazing suite of carnivorous plants, which trap insects to supplement spare nutrients in the soil. The trumpets of pitcher plants broadcast their sweetness through the air, attracting flies. Bladderworts bloom in purple sheets in the water; along their roots are raindrop-sized bladders that traps microorganisms. On wet land, sundews with their buttery, slick leaves entice small insects.

By the third day, the paddling becomes hypnotic, and the glens and glades start to feel like home. This is the effect the Okefenokee has on just about everyone. Long after you leave, you'll be able to close your eyes and summon images from your journey: gator wallows, branches of cypress hung with moss, bear trails leading through hammocks of titi, and floating schools of yellow-blooming spatterdock.

TRAVEL TIPS

DETAILS

When to Go

Fall, winter, and spring are the best times to paddle here, as summer brings heat, insects, and thunderstorms. Spring is the most popular time, when flowering plants are at their peak, and temperatures are in the 70s and 80s. Fall brings marsh hawks, sandhill cranes, migratory robins, feeding black bears, and a slight autumnal hue to the cypress and sweet-gum leaves. Winter, with flocks of migratory birds and generally low rainfall, can range widely in temperature from 80°F to below freezing, but the 50s and 60s are typical. The driest time of year is from late September through May, not counting occasional tropical storms that blow in from the Gulf of Mexico.

Getting There

The refuge is headquartered in Folkston, Georgia, about 35 minutes from Jacksonville, Florida. There are three main entry points for canoeists: East Entrance, 11 miles southwest of Folkston; West Entrance at Stephen Foster State Park, 17 miles east of Fargo, Georgia; and Kingfisher Landing, on the northeast side of the swamp. The nearest airports are the Glyncoo Airport, about an hour's drive away, and Jacksonville International.

Permits

Advance reservations are required for overnight paddling trips. Paddlers are charged $10 per person per night. Late winter and spring are the most popular times. Reservations are accepted no more than two months in

INFORMATION

Okefenokee Chamber of Commerce
P. O. Box 756, 202 West Main Street, Folkston, GA 31537; tel: 912-496-2536.

Okefenokee National Wildlife Refuge
Refuge Manager, Route 2, Box 3330, Folkston, GA 31537; tel: 912-496-7836.

Georgia Tourism
285 Peachtree Center Avenue, Suite 1000, Atlanta, GA 30303; tel: 404-656-3590 or 800-847-4842.

CAMPING

Camping along canoe trails is permitted only at seven designated sites built on platforms. They must be reserved well in advance; call 912-496-7836.

Laura S. Walker State Park
5653 Laura Walker Road, Waycross, GA 31501; tel: 912-287-4900.

This wooded park has 44 campsites in a grassy area near a lake.

Okefenokee Pastimes
Route 2, Box 3090, Folkston, GA 31537; tel: 912-496-4472.

RV and tent camping are available near the east entrance to the Okefenokee; canoe and kayak rentals are also offered.

Stephen C. Foster State Park
Route 1, Box 131, Fargo, GA 31631; tel: 912-637-5274.

Set in a remote corner of the swamp 20 miles east of Fargo, this park is a hub of activity. There are 66 campsites with showers, nature trails, and a small store.

LODGING

PRICE GUIDE – double occupancy

$ = up to $49 $$ = $50–$99

$$$ = $100–$149 $$$$ = $150+

Brunswick Manor
825 Egmont Street, Brunswick, GA 31520; tel: 912-265-6889.

This Victorian bed-and-breakfast is in the Old Town area of Brunswick about an hour east of the swamp. The inn has seven rooms (most with private baths) in two late-19th-century buildings. $$

Holiday Inn
1725 Memorial Drive, P.O. Box 1357, Waycross, GA 31501; tel: 912-283-4490 or 800-465-4329.

This 145-room chain motel is in the busy commercial district of Waycross north of the swamp. There is a pool, playground, lounge, and restaurant.

Inn at Folkston
509 West Main Street, Folkston, GA 31537; tel: 912-496-6256 or 888-509-6246.

This bed-and-breakfast is housed in a restored 1922 bungalow with antiques, oriental rugs, and a grand veranda. The four guest rooms all have period furnishings, private baths, and air conditioning. $$–$$$

Stephen C. Foster State Park
Route 1, Box 131, Fargo, GA 31631; tel: 912-637-5274 or 800-864-7275 (reservations).

In addition to camping, this state park rents nine two-bedroom cottages that sleep eight people each. This is the only lodging at a canoe trail access point. $$

TOURS AND OUTFITTERS

Kingfisher and Beyond Canoe Outpost
Route 3, Box 973, Folkston, GA 31537; tel: 912-496-4834.

Guided canoe trips can be arranged throughout the swamp and surrounding area. Shuttle service and canoe and equipment rentals are also available.

Okefenokee Pastimes

Route 2, Box 3090, Folkston, GA 31537; tel: 912-496-4472.

This outfitter offers canoe rentals, guided trips, shuttle service, and a campground.

Southeast Adventure Outfitters

313 Mallory Street, St. Simons Island, GA 31522; tel: 912-638-6732.

Guides lead canoe trips in the Okefenokee Swamp and nearby destinations.

Suwannee Canal Recreation Area

Route 2, Box 3325, Folkston, GA 31537; tel: 912-496-7156 or 800-792-6796.

Guided canoe trips, canoe and equipment rentals, and shuttle service are offered.

Up the Creek Expeditions

111 Osborne Street, Marys, GA 31558; tel: 912-882-0911.

Guided kayaking trips include sea kayaking, surf kayaking, and whitewater.

Weatherbee's Botanical Trips

11405 Patterson Lake Drive, Pinckney, MI 48169; tel: 318-878-9178.

Guided swamp trips focus on flora and fauna.

Excursions

Cumberland Island National Seashore

National Park Service, Box 806, St. Marys, GA 31558; tel: 912-882-4335.

Once privately owned by the Carnegie family, 16-mile-long Cumberland Island is now a national seashore and a premier sea-kayaking destination. There are 18 miles of beach and 30 miles of trails, along with historic plantations and the ruins of a settlement built by freed slaves. Now the island is home to wild horses, loggerhead turtles, and other wildlife. Only 300 visitors per day, including 120 campers, are permitted. Reservations are required and can be made up to six months in advance.

Little Tybee Island

Chamber of Commerce, 301 Martin Luther King Boulevard, Savannah, GA 31402; tel: 912-944-0455.

Just a short paddle from Savannah, this uninhabited island offers sea kayakers a place under the palms. Paddlers have a choice of ocean swells and beaches on the east side of the island or tidal creeks and marshes on the west. Raccoons, ospreys, eagles, and river otters are often seen. Little Tybee is less than an hour from Savannah by paddle, so it makes a good overnight or day trip, and can be enjoyed year-round.

Suwannee River Canoe Trail

Suwannee River Water Management, 9225 County Road 49, Live Oak, FL 32060; tel: 904-362-1001.

The mostly tranquil Suwannee River, made famous by the Stephen Foster tune, offers canoe trips of up to two weeks in both Georgia and Florida. Cypress groves festooned with Spanish moss and a field guide's worth of animals and plants thrive along its banks. Riverside attractions include fossil-bearing limestone grottoes and huge crystal springs, where flowers flourish and swimmers can splash around in astoundingly clear water.

Boundary Waters
Canoe Area Wilderness
Minnesota

CHAPTER
11

t has a thousand sun-kissed lakes, hundreds of miles of rivers and streams, a million acres of boreal forest, abundant wildlife, superb fishing, and some of the best flatwater paddling in North America. With all this going for it, it is easy to see why Minnesota's **Boundary Waters Canoe Area Wilderness** is one of the most popular paddling destinations in the United States. Each year, some 200,000 visitors sample this maze of waterways, and few go away disappointed. ◆ The lakes of the Boundary Waters are the liquid remains of glaciers two miles thick that once gouged this country to the bedrock. Situated about two hours north of **Duluth**, Minnesota, the canoe area is on the southern edge of the Canadian Shield, a vast exposure of Precambrian stone that sweeps from eastern Manitoba to the Atlantic Ocean. With the frigid waters of **Lake Superior** just to the south generating a chilly microclimate, the forest and plants are more typical of those found farther north – vast stretches of black spruce, balsam fir, and jack pine. Owing to its position on the edge of several eco-types, the southern part of the Boundary Waters also has trees of the northern hardwood forest – birch, aspen, maple, and Norway and white pine. ◆ The constellation of lakes in this glacially wrought landscape is ideal for canoe travel and was used for centuries by Native people, most recently the Ojibwa. One can still see the mysterious rock art, or pictographs, that they painted on sacred cliffs. By the late 18th century, these waters were also being plied by French-Canadian traders known as voyageurs who followed a route along the present Minnesota–Ontario border to reach the fur wealth of the Northwest.

A canoe grants entry to the great North Woods, where wildlife and solitude abound.

A classic canoe and "Duluth" pack await on Little Saganaga Lake. The canoe area is true wilderness, with little development and few trail signs.

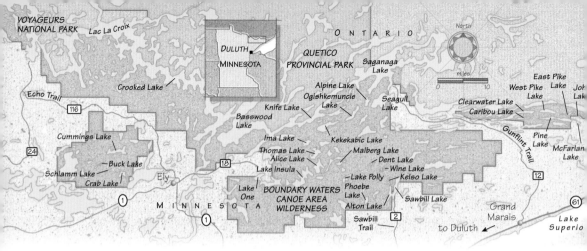

Wildlife also uses lakes and shorelines as travel corridors or as places to feed, resulting in frequent encounters. Among the animals most visitors hope to see are moose, which are fairly common and relatively easy to find, and timber wolves, also common but rarely seen. Other large mammals in canoe country are black bears, white-tailed deer, lynx, fishers, beavers, and otters.

Choosing a Route

Flanked to the west by **Voyageurs National Park**, and to the north by **Quetico Provincial Park**, the canoe area offers hundreds of possible routes for the paddler, reached by no fewer than 74 entry points scattered around its periphery. Where the water runs out, canoeists use the same portages that the Ojibwa and voyageurs used to carry their gear overland.

Local paddlers measure portages in rods – a distance of 16.5 feet, about the length of a canoe. A long portage is one that approaches a mile in length, but the majority rarely exceeds 40 rods, or a couple of hundred yards. Nevertheless, visitors should pack wisely, for the land is rugged, and your ability to penetrate into the Boundary Waters' lonely heart depends upon how far and fast you can travel.

With so many entry points to choose from, where you start should be determined by what you want to do or see. Entry points on the east end of the Boundary Waters lead paddlers into an area of dramatic topographic relief. Ridges rise hundreds of feet on each side of this region's long, narrow lakes, which lie along geologic faults. The most popular loop route in this part of the Boundary Waters begins at **John Lake**. Choosing a counterclockwise, westerly route, you'll pass through beautiful **East** and **West Pike Lakes** to **Clearwater**, connected by fairly long but level portages. A steep jaunt from Clearwater to **Caribou Lake** reverses the loop to the east, with a glorious paddle down the 10 miles of **Pine Lake** through **McFarland** and back to John.

John Lake is also where many canoeists begin their journey along the famous **Border Route**, which extends nearly 150 miles west to **Crane Lake**. The route meanders through a series of huge lakes, including **Saganaga, Basswood, Crooked,** and **La Croix**, and passes scenic waterfalls and stunning vistas. This is a challenging paddle; the lakes can be whipped into a frenzy by prevailing westerly winds, and some, like Crooked and La Croix, test one's map-reading and compass skills with their myriad islands and bays. Portages, however, are infrequent, which is why the voyageurs loved to come this way.

Paddling in Circles

For those who want to wander at will and enjoy the tranquillity of small- to medium-sized lakes, the central part of the wilderness – bounded on the east by the **Gunflint Trail** and on the west by the town of **Ely** – offers untold opportunities for exploration, albeit with more portaging. About midway between these two landmarks is the **Sawbill Trail**, a gravel highway that pokes north to the Boundary Waters' southern edge. Dozens of entry points provide paddlers with choices of both loop routes and linear trips to hundreds of lakes. Those in search of solitude will find plenty of remote areas off the well-traveled routes.

Circle routes are popular here. One of the best, just east of Ely, leads paddlers through medium-sized **Lake One** and **Lake Insula**, and **Alice**, **Thomas**, **Ima**, and **Snowbank Lakes**. An equally challenging route near the Sawbill Trail starts at **Sawbill Lake** and passes through **Alton**, **Phoebe**, **Polly**, **Malberg**, **Dent**, **Wine**, and **Kelso Lakes** before returning to Sawbill. This is an especially good choice for paddlers

Ancient pictographs (left) adorn a rock face on North Hegman Lake.

Wood canoes (opposite) have a timeless beauty, but updated models are typically lighter and faster.

A refreshing leap (below) into Saganaga Lake is a perfect break on a warm summer afternoon.

seeking the intimacy of small creeks and lakes. From the north end of the Gunflint Trail – a paved highway – many canoeists head west down **Seagull Lake** through **Alpine**, **Ogishkemuncie**, and **Kekekabic Lakes** before portaging north to **Knife Lake** and paddling east down the Border Route to their vehicles.

The western end of the Boundary Waters offers exceptional paddling as well. West of Ely and north of **Echo Trail** are routes to the large border lakes of Crooked Lake or Lac La Croix. A lovely route south of Echo

Trail begins and ends at **Crab Lake** and passes through **Cummings**, **Buck**, **Schlamm**, and other small lakes. Of course, a loop trip isn't your only option. In fact, some of the lonelier spots in the Boundary

The loon (left), known for its haunting call, is found throughout canoe country.

A canoeist (below) tackles the rapids at Clove Lake Portage. He has wisely unloaded his gear; a mishap in such a remote location could have serious consequences.

Waters can be found on "dead-end" journeys, where you'll enter and exit by much the same route. Visitors in search of privacy should seek such trips or choose to portage a lake or two away from main travel corridors. As a rule, the nearer you stay to a road, entry point, or major route, the more people you're likely to encounter.

Base camping also offers an alternative to loop trips. Take a day or two to find the right spot to set up camp, and then explore the area unencumbered by heavy packs. And if the lakes you want to visit don't offer a circle route, but you wish to avoid paddling back over the same waters, most outfitters will provide shuttle service back to your vehicle.

Wildlife Encounters

If you're hoping to encounter wildlife during your explorations, keep in mind that different habitats attract different species. At water's edge, for example, you may find nesting birds such as black ducks, ring-billed ducks, and common mergansers. Mink and fishers dart among the dark rocks, and otters travel on the banks or swim near them. Ospreys

nest in large Norway or white pines along the shore, where they can find a supply of fish to feed their young.

Slow waterways – especially those with lots of water lilies, a favorite moose food – are always excellent places to watch for this largest member of the deer family. On hot summer days, you may find them submerged in shallow back bays where they feed and stay cool. Waterways near young forest are prime locations for observing industrious beavers. Telltale signs are easily spotted: mounded lodges of sticks along banks and dams that frequently cross the creeks on which you're traveling. The great blue heron favors shallow waters and marshy areas where it can wade along on its spindly legs looking for frogs and minnows. Signs of the reclusive timber wolf can be spotted along high ridges. In winter, wolves feed primarily on moose or deer, consuming the entire animal, hide and all. The indigestible hair passes through the wolf and, when found months later on a summer day, looks like a twisted chunk of rope about five inches long and an inch thick. And while black bears tend to be shy by nature, it's not unheard of for paddlers to come across one swimming far out in a lake, intent on raiding an island campsite.

Such encounters with wildlife are a part of the magic of the Boundary Waters, and all it takes to experience it is time and patience. Give yourself at least four days to explore the wilderness, though you could stay for a month or longer and never paddle the same lake twice. Groups are limited to nine people, but you'll see more wildlife, be less obtrusive to other visitors, and have less impact on the fragile environment if you keep your party smaller.

The (Almost) Painless Portage

It's inevitable. You will have to carry your canoe at some point during your adventure in the Boundary Waters. Here are some tips to lighten the load:

● It may seem surprising, but the easiest way to carry a canoe is usually by yourself. Hold the boat upside down over your head, placing the center thwart across your shoulders and a hand on a forward thwart. Other members of your party should walk ahead and warn of obstacles but shouldn't try to help with the canoe unless asked, lest they throw off your balance.

● Picking up a canoe solo is easy once you get the timing and technique down. Lean the boat on its side with its bottom against your thighs. With your knees slightly bent, reach over and place both hands on the center thwart, knuckles facing forward. In one movement, "bounce" the canoe on your thighs and swing it overhead onto your shoulders. If help is available, it may be easier to simply walk under a boat held up at one end by a companion.

● Try padding your shoulders with extra clothes or a life jacket, and watch for "canoe rests" built along many portage trails that allow you to set the boat down in the "ready" position.

● Consider leaving one person behind to guard the food bags, or hang them out of reach of savvy bears who have been known to wait near portage trails for temporarily abandoned treats.

● Pack lightly. Fit all your gear into easy-to-carry packs or duffels (preferably with shoulder straps) and avoid the temptation to hang loose gear on the canoe or the outside of your pack.

● Wear sturdy boots. Rafting sandals and neoprene paddling boots provide little support on rugged portages.

● Pace yourself, and allow plenty of time for rest. Overexertion will only lead to fatigue, frustration, and injury.

Portage trails can vary from wide thoroughfares (right) to overgrown tracks.

TRAVEL TIPS

DETAILS

When to Go

Summer brings the most visitors as well as the region's infamous mosquitoes and blackflies. Daytime temperatures rise into the 80s, with evenings in the 50s and 60s. By late August the mosquitoes have faded, and after Labor Day the crowds thin considerably, too, making the pre-frost, fall-foliage weeks of September a favorite time for Boundary Waters aficionados. September temperatures usually range between 45° and 65°F. Try spring for solitude, though cold lake water and rain put a damper on swim breaks.

How to Get There

Two towns serve as the gateways to the Boundary Waters: Ely, Minnesota, about five hours north of Minneapolis and two hours north of Duluth, and Grand Marais, about three hours east of Duluth. Northwest Airlines (800-225 2525) provides direct service to Ely from Minneapolis in summer.

Permits

Permits are required year-round. A daily quota restricts the number of overnight visitors at each of the various entry points from May 1 to September 30. To make reservations, write the Reservation Office at P.O. Box 462, Ballston, NY 12020, or call 877-550-6777.

INFORMATION

Ely Chamber of Commerce

1600 Sheridan Street, Ely, MN 55731; tel: 800-777-7281.

Gunflint Ranger District

P.O. Box 790, Grand Marais, MN 55604; tel: 218-387-1750.

Superior National Forest

Supervisor's Office, 8901 Grand Avenue Place, Duluth, MN 55808; tel: 218-626-4300.

CAMPING

All of the lakes in the Boundary Waters have designated camp-sites available on a first-come, first-served basis. The sites are primitive, with pit toilets.

Bear Head Lake State Park

9301 Bear Head State Road, Ely, MN 55731; tel: 218-365-7229 or 800-246-2267 (reservations).

About 10 miles west of Ely, the park has 78 wooded campsites, including five that can be reached only by foot.

Cascade River State Park

3481 West Highway 61, Lutsen, MN 55612-9535; tel: 218-387-3053 or 800-246-2267 (reservations).

This park makes a good stopover for travelers headed to the east side of the Boundary Waters. Forty-five campsites are on Lake Superior about 10 miles southwest of Grand Marais; reservations are accepted.

LODGING

PRICE GUIDE – double occupancy

$ = up to $49 $$ = $50–$99

$$$ = $100–$149 $$$$ = $150+

Blue Heron Bed-and-Breakfast

827 Kawishiwi Trail, Ely, MN 55731; tel: 218-365-4720.

This log lodge on the edge of the Boundary Waters features lake views from all three guest rooms. Amenities include a wood-fired sauna, canoes, and a restaurant. $$

Burntside Lodge

2755 Burntside Lodge Road, Ely, MN 55731; tel: 218-365-3894.

Six miles from Ely on the shore of Burntside Lake, this lodge was built as a hunting camp in 1913 and has been in the National Register of Historic Places since the 1970s. Housekeeping cabins (one to three bedrooms) are available on a weekly or nightly basis. A restaurant, lounge, cappuccino bar, sauna, and marina are also available. $$–$$$$

Gunflint Lodge

143 South Gunflint Lake, Grand Marais, MN 55604; tel: 218-388-2294 or 800-328-3325.

The Gunflint was started as a trading post and has been run by the same family since the 1930s. The lodge emphasizes "wilderness elegance," with native-wood construction and regional artifacts. A year-round schedule of special programs ranges from "howl with the wolves" seminars to family canoe instruction, outfitting, and guided tours. More than 20 one- to four-bedroom cabins are spread around the property, all with fireplaces, some with a hot tub or sauna. "Rustic canoer cabins" provide a budget option. $–$$$$

Silver Rapids Lodge

HC 1, Box 2992, Ely, MN 55731; tel: 218-365-4877 or 800-950-9425.

Set on a 59-acre peninsula, the lodge has 11 lakeside guest rooms and 14 housekeeping cabins, each with two to eight bedrooms, a fireplace, and out-door grill. Campsites and banquet facilities are also on the premises. $$–$$$$

TOURS AND OUTFITTERS

The following companies offer guided trips and outfitting services, and many rent one-, two-, or three-person canoes in a choice of materials. In some cases, they will also arrange fly-in trips to Quetico Provincial Park in Canada or motorboat tows for quick access to remote locations.

Bear Track Outfitting Company
P.O. Box 937, Grand Marais, MN 55604; tel: 218-387-1162 or 800-795-8068.

Border Lakes Wilderness Canoe Trips
5865 Moose Lake Road, Ely, MN 55731; tel: 218-365-5811 or 800-569-4151.

Canadian Border Outfitters
P.O. Box 117, Ely, MN 55731; tel: 800-247-7530.

Canoe Country Outfitters
629 East Sheridan Street, P.O. Box 30, Ely, MN 55731; tel: 218-365-4046 or 800-752-2306.

Gunflint Northwoods Outfitters
143 South Gunflint Lake, Grand Marais, MN 55604; tel: 800-362-5251 or 800-226-6346.

Hill's Wilderness Trips
2030 East Sheridan Street, Ely, MN 55731; tel: 218-365-3149 or 800-950-2709.

Piragis Northwoods Outfitters
105 North Central Avenue, Ely, MN 55731; tel: 218-365-6745 or 800-223-6565.

Tom and Wood's Moose Lake Wilderness Canoe Trips
Box 358, Ely, MN 55731; tel: 218-365-5837 or 800-322-5837.

Wilderness Outfitters
1 East Camp Street, Ely, MN 55731; tel: 218-365-3211 or 800-777-8572.

Excursions

Isle Royale National Park
800 East Lakeshore Drive, Houghton, MI 49931; tel: 906-482-0984.

Sea kayakers and canoeists can spend weeks exploring the wetlands, rocky coves, and beaches along the shores of this wild island in Lake Superior, where campers sometimes hear the howls of resident wolves. The island, some 45 miles long and nine miles wide, is reachable only by boat or seaplane, and open only from mid-April through October. For those who crave civilized comforts, historic Rock Harbor Lodge (906-337-4993 or in winter 502-773-2191) offers guest rooms, cabins, and a log dining room overlooking the lake.

St. Croix National Scenic Riverway
P.O. Box 708, St. Croix Falls, WI 54024; tel: 715-483-3284.

One of the eight original Wild and Scenic Rivers designated by Congress, the St. Croix flows from the gently rolling forests and wetlands of Wisconsin past the sandstone banks, pristine parks, and quiet wooded countryside of the Minnesota–Wisconsin border. Virtually the entire stretch is ideal for easy to moderate canoe tours ranging from a day to a week or more.

Voyageurs National Park
3131 Highway 53, International Falls, MN 56649; tel: 218-283-9821.

It's easy to imagine the chants of 18th-century voyageurs ringing through the mist in this North Woods wilderness. Named for the French-Canadian fur traders who once paddled these waters in birch-bark canoes, the park encompasses more than 30 lakes and 170 boat-in campsites. Though much of the park is open to motorized vessels, sea kayakers and canoeists will easily find solitude in the maze of small coves, lakes, and waterways. Lodging is available at the Kettle Falls Hotel (888-534-6835), a former logger's hostel (and brothel), and several outfitters offer kayak and canoe tours into the park.

Apostle Islands
National Lakeshore
Wisconsin

CHAPTER 12

Prettily described as "an emerald necklace on blue velvet," northern Wisconsin's **Apostle Islands** cluster off the tip of Lake Superior's **Bayfield Peninsula**. French missionaries named the islands to celebrate the disciples of Christ – never mind that there are actually 22 islands, not 12, in the archipelago. In any case, 21 of the Apostles, plus an 11-mile strip of the mainland, are now part of **Apostle Islands National Lakeshore** and one of the Midwest's foremost sea-kayaking destinations. ◆ Early French fur traders called this region the Chequamegon (She-wah-me-gon), a Chippewa word meaning "soft beaver dam." And indeed, commerce in beaver pelts was the area's premier enterprise for generations, with vast cargoes of skins leaving island trading posts for Montreal and, later, New Orleans and Europe. ◆ The huge *canots du maître* laden with five tons of furs and powered by 10 hardy voyageurs are gone now. Today's

A cluster of islands in Lake Superior lures paddlers with secluded beaches, historic lighthouses, and fascinating sea caves.

adventurers paddle sleek, modern sea kayaks, and there are few places better suited to these craft. Lying between one and 16 miles offshore, the islands' sheltered waters beckon the novice, while the open stretches offer a challenge comparable to ocean paddling for the expert. ◆ The gateway to the Apostle Islands is the small town of **Bayfield**, less than two hours from Duluth, Minnesota, on Lake Superior's **Chequamegon Bay**. The national lakeshore visitor center is housed in the old Bayfield County Courthouse, built in 1883 and now in the National Register of Historic Places. ◆ Ranging in size from three-acre **Gull Island** to 10,054-acre **Stockton Island** (notable for one of the heaviest concentrations of black bears in North America), the

A sandy beach at Squaw Bay on the Wisconsin mainland makes a convenient landing site. Lake Superior is famous for inhospitable conditions, but there is plenty of protected paddling around the Apostle Islands.

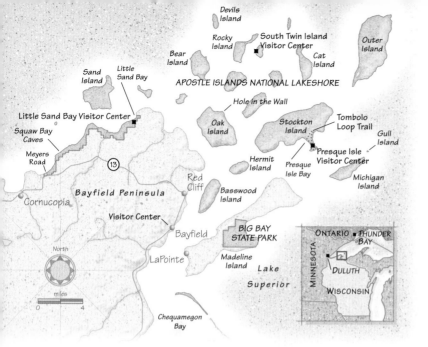

varied history, and plenty of solitude (after all, the island is named for a recluse who holed up here for more than a decade in the mid-19th century). Like Hermit, **Basswood** and **Oak Islands** are relatively easy to reach from the mainland. Basswood offers good camping and fishing and is only a mile from the Bayfield Peninsula. Here, low cliffs of brown sandstone or banks of broken stone and red clay meet **Lake Superior** along a picturesque shoreline. Oak, on the other hand, rises 480 feet above the lake level and is the tallest of the Apostles. On its northern tip you'll be able to paddle along the highest cliffs on Wisconsin's Lake Superior shoreline and view a remarkable archway called the **Hole-in-the-Wall** that was formed by erosion. Except for widely spaced backcountry campsites and about 12 miles of hiking trails, the 5,078-acre island is largely undeveloped.

Agates and Sea Caves

Stockton Island is a favorite among sea kayakers, and for good reason. The exposed sandstone bedrock along the shoreline has been shaped into graceful arches, caves, columns, and cliffs. Poke through the pebbles on the beaches and you may find a semi-precious agate – a smooth, lustrous stone that displays concentric rings when split open and polished. For a nice hike, follow the **Tombolo Loop Trail** about four miles from the island's camping area through a variety of habitats – towering pines, old and new bogs, a lagoon, and sand dunes. Almost hidden are signs of previous human occupants. Native people fished, hunted, harvested berries, and made maple syrup here. By the late 1800s, the island lured commercial interests such as fishing camps, a brown-

island chain presents a multitude of options for paddlers. There are secluded white-sand beaches, striking, eroded cliffs, 22 documented shipwrecks, six lighthouses built in the last century, abandoned fishing camps, and a history rich with Indian and voyageur lore.

Although similar in many ways, each island offers some special feature. Tiny **Devils Island** (318 acres) lies the farthest north, about 20 miles from Bayfield. It has a lighthouse, spectacular sea caves, and only one campsite – and when you get there, you'll find yourself alone at the tip of Wisconsin. But if time is short, any one of the near-shore islands will serve as an idyllic getaway.

For example, **Hermit Island**, two and a half miles east of the mainland, has sandy beaches, scenic rocky cliffs, a colorful and

stone quarry, and lumber camps. Today, however, Stockton is uninhabited; only in the summer do park rangers staff a small visitor center at **Presque Isle Bay**.

The islands themselves deservedly get

The hull of the ***Ottawa*** (left), shipwrecked in 1909, lies in shallow water in Red Cliff Bay.

The sea caves at Squaw Bay (opposite) are easily explored with a sea kayak.

Sunlight plays on the walls of the Swallow Point sea caves on Sand Island (below).

Camping is allowed on most of the Apostle Islands, ranging from developed sites to designated wilderness zones. Permits are required. You can call ahead for one, or pick a permit up at park visitor centers in Bayfield or at **Little Sand Bay**, 13 miles north along the coast.

If you camp in late summer or fall, be sure to walk out to the lake before turning in for the night. The open vista to the north often provides glorious views of the northern lights. But if you arrive during the warm period of June and July, be prepared for biting insects. A liberal supply of repellent, proper attire, and an open, breezy campsite generally reduce the annoyance to a tolerable level.

The islands themselves deservedly get most of the attention in this park, but don't neglect the mainland section. This coastal strip extends 11 miles from Little Sand Bay on the east to **Squaw Bay** on the west. In summer, kayakers leave from the **Little Sand Bay Visitor Center** to tour the colorful cliffs, sea caves, and historic lighthouse on **Sand Island**.

Also on the mainland, several miles from Little Sand Bay, are the **Squaw Bay Caves**, one of the most beautiful features of the national lakeshore. They can be reached from a launch point at the end of

Night Lights

Best known of the national lakeshore's historic sites are its lighthouses. Between 1857 and 1891, six light stations were established on the Apostle Islands to aid ships navigating the dangerous, often stormy channels. Although modernized and automated, all stations are still in use and remain major landmarks along the trans-Superior shipping lanes.

Five of the stations are staffed through the summer. The **Raspberry Island** light, completed in 1863 to mark the west channel through the Apostle Islands, is the most popular with visitors. The building's exterior and grounds have been restored to their 1920s appearance. Visitors can follow park personnel on guided tours through the quarters where the keeper lived and up spiral stairs to the top of the tower for a thrilling view of the lake.

Park Service volunteers also occupy light stations at **Sand**, **Devils**, **Michigan**, and **Outer Islands**, and paddlers are welcome to dock or beach their boats and stroll around the grounds. The lighthouses themselves are closed unless Park Service staffers are there to lead tours.

A Park Service volunteer (above) inspects the Devils Island Lighthouse; the lens was made in 1901.

Sand Island Lighthouse (left) was built of native sandstone in the 1880s.

"The Crack" (right) towers over kayakers at the entrance of the Squaw Bay Caves.

People without their own boats can visit the island-based lighthouses on a cruise. Packages offer a chance to see several lighthouses from afar, or participants can stop in at one lighthouse for a close-up look.

Meyers Road, about four miles east of the tiny village of **Cornucopia**. If the weather is right (calm, with a favorable forecast), it's possible to paddle into some of these caves with their twisting sandstone pillars and arches sculpted by the lake's waves. Kayakers call it "yak-spelunking."

Perilous Waters

Operating small craft on Lake Superior is fun and exciting, but it can also be hazardous. This is what one chronicler had to say about the lake in 1872, and the words ring just as true today: "Those who have never seen Superior get an inadequate, even inaccurate idea of hearing of it spoken as a lake. Though its waters are fresh and crystal, Superior is a sea. It breeds storms and rain and fog, like the sea. It is cold in midsummer as the Atlantic. It is wild, masterful, and dreaded."

Experienced kayakers use wet suits or dry suits when paddling the Apostles. This is especially important in spring and fall when the risk of hypothemia is high. Even in summer, Lake Superior is seldom warm enough for comfortable swimming except in shallow, protected bays. Boaters should also monitor radio marine weather forecasts and be constantly alert to changing conditions. Prepare for possible severe weather by packing provisions for an extra day or two. Sitting out a storm in a snug camp is far better than chancing a crossing in conditions beyond your paddling abilities.

If you're short on time or kayaking skills, consider taking one of the concession-operated cruise and shuttle vessels to the outlying islands. Water taxis will transport kayaks as well as campers on a prearranged basis. Another option is to go with one of the full-service outfitters in Bayfield; they will be happy to provide everything from paddling instruction to sea-kayak rentals, and they offer both short and extended guided kayak tours around Lake Superior's "emerald necklace on blue velvet."

TRAVEL TIPS

DETAILS

When to Go

Late spring through early fall is the best time to paddle in the Apostle Islands. Daytime temperatures in May and September average around 60°F; July temperatures reach only the upper 70s. Wind adds a chill out on the water, blowing from five to 20 knots in summer. Lake Superior is notorious for bad weather; paddlers should be alert to changing conditions and rough seas. Four-foot waves are not uncommon; 12-foot seas are possible under extreme conditions.

Getting Around

The islands are situated off the southwest shore of Lake Superior, 90 miles east of Duluth, Minnesota, and 13 miles north of Bayfield, Wisconsin. Ferries run by Apostle Islands Cruise Service (715-779-3925 or 800-323-7619) will transport kayakers and their equipment to select portions of the park and will arrange water taxis to less-visited areas. Docks are located in downtown Bayfield. The service also operates cruises throughout the islands and rents equipment.

Permits

No permits are required for sea kayaking within the national lakeshore, but camping permits are necessary.

INFORMATION

Apostle Islands National Lakeshore

Route 1, Box 4, Bayfield, WI 54814; tel: 715-779-3397.

Bayfield Chamber of Commerce

P.O. Box 138, Bayfield, WI 54814; tel: 715-779-3335 or 800-447-4094.

Bayfield County Tourism and Recreation

Box 832, Courthouse, Washburn, WI 54891; tel: 715-373-6125 or 800-472-6338.

CAMPING

Apostle Islands National Lakeshore

Route 1, Box 4, Bayfield, WI 54814; tel: 715-779-3397.

Camping is allowed on 18 of the Apostle Islands. Campsites may be reserved by calling headquarters; a fee and permit are required. It is essential to plan paddling itineraries around reserved sites.

Apostle Islands Area Campground

Atar Route Box 8, Bayfield, WI 54814; tel: 715-779-5524.

This campground has 56 sites and a separate tent area about half a mile south of Bayfield. Two log cabins with no water or electricity are also available.

Big Bay State Park

Department of Natural Resources, P.O. Box 589, Bayfield, WI 54814; tel: 715-779-4020 or 888-947-2757 (reservations).

A 20-minute car ferry from Bayfield takes you to this popular state park on Madeline Island south of the Apostles. The park has a long sandy beach, five miles of hiking trails, and sandstone bluffs and caves. Only primitive campsites are available.

Dalrymple Campground

City of Bayfield, North Highway 13, Bayfield, WI 54814; tel: 715-779-5712.

The city of Bayfield operates a 30-site campground for both tents and RVs in a pine forest overlooking Lake Superior a mile north of town.

Little Sand Bay Campground

Little Sand Bay Road, Russell, WI.

This 16-site campground is adjacent to the lakeshore's Little Sand Bay Visitor Center. Maintained by volunteers, it operates on a first-come, first-served basis. The sites are arranged in a circle and sometimes feel congested, but this is the most convenient camping for kayakers launching from Sand Bay or who want to explore the mainland sea caves.

LODGING

PRICE GUIDE – double occupancy

$ = up to $49 $$ = $50–$99
$$$ = $100–$149 $$$$ = $150+

Cooper Hill House

33 South 6th Street, Bayfield, WI 54814; tel: 715-779-5060.

An in-town bed-and-breakfast with four rooms, this 1888 antique-filled house features a central fireplace and private baths. $$

Old Rittenhouse Inn

301 Rittenhouse Avenue, P.O. Box 584, Bayfield, WI 54814; tel: 715-779-5111 or 888-611-4667.

This Victorian mansion was built by a Civil War general. The big wraparound porch overlooks Lake Superior, and nearly all of the 20 guest rooms have private baths and working fireplaces. The property also includes three turn-of-the-century buildings. Fine dining is available. $$–$$$$

Pinehurst Inn at Pike's Creek

Route 1, Box 22, Bayfield, WI 54814; tel: 715-779-3676.

Once owned by a lumber baron, this large home three miles south of Bayfield was built of sandstone in 1885. There are six guest rooms, each with a private bath, and a three-room suite with a Jacuzzi. A two-night stay is required during the summer. $$–$$$$

Thimbleberry Inn

15021 Pageant Road, P.O. Box 1007, Bayfield, WI 54814; tel: 715-779-5757.

This contemporary bed-and-breakfast is set on 40 lakeshore acres. The three bedrooms have private baths and fireplaces. The innkeepers offer a full- or half-day sail in a 35-foot wooden ketch. $$–$$$

Trek and Trail Cabins

100 North Limits Avenue, Bayfield, WI 54814; tel: 715-779-3595 or 800-354-8735.

Cabins with kitchen facilities and views of Lake Superior are in a wooded setting within walking distance of Bayfield. $$

Winfield Inn

100 Lynde Avenue, Bayfield, WI 54814; tel: 715-779-5558.

This lakeshore inn offers more than 30 motel rooms, two-bedroom suites with kitchens, and Stonehearth, a rustic cabin with a stone fireplace and wraparound deck that sleeps up to eight people. $$–$$$

TOURS AND OUTFITTERS

Apostle Islands Kayaks

19 Front Street, P.O. Box 990, Bayfield, WI 54814; tel: 715-779-9575 or 800-779-4487.

Associated with the Apostle Islands Cruise Service, this company rents kayaks for unguided day or overnight trips. Kayaks may not be paddled from island to island and are limited to within 100 yards of shore. Water-taxi service to the islands and a short orientation session are included.

Trek and Trail Outdoor Adventure Specialists

222 Rittenhouse Avenue, P.O. Box 906, Bayfield, WI 54814; tel: 800-354-8735.

Trek and Trail provides outfitting services and guided kayak trips from one to seven days in the Apostle Islands.

Excursions

Flambeau River

Flambeau River State Forest, Coney Road West, Winter, WI 54896; tel: 715-332-5271.

About three hours east of Minneapolis, the two forks of the Flambeau River are a good choice for canoe trips of one to five days. The North Fork is the more popular of the two: a shallow, easy river with rapids and riffles up to Class II. Forty miles of the North Fork flow through Flambeau State Forest, with quiet, canoe-access-only campsites along the way. Longer trips may require several portages around dams. The South Fork is more challenging, with rapids up to Class III and one Class IV drop that canoeists should portage.

Sylvania Wilderness Area

Ottawa Visitor Center, P.O. Box 276, Watersmeet, MI 49969; tel: 906-358-4724.

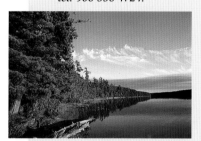

An 18,000-acre "pocket wilderness" of virgin hardwood forest and more than 35 picturesque lakes, the Sylvania Wilderness Area is a miniature Boundary Waters, ideal for two days to a week of peaceful exploration by paddle and portage. It is located on Michigan's Upper Peninsula along the Wisconsin border, about a five-hour drive north of Green Bay. Canoeists and hikers use designated campsites on eight of the lakes. Powerboats are forbidden on all but the largest, two-mile-long Clark Lake, where electric motors are permitted. Advance reservations, taken January through May, are highly recommended.

Wolf River

Whitewater Specialty, N3894 Highway 55, White Lake, WI 54491; tel: 715-882-5400.

The tea-colored Wolf River is a mecca for whitewater paddlers in the upper Midwest and a great place to hone whitewater skills. Over its 30-mile course, the Wolf passes through four short sections that get progressively more difficult. The upper reach, starting at Post Lake, is a flatwater float excellent for wildlife watchers. By the fourth stretch, the river has changed character, dropping over waterfalls and Class IV rapids. There is ample access and plenty of scenery but no camping along the river. Several guides and outfitters provide canoe and kayak instruction, equipment, and guided raft trips.

Upper Missouri River
Montana

CHAPTER **13**

They were the pathfinders for a nation. In 1804, immediately after completing the Louisiana Purchase, President Thomas Jefferson sent two U.S. Army officers on an epic journey of exploration up the Missouri River and thence to the Pacific Ocean at the mouth of the Columbia. Captains Meriwether Lewis and William Clark and their 30-man Corps of Discovery traveled 7,689 arduous miles out and back, and when they returned in triumph to St. Louis after two years, four months, and 10 days, they had opened the way west for legions of Americans to come. ◆ Now, two centuries after Lewis and Clark's exploit, modern-day adventurers can savor their own sense of discovery by voyaging along a segment of the route that remains much as it was when the explorers first poled their dugouts and keelboats westward. This is a 149-mile stretch of the **Upper Missouri** in central Montana (starting at U.S. Highway 191 and ending at **Fort Benton**) that has been designated a national wild and scenic river. Watched over by the Bureau of Land Management (BLM), this historic, riparian highway marks the point where Lewis and Clark first beheld what they thought were the snow-draped Rocky Mountains, beyond which, the Indians had told them, lay the passageway to the Pacific waters. (In hindsight, the peaks they saw were more likely the Belt Mountains southeast of the Rockies.) ◆ Flat, wide, and gleaming, the untamed Upper Missouri slices through a semiarid prairie landscape punctuated by elaborately eroded hills and gullies called the **Missouri River Breaks**. It is virtually unequaled as a canoe destination. Multiple access points allow trips of varying lengths, from weekend outings to the seven or

Follow in the wake of Lewis and Clark on a gentle paddle through the Missouri River Breaks.

A hiker takes in the view of Woodhawk Bottom. Now quiet, the Upper Missouri was once a busy frontier highway.

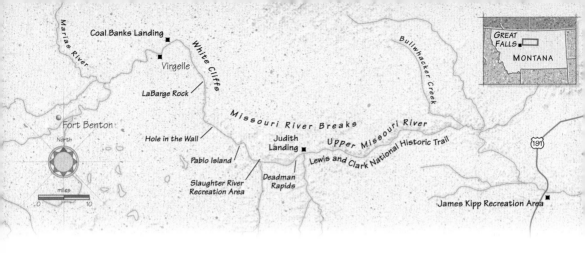

eight days needed to cover the full 149 miles.

There are no rapids or portages on the "Upper Mo'." Still, it's much easier to travel downstream than to travel upstream as the Corps of Discovery did on its outbound journey. Meriwether Lewis described the exhausting work required to push past Pablo Island at the height of the spring runoff: "The men are compelled to be in the water even to their armpits, and the water is yet very could ... added to this the banks and bluffs along which they are obliged to pass are so slippery and the mud so tenacious that they are unable to wear their mockersons ... in short their labour is incredibly painfull and great, yet those faithfull fellows bear it without a murmur."

Each uncomplaining fellow received a dram of liquor (about an ounce) that noon as a reward.

Reading the Stars

Paddling easily, with no rocks or rapids to worry about, modern explorers can sit back and watch the miles slide by. Despite their grueling assignment, the Corps of Discovery found time to appreciate the scenery, too. Lewis wrote in 1805 that the river "passes through a rich, fertile and one of the most beautifully picteresque countries that I ever beheld, through the wide expanse of which, innumerable herds of living animals are seen."

It's almost uncanny the way his reports match a visitor's impressions two centuries later. Gliding across water that's been stirred to a cream-and-coffee color by the spring runoff, you can easily imagine what it was like when Blackfeet horsemen and 60 million bison roamed the surrounding plains. Cattle have replaced the bison, and the grizzly bears and wolves are gone, but virtually every other animal species that Lewis and Clark encountered can be seen by present-day travelers. Bighorn sheep are frequently spotted by canoeists, along with mule deer, white-tailed deer, and pronghorn antelope, not to mention elk, coyotes, badgers, prairie dogs, herons, and bald and golden eagles.

Names like **Slaughter River**, **Bullwhacker Creek**, **Deadman Rapids**, and **Hole in the Wall**, on your BLM river map, evoke powerful images and give you landmarks that help determine your whereabouts. Since Lewis and Clark took readings from the stars when they stopped at night, the locations of many of their campsites are known and are marked on the map.

Straggly cottonwood groves similar to those under which the explorers pitched their tents offer shade to travelers today.

Camped at the mouth of the **Marias River** (mile 22 from Fort Benton on the BLM map), where Lewis and Clark stopped on June 3, 1805, you can read from their journals as you sit by a fire, listening to the wind move through the cottonwoods and coyotes bark in the distance. It was here that the Corps of Discovery had to make one of the most critical decisions of its entire journey.

Turbid or Clear?

Upon reaching the Marias, the explorers didn't know which waterway to follow. At the time, the Marias closely resembled the slow and turbid part of the Missouri the party had already traversed, and the crew felt it would lead them to the Pacific. The other fork, which we know today as the

Easy paddling and abundant wildlife make the Upper Missouri an excellent family destination (left).

Bighorn sheep (opposite) are one of 60 mammal species found in the river corridor.

The White Cliffs (below) loom over the river. Lewis and Clark first passed them in the last week of May 1805.

Missouri, was clearer and seemed to lead toward the mountains. This is the route that the two captains favored.

Think of the anxiety. With no maps or global positioning systems to pinpoint their location, and no reliable knowledge of the path ahead, their lives and the lives of all those in their party hung in the balance. Delving into the journals, which brim with vivid imagery, anecdotes, and drama, you can almost feel the pressure facing the two men. If they had followed the Marias, they might have had to retrace their path, which

to get out and stretch your legs (as well as the most scenic and popular canoe route) is the 47-mile run from **Coal Banks Landing** to **Judith Landing**. Here the big sky of the prairie is replaced with tiers of light-colored sandstone spires and vertical bluffs known as the **White Cliffs**.

The gallery of curious formations captured the imaginations of Lewis and Clark. They wrote poetically of "eligant ranges of lofty freestone buildings, having their parapets well stocked with statuary." Other formations resemble giant sandstone toadstools, gargoyles, and tabletop rocks that seem ready to topple.

would have meant a late, dangerous journey over the Rockies in November. Only after more than a week of fitful consideration did Lewis and Clark make the right choice to continue up the Missouri.

About 40 miles downstream of its confluence with the Marias, the Missouri offers some of the best hiking along any western river. The valley grows increasingly wild – typical Missouri River Breaks scenery with an array of side canyons, rolling rangeland, and eroded buttes. An excellent section in which

There are several notable side hikes in the White Cliffs area. One is **Neet Coulee** (mile 56), on the north side of the river not far from the spot where Lewis and Clark camped in 1805. Across the river, **LaBarge Rock**, an igneous plug that towers above the adjacent terrain, confirms that you're at the right place. Here, camped among the cottonwoods, you may want to set out at

"Old Muddy" by Steamboat

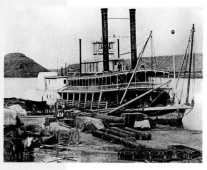

The Missouri was once one of the busiest "highways" in the West. First came keelboats, flat-bottomed vessels propelled by oars, poles, and sails, but by the mid-19th century they were too small and slow to accommodate the burgeoning frontier trade. A new era dawned on July 2, 1860, when the sternwheeler *Chippewa* became the first steamboat to journey upriver from St. Louis, Missouri, to Fort Benton, Montana.

The *Chippewa* was well designed for the shallows of Old Muddy, as the Missouri was known. Thirty feet wide and 165 feet long, the vessel could handle 350 tons of cargo and operate in as little as one foot of water. After gold was discovered in Montana in 1862, dozens of similar boats plied the river. Unlike the plush steamboats of the Mississippi, however, they were not a particularly pleasant mode of transportation. Passengers had to contend with loud and smoky engines and the enervating vibrations of the paddle wheels, not to mention the very real possibility of a boiler explosion or foundering on a sandbar or snag. Creature comforts were few and primitive. Many passengers slept below deck amid piles of cargo and dragged drinking water from the silty river.

Though the heyday of the sternwheelers lasted only until the late 1880s, the era left its mark. "Woodhawks" deforested much of the area in order to supply the vessels with fuel, and modern paddlers pass former landings such as **Cow Island** and **Judith Landing**. The **Museum of the Upper Missouri** in Fort Benton (406-622-5316) exhibits photographs and scale models of the boats.

The *DeSmet* (above) was one of dozens of steamboats that transported passengers and cargo between St. Louis, Missouri, and Fort Benton, Montana, in the late 1800s.

Camping (opposite, top) is permitted on public lands along the river.

Paddler and dog (opposite, bottom) enjoy a quiet float below Fort Benton.

dawn and head up the side canyon. The shortgrass and wild rose of the river bottom changes to silvery sage and greasewood along the valley slopes. Farther into the dry coulee, pockets of ponderosa and limber pine appear, along with Douglas fir and juniper. The chasm narrows, and the sandstone cliffs become so close and sheer that you can touch both walls with outstretched arms. Eventually you'll reach the end of the slot canyon and clamber up onto the flat rim above for a look around.

"Visionary Inchantment"

Perhaps the most notable hike in the White Cliffs area is just upstream of LaBarge Rock. Until recently, an objective here for canoeists was to peer through the **Eye of the Needle**, an unusual sandstone arch perched on a 200-foot cliff directly above the river. Framed through the delicate arch was a landscape without walls, a hundred square miles of the northern plains through which the tranquil Missouri flows. Lewis wrote that the sight was one of "visionary inchantment."

But the arch is no more. On Memorial Day weekend in 1997, vandals destroyed the Eye of the Needle, leaving the wind-shaped stones in a scattered pile on the ground. Like the Grand Canyon or Devil's Tower, this formation was a monument to the artistic powers of nature, a landmark that had withstood the fury of countless storms. In perhaps 30 minutes or less, it was gone.

Canoeists and concerned citizens everywhere were deeply saddened. Peering through the Eye of the Needle was the finest of the many extraordinary vistas along the Upper Missouri. Now the decision has been made to leave what remains of the Eye of the Needle as it is – two six-foot-high sandstone pillars overlooking the river. A full replica of the arch will be constructed on a promontory just downstream from Fort Benton. The remains will serve as a reminder to future travelers that the West, as seen by Lewis and Clark, needs to be preserved for history's sake as well as our own.

DETAILS

When to Go

Summer, the most popular time to float the Upper Missouri, is quite warm, with daytime temperatures in the 80s or 90s and cool evenings. Be prepared for afternoon winds, thunderstorms, and pesky mosquitoes. Water levels drop by early fall, so add a day or two to your itinerary and expect to paddle a bit harder.

How to Get There

Fort Benton, near the starting point for most Upper Missouri canoe trips, is about 45 miles northeast of Great Falls, Montana. The take-out is 70 miles north of Lewistown, Montana. Both Great Falls and Lewistown are served by Big Sky Airlines (800-237-7788).

Permits

No permits are required to float this section, but boaters are asked to register at their put-in location.

INFORMATION

Bureau of Land Management

River Manager, Lewistown District Office, Airport Road, Lewistown, MT 59457; tel: 406-538-7461.

Fort Benton Visitor Center

1718 Front Street, P.O. Box 1389, Fort Benton, MT 59442; tel: 406-622-5185.

CAMPING

Camping is allowed on public land along the river; there are some fine spots in cottonwood groves and at the mouths of side canyons. In addition, the Bureau of Land Management has developed 11 campsites with toilets, some with simple shelters. Though fires are permitted, firewood is scarce; paddlers are encouraged to bring portable stoves for cooking and gather driftwood from the riverbanks as they float. Drinking water is available at only two boat launches.

Camp Creek Campground

Bureau of Land Management, 501 South 2nd Street East, HC 65, Box 5000, Malta, MT 59538; tel: 406-654-1240.

This wooded mountain campground near Zortman has a pleasant creekside location with 21 primitive sites.

Coal Banks Landing Campground

Bureau of Land Management, Airport Road, Lewistown, MT 59457; tel: 406-538-7461.

Situated in tiny Virgelle, this campground has about a dozen sites with drinking water and vault toilets.

James Kipp Recreation Area

Bureau of Land Management, Airport Road, Lewistown, MT 59457; tel: 406-538-7461.

This recreation area is in the Charles Russell National Wildlife Refuge at the point where Route 191 crosses the Missouri River. There are 30 sites in a grove of cottonwoods, plus a separate, grassy "floaters camp" set aside for canoeists.

LODGING

Great Falls Inn

1400 28th Street South, Great Falls, MT 59405; tel: 406-453-6000.

This pleasant hotel has 45 generously sized rooms with a touch of western styling and a fireplace in the lobby. $$

Pioneer Lodge

1700 Front Street, Fort Benton, MT 59442; tel: 406-622-5441.

This two-story motel in the center of Fort Benton is a converted shop originally built in 1916. The 12 guest rooms are simple and spacious; some have lofts. A sitting area in the lobby overlooks the Missouri River. $–$$

Virgelle Mercantile

HC 67, Box 50, Loma, MT 59460; tel: 406-378-3110 or 800-426-2926.

Situated at Coal Banks Landing, the Mercantile is an old country store that now houses a canoe outfitter, antique shop, and accommodations. Choose from three "homestead" cabins outfitted as they would have been a hundred years ago, with no running water or electricity, a wood-burning cook stove, a kerosene lamp, and an outhouse (described as "rustic but romantic"). There are also four guest rooms above the shop. $–$$

Wicks Bed-and-Breakfast

220 West Boulevard, Lewistown, MT 59457; tel: 406-538-9068.

This sandstone house in the old part of Lewistown was built around the turn of the century and features hardwood floors, high ceilings, a large stained-glass window, and exposed woodwork. There are five guest rooms, one with a private bath. $$

TOURS AND OUTFITTERS

Adventure Bound Canoe and Shuttle Service

607 East Boulevard, Lewistown, MT 59457; tel: 406-538-4890.

Canoe rentals and logistical support are provided for self-guided trips.

Missouri River Canoe Company

Virgelle Mercantile, HC 67, Box 50, Loma, MT 59460; tel: 406-378-3110 or 800-426-2926.

This company offers guided canoe trips from four to 12 days long, fully outfitted self-guided trips, and canoe rentals.

Montana River Outfitters

1401 Fifth Avenue South, Great Falls, MT 59405; tel: 406-761-1677.

Guided canoe, kayak, or raft trips on the Missouri are available, as well as rentals for self-guided trips. Shuttle service is provided with rentals.

River Odysseys West

P.O. Box 579, Coeur d'Alene, ID 83816; tel: 208-765-0841 or 800-451-6034.

ROW offers trips down the Missouri in 34-foot voyageur canoes, each capable of carrying 14 paddlers. The scheduled trips last four to six days and feature guest historians and writers to bring the region's history to life.

Upper Missouri River Guides

315 West 4th Street, Anaconda, MT 59711; tel: 406-563-2770.

Guided canoe trips last one to seven days; rentals of light-weight Kevlar and fiberglass canoes are also available.

Wild Rockies Tours

P.O. Box 8184, Missoula, MT 59807; tel: 406-728-0566.

Guided or outfitted canoe trips on the Missouri River and other Montana waterways range from three to eight days. Women-only trips and customized itineraries are also available.

Excursions

Alberton Gorge, Clark Fork River

10,000 Waves Raft and Kayak Adventures, P.O. Box 7924, Missoula, MT 59807; tel: 800-537-8315.

Forty miles west of Missoula, this popular one-day whitewater run flows past dramatic red and purple cliffs and through a series of Class III and IV rapids. Calm stretches between the rapids allow time to spot elk, bears, eagles, and other wildlife. Alberton Gorge is the rowdiest section of the Clark Fork; in all, more than 200 miles can be floated. Several outfitters offer raft and kayak trips, as well as tranquil float trips ranging up to five days on the more remote downstream sections.

Gallatin River

Montana Whitewater, P.O. Box 1552, Bozeman, MT 59715; tel: 406-763-4465.

The Gallatin River barrels out of the mountains near Yellowstone National Park toward its confluence with the Missouri, its clear water roiling into terrific Class II and III rapids through narrow canyons bristling with spruce, hemlock, and lodgepole pine. Several outfitters offer half- and full-day raft trips. The fly-fishing is among the best in the Rockies, and the mountain scenery is nothing short of splendid.

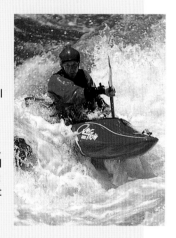

Red Rock Lakes National Wildlife Refuge

Monida Star Route, Box 15, Lima, MT 59739; tel: 406-276-3536.

Two high-elevation lakes nestled at the foot of southwest Montana's remote Centennial Range are home to more than 250 species of birds, including pelicans, sandhill cranes, and rare resident trumpeter swans. Canoeists can travel between Upper and Lower Red Rock Lakes by way of the intricate River Marsh channel that connects them, a long day of paddling. To protect nesting habitats, canoeing is prohibited on Upper Lake before July 15 and on Lower Lake before September 1, making this a late summer and early fall destination. By then the mountains are colored by a delicate spray of autumn hues.

Middle Fork of the
Salmon River
Idaho

CHAPTER **14**

t's a dazzling Idaho morning at mile-high **Boundary Creek** campground. Like an orchestra tuning up for a concert, a congenial, disorderly buzz prevails. Blue, orange, and gray rafts take shape as air pumps whine; paddlers toting life jackets and coolers parade by en route to the steep wooden ramp that slopes to the river; tanned guides in faded nylon shorts and river sandals scurry between growing piles of gear; and Forest Service employees with clipboards check permits and assign downstream campsites. ◆ At some point in the commotion, almost all of the people assembled here will stop for a moment, paddles, dry bags, and other gear balanced in their arms, and regard the river below. Beer-bottle green and intensely clear, it sweeps to the right and out of view – the first bend of many in the 100-mile, five- to eight-day trip that has brought them to this remote canyon. ◆ The Middle Fork of the Salmon is one of the jewels in the

Big water, jaw-dropping scenery, and inviting hot springs are just a few of the highlights of this brawny mountain stream in central Idaho.

national system of wild and scenic rivers. Flanked by the Sawtooth and Salmon River Ranges, it flows through dozens of Class III and IV rapids through the heart of the 2.3-million-acre **Frank Church–River of No Return Wilderness**, the largest federally designated wilderness area in the continental United States. ◆ Though Boundary Creek may seem like a mob scene, only seven parties – typically three commercial and four private – launch each day. They have all scored one of the coveted permits that the Forest Service distributes by lottery. The competition for permits is all the more heated because of the river's short paddling season. Fed primarily by snowmelt, the Middle Fork peaks in June with flows of about 5,000 to 6,000

The clear, green Middle Fork, among the nation's most revered wilderness runs, was one of eight original wild and scenic rivers designated by Congress in 1968.

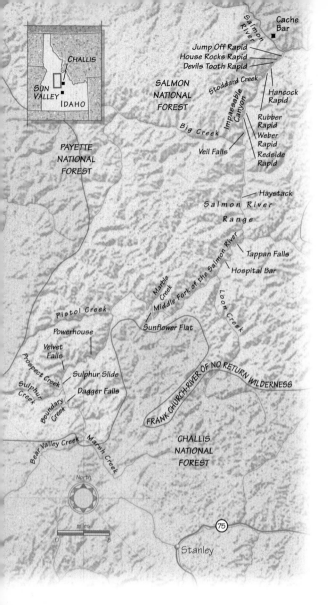

water – hesitantly at first, as if petting a nervous animal, then more and more decisively.

The river, too, seems eager to get started. It rushes downhill, leaving few calm stretches or eddies where paddlers can catch their breath. A patchwork of colorful river rocks zips under the boats; Douglas firs and meadows cloaked in purple lupine and white beargrass fly past in a fragrant blur; boaters catch glimpses of what appear to be elk or even black bear in the steep, wooded canyon.

The first serious face-shot comes at Class III **Sulphur Slide**, a long, rocky drop just a few miles downstream. It wasn't much until 1936, when a flash flood from a side stream plugged the river with boulders. Now the rocks have spread downstream like a sloping maze of bowling balls. The next rapid, **Velvet Falls** (named for the way it sneaks up on unwary paddlers), comes up quickly. It's a river-wide ledge with a nasty, boat-eating reversal at the bottom. Depending on the water level, paddlers try to catch an elusive eddy just above the ledge, then squeeze down the relatively safe chute on the left.

Camp is made later that afternoon in a sunny grove of pine trees or on a sandbar about the size of a volleyball court. The Forest Service assigns campsites to each party before the trip, so there's no need to race others down the river for the best spots. This arrangement gives the whole experience a more relaxed atmosphere and assures your group relative solitude. Take a hike, or just break out a cold drink and a handful of chips and contemplate the next 90 or so miles: more great scenery and wildlife, sun-dappled campsites, hot springs, and of course, plenty of whitewater.

Hot Springs and History

Powerhouse, about 12 miles downstream, becomes Class IV at higher water levels. A quick 10 miles farther down comes Class III–IV **Pistol**, constricted in a narrow gorge, where failure to make the tight S-turn at the bottom can result in a close encounter with a huge rock.

The 56 miles from Pistol Creek to **Big**

cubic feet per second and by mid-August is often too low to run. Though a permit is required of all groups who paddle the river, you can bypass the process by signing on with an outfitter, who will have already acquired one. While some people bemoan such tight regulations (the Forest Service also requires that boaters carry out all trash, including ashes and human waste), most understand the benefits of diligent management.

Rapid Transit

Your group is finally in the boats and ready to go. Oars and paddles are dipped into the

Creek make up the middle portion of the run. The canyon broadens; jagged peaks come into view; the forest thins out into stands of stately Ponderosa and western yellow pine. Though the whitewater mellows a bit (this section includes only about a dozen of the river's 40 or so major drops), the Middle Fork provides an equally interesting, if more relaxing, diversion: about half a dozen hot springs. It is in this middle section, too, that abandoned cabins and ghostly garden plots remind visitors of those who made their homes here not too long ago.

In 1942 a Yale junior named Eliot DuBois paddled the river looking for one last adventure before joining the Marines. His whitewater exploits, recounted in his book *An Innocent on the Middle Fork*, are truly impressive, but it's the stories of the people

The grave (left) of miner Whitie Cox is a grim reminder of the settlers who scratched out a living along the river.

A paddler in an oar raft (below) scans the river ahead.

who lived along the river, connected to the world only by pack trail and to each other by crank telephone, that are the most poignant. He tells of trapper and prospector Ed Buddell, living alone in an immaculately kept cabin near Pistol Creek; the Hood family, who cultivated vegetables at their homestead a few miles below Marble Creek; Frank Allison at Loon Creek, a prospector and occasional fishing guide who made the best pancakes DuBois ever ate; and the Crandall family, in the process of establishing the Flying B guest ranch above Haystack Rapid. Their cabins and others are worth a look.

A Warm Soak On the River

A trip down the Middle Fork isn't complete without a few dips in the hot springs that are scattered along the river's edge. Some are little more than seeps, but others are bigger and hotter than your bathtub at home.

Sunflower Hot Springs is on river right 36½ miles from Boundary Creek. A cozy, simmering pool can be found up a short trail to the top of a cliff above the river, or you can shower yourself in the rivulets of warm water that cascade over a ledge.

Loon Creek Hot Springs require about a mile-long hike, but it's worth the effort. Roughly 50 miles into the trip on river right, the trail follows Loon Creek to a large wooden enclosure. A pipe feeds the hot spring into the pool, which can easily accommodate a dozen people.

Another fine soaking spot is at **Hospital Bar** just 2½ miles below Loon Creek. If the spring gets too hot, you simply swim into the cool river before returning to the steaming water.

Hot springs (left) are the perfect place to soothe achy muscles. The Forest Service assigns each party at least one campsite with a hot spring.

A paddle raft (below) careens through a battery of rapids.

Quiet moments in camp (right) balance whitewater thrills and give paddlers an opportunity to enjoy the river's soothing flow.

Canyon walls (opposite, bottom) dwarf rafts on a gentle stretch of water.

If you're feeling grimy after three days on the river, treat yourself to a hot shower at **Sunflower Flat**, where hot springs cascade down a cliff above the river about 12 miles downstream of Pistol Creek. Follow up with a cold drink or ice cream a little farther along at the Flying B Ranch, which runs a small concession for paddlers.

It was along **Loon Creek**, where a short hike leads to another hot spring, that the Middle Fork's saddest episode began. In February 1879, five Chinese miners living along its banks were murdered. Whites blamed a band of Sheepeater Indians, cousins of the Shoshone and Bannock tribes. "The result," wrote historian Roderick Nash in *The Big Drops*, "was one of the most ill-conceived and unnecessary campaigns in the history of the Indian wars." A detachment of 56 U.S. soldiers arrived from Boise in early summer to capture the alleged murderers. The troops were nearly done in by the rugged terrain, but they eventually managed to find the Sheepeaters and steal their cache of food and supplies. With no hope of surviving

narrow for pack trails, leaving boaters alone in the deepening chasm. This is the third section, the dramatic grand finale of the Middle Fork, with the river's most challenging rapids. Its name is **Impassable Canyon**.

Though ominous, the cliffs of Impassable Canyon harbor some surprises. Not far from Big Creek, you can follow a trail up to delicate **Veil Falls**. The view upstream is breathtaking, and dozens of ancient pictographs record the presence of those who came here long before. More pictographs, such as those at **Stoddard Creek**, are found on the walls of caves and cliffs throughout the canyon.

About 10 miles downstream of Veil Falls, you may notice an old cabin near river level. It was built in the 1920s by Earl Parrott, who used ladders to climb the canyon wall

the winter, the 51-member band was forced to surrender and promptly escorted to a reservation. The truth about the Sheepeaters' innocence was revealed only years later: the miners had been murdered by white thieves who were after their gold.

The Hermit's Canyon

As you drift past **Hospital Bar** (named by ranchers who grazed their ailing livestock on its expansive meadows) or enjoy its riverside hot spring, scan the cliffs on the left for bighorn sheep, who seem to be as fond of watching people soak in the springs as they are of cavorting on the perilous ledges. Three-part **Tappan Falls** follows shortly. One of the most significant drops in the middle section, Tappan is a steep, rocky ledge notorious for chewing up kayaks and tearing rafts. **Haystack**, a long Class III rapid, is next.

Aptly named **Big Creek** adds its considerable volume to the waterway 18 miles above its confluence with the main Salmon River. At this point, the Middle Fork is no longer an impetuous mountain creek but a fully grown, rolling river capable of more than merely toying with boaters. The canyon walls close in. Gray granite cliffs, the geologic core of central Idaho, loom overhead, and ghostly black tree trunks bear witness to past forest fires. The canyon is too

to his mine some 2,000 feet above the river. It was rumored that the old hermit hibernated like a bear, sleeping as much as 22 hours a day in winter.

The Big Finish

After Veil Falls, the guides ready the bail buckets and spare oars. They tug down their baseball caps and check that everything is securely tied down. Kayakers lay their paddles across cockpits and wordlessly drift downstream, sitting tall as they strain to see ahead.

Redside Rapid is first; three huge midstream rocks are the giveaway. Beyond them the river crosses the characteristic dense white lines that mark particularly bad holes. The water pours between the big rocks and their attendant holes, shoving boats around violently. At high water levels, there is barely enough time to regain your bearings before the next two hole-studded drops, **Weber** and **Rubber**, are upon you. Rubber is notorious for having the biggest waves on the river, including an oblique monster that can stall a raft or kayak and spill its human contents like apples off a cafeteria tray. **Hancock**, **Devils Tooth**, **House Rocks**, and **Jump Off**, all different, all significant, follow in short order.

Then, a gust of warm air blows upstream, a welcome sensation after one is doused by cold water. "I found myself looking down a mile-long dark corridor of canyon toward a sunlit wall that seemed to block the far end," wrote Eliot DuBois of the Middle Fork's final stretch, exulting in his own survival. The main Salmon River, as big and powerful as an older brother, appears from the right and the Middle Fork gracefully acquiesces. No one says much for the last two miles to **Cache Bar**. The end of this river has come far too soon.

An angler (above) casts a line from an oar raft. The Middle Fork offers superb fishing for Dolly Varden, cutthroat, and rainbow trout.

A rafter (left) muscles through a section of whitewater.

A flotilla of rafts (right) rounds a bend. More than 10,000 people float the Middle Fork annually.

TRAVEL TIPS

DETAILS

When to Go

The Middle Fork is a late spring and summer run. The river is typically quite low by early August, and though it may be runnable, rafts may have to be flown to a downstream launch point. Summer days are usually around 85°F, with cool evenings. Water levels are higher in early spring, but weather can be cold and unpredictable. It's not unusual for the road to the Boundary Creek put-in to be closed by snow until mid-May.

How to Get There

Drive to the Boundary Creek put-in on a gravel road from Stanley, Idaho, about 140 miles northeast of Boise. Major airlines, including Horizon Air, Southwest, and Delta, serve Boise. Many outfitters will arrange transportation from Boise for their guests. The take-out is at the end of another gravel road near North Fork, 20 miles north of Salmon, Idaho.

Permits

A permit to run the Middle Fork is required between June 1 and September 10 and is very difficult to obtain. Applications are accepted from December 1 to January 31 at the Middle Fork Ranger District; the chances of getting one are about one in 26. Paddlers can bypass the permit process by signing up with an outfitter.

INFORMATION

Challis National Forest

Middle Fork Ranger District, Highway 93, P.O. Box 750, Challis, ID 83226; tel: 208-879-4101.

CAMPING

Camping along the Middle Fork is allowed at designated campsites assigned to each group at the put-in. All groups must carry self-contained toilet systems.

Salmon River Campground

Stanley Ranger District, Stanley, ID 83340; tel: 208-774-3681.

Six miles east of Stanley, this is one of 37 campgrounds in the Sawtooth National Recreation Area. Thirty-two sites are on the banks of the river. Drinking water, pit toilets, and picnic tables are provided. Sites are allotted on a first-come, first-served basis.

Stanley Lake Campground

Stanley Ranger District, Stanley, ID 83340; tel: 208-774-3681.

Eight miles northwest of Stanley, at an elevation of 6,400 feet, this 33-site campground is set in a conifer forest on the shores of a mile-long lake ringed by the jagged Sawtooth Mountains. Drinking water, vault toilets, grills, and picnic tables are available. Sites are allotted on a first-come, first-served basis.

Tower Rock Campground

Bureau of Land Management, Route 12, Box 610, Salmon, ID 83467; tel: 208-756-5401.

Tower Rock is a small riverside campground 11 miles north of Salmon, at the site of a Lewis and Clark expedition camp. Six sites, with vault toilets and picnic tables, are set on the Salmon River.

LODGING

PRICE GUIDE – double occupancy

$ = up to $49 $$ = $50–$99

$$$ = $100–$149 $$$$ = $150+

Hundred Acre Wood at North Fork

P.O. Box 202, North Fork, ID 83466; tel: 208-865-2165.

Three miles north of North Fork, the closest settlement to the take-out, this bed-and-breakfast has six rooms (four with private bath) and a restaurant. Guests enjoy 22 acres of forest, a catch-and-release trout pond, and an outdoor hot tub. $$–$$$

Idaho Rocky Mountain Ranch

HC 64, P.O. Box 9934, Stanley, ID 83278; tel: 208-774-3544.

Built in the 1930s as a private hunting lodge, this log ranch house is set on 1,000 acres and is listed on the National Register of Historic Places. There are four lodge rooms and 17 log cabins with fireplaces and rustic furniture; the swimming pool is fed by a natural hot spring. Stays of several nights are preferred. $$–$$$

Jerry's Motel

Highway 75, HC 67, P.O. Box 300, Lower Stanley, ID 83728; tel: 208-774-3566 or 800-972-4627.

This motel has a woodsy feel. Each of the nine rooms has a kitchenette and private balcony overlooking the river. $$

Mountain Village Resort

Route 21 at Route 75, Stanley, ID 83278; tel: 208-774-3661 or 800-843-5475.

The resort has 60 log cabins, some with kitchens, and features a natural hot spring tub. $$

Stagecoach Inn Motel

201 Route 93 North, Salmon, ID 83467; tel: 208-756-4251.

This three-story, riverfront motel offers simple accommodations at a reasonable price. A pool is on the premises. $$

TOURS AND OUTFITTERS

Canyons Incorporated

P.O. Box 823, McCall, ID 83538; tel: 888-634-2600.

Canyons is run by one of the nation's most respected whitewater experts, Les Bechdel. The guided raft trips will also support experienced kayakers and canoeists.

Hughes River Expeditions

P.O. Box 217, Cambridge, ID 83610; tel: 208-257-3476 or 800-262-1882.

Hughes runs trips on the Middle Fork and other Idaho rivers, including the Owyhee and Bruneau.

Mackay Wilderness River Trips

3190 Airport Way, Boise, ID 83705; tel: 208-344-1881 or 800-635-5336.

The company offers lodging, flight packages, and transportation from Boise. A wilderness airstrip near the river's midpoint is used for customers who have time for only a partial trip. Arrangements can be made for ranch stays before or after a river trip.

River Odysseys West

P.O. Box 579, Coeur d'Alene, ID 83816; tel: 208-765-0841 or 800-451-6034.

River Odysseys West runs outfitted trips on a variety of western rivers but specializes in Idaho streams.

Rocky Mountain River Tours

P.O. Box 8596, Boise, ID 83707; tel: 208-345-2400 or 208-756-4808 (summer).

The company offers guided raft trips on the Middle Fork. Customers are also given the option of crewing a paddle boat or paddling inflatable kayaks. Excellent Dutch-oven cooking is a highlight of the trip.

Solitude River Trips

P.O. Box 907, Merlin, OR 97532; tel: 541-476-1876 or 800-396-1776.

River trips are designed for paddlers who want to take advantage of the Middle Fork's excellent fishing. The company uses river-worthy rowing vessels known as McKenzie boats, which are particularly well suited for fly-fishing.

Excursions

Flathead Lake

Glacier Sea Kayaking, 390 Tally Lake Road, Whitefish, MT 59937; tel: 406-862-9010.

Sea kayakers have begun to discover this enormous lake just south of Glacier National Park. To the east, dense forest yields to the snowy peaks of the Swan Range. To the north and west is a broad landscape of meadows, rolling mountains, and fragrant pine forests. Head out for a day or overnight trip. For a real treat try a moonlight or sunset paddle, and watch the changing light cast a magic glow over some of Montana's finest scenery.

Payette River

Payette National Forest, McCall Ranger District, 800 West Lakeside Avenue, P.O. Box 1026, McCall, ID 83638; tel: 208-634-0700.

The forks of the Payette give canoeists, rafters, and the world's best kayakers a treasure trove of options. The popular nine-mile run on the North Fork from Cabarton Bridge to Smiths Ferry flows through a secluded canyon with a sprinkling of Class III rapids. It's a great run for intermediate kayakers and advanced canoeists, and very popular with rafters. The Main Payette downstream of Banks is a Class III run punctuated by an infamous reversal known as Mike's Hole and a big wave tellingly dubbed Mixmaster. The lower South Fork, from Deer Creek Turnout to Banks, is usually called the Staircase Section for its most formidable drop. This Class III-IV run is home to the annual Payette whitewater rodeo, one of the nation's premier whitewater competitions.

Snake River Birds of Prey Area

Bureau of Land Management, Boise District Office, 3948 Development Avenue, Boise, ID 83705; tel: 208-334-1582.

The Snake River canyon and surrounding plateaus support the densest concentration of nesting raptors in North America. Paddlers have the best view as prairie falcons, red-tailed hawks, golden eagles, northern harriers, and American kestrels soar overhead. The deep desert canyon makes an excellent half- to two-day float by canoe or raft. Put in above Swan Falls Dam for a calm two-day trip or just below the dam for a few hours to a couple of days of Class I-II paddling.

Snake River
Wyoming

CHAPTER **15**

As dawn comes to **Grand Teton National Park**, a solitary paddler shoves off from the bank of the Snake River and glides out onto the glassy surface. He takes a couple of casual strokes to reach the channel, then swings the bow upstream and settles back, paddle dripping, to admire the view. Far above the river, the jagged Teton crest catches a crease of golden light that slowly works its way down the flanks of the range, warming cliffs and canyons mantled in snow and evergreens. ◆ The canoe drifts downstream, its graceful lines reflected in the mirrored surface. The canoeist glances over, smiles at another person up at this virtuous hour, and paddles on, eyes crinkling with silent joy. ◆ The lucky stiff. He's timed this trip perfectly. While most campers are still snoozing in their tents, he'll be slipping through one of the park's richest wildlife areas just when moose, beaver, and bison are most

A verdant waterway rich with wildlife meanders past the majestic Teton Range.

active. Then, as the full warmth of morning comes on, he'll make the big southwestern curve near **Moran Junction** and ride the Snake through the deep, meandering furrow it has etched into the gravel floor of **Jackson Hole**. From time to time, grand vistas of the Tetons will swing into view as he threads through the braided channels of the river and lines up for the few mild rapids. By noon, he'll reach **Deadman's Bar**, where he might doze for an hour or so before setting off for **Moose**. If he dawdles, he'll make the take-out in time to watch the sunset and maybe drive over to Jackson for a burger. ◆ This amazing stretch of water, from **Jackson Lake Dam** to **Moose Landing**, runs for roughly 25 miles through one of North America's most compelling landscapes. With the awesome

Sea kayaks are suitable for the upper Snake River, but canoes and rafts offer the maneuverability required downstream.

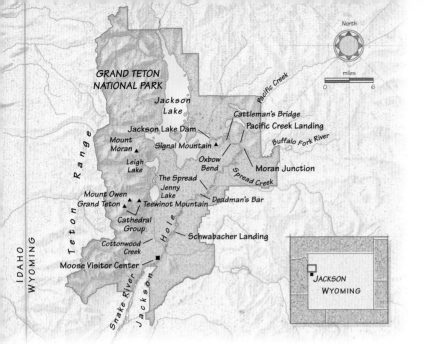

North

GRAND TETON
NATIONAL PARK

Jackson
Lake

Pacific Creek

miles

0   6

Cattleman's Bridge

Jackson Lake Dam

Pacific Creek Landing

Mount
Moran ▲   Signal Mountain ▲

Buffalo Fork River

Leigh
Lake

Oxbow
Bend

Moran Junction

The Spread

Spread Creek

Jenny
Lake

Mount Owen ▲ ▲
Grand Teton ▲ ▲ Teewinot Mountain

Deadman's Bar

Cathedral
Group

Schwabacher Landing

Cottonwood
Creek

Moose Visitor Center

JACKSON
WYOMING

Teton Range

Jackson Hole

Snake River

IDAHO

WYOMING

several intermediate landings make it possible to plan more leisurely trips. The initial five-mile stretch from Jackson Lake Dam to **Pacific Creek** is suitable for beginners; the 10½-mile stretch from Pacific Creek to Deadman's Bar is best for intermediate paddlers; and the 10 miles from Deadman's Bar to Moose should be attempted only by seasoned canoeists.

Whatever your skill level, the calm sections of the river below Jackson Lake Dam are not to be missed. You'll find a parking lot and put-in along the north bank near the dam. Before you clamber down to the river, scan the willow flats around the parking area for moose and listen for the throaty chuckle of sandhill cranes.

As you drift downriver, turn upstream to savor the Tetons. The great hulking dome of gray rock dominating your view is **Mount Moran** (elevation 12,605 feet), which rises more than a vertical mile above the water.

The Tetons are what geologists call fault-block mountains. As the rock on one side of the fault was thrust skyward, the other side

ramparts of the Tetons nearly close enough to touch, the river bends around darkly forested hills, sagebrush flats, wildflower meadows, willow marshes, and long, inviting gravel bars. It is a crucial riparian zone, a priceless corridor of running water and moist soil that supports a nearly continuous ribbon of forest in a semiarid valley.

Fast, cold, and clear as glass most of the year, the river should pose no great challenges to experienced paddlers. Even beginners can set off with confidence for a half-day trip starting from the dam. Still, the Snake is easy to underestimate. Currents aren't always what they seem, and toppled trees, or snags, can flip canoes, puncture rafts, and trap people beneath the surface in a tangle of roots and branches. There are accidents every summer, and even park rangers have had close calls.

Grand Views and Wildlife

Though paddlers familiar with the river can run the full route in a single day,

The Tetons (right) are a fault-block range. As one side of the fault rose and tilted, the other sank, producing mountains that rise abruptly with virtually no foothills.

A bull moose (opposite) grazes near the river.

subsided, creating the precipitous rise from valley to peak we see today. Glaciers finished the job, sharpening ridges, widening canyons, and gouging out a string of lakes at the mountains' base.

The view of Moran is soon eclipsed by the forested slopes of **Signal Mountain**, which rises from the south bank of the river. As you paddle this stretch, look for ospreys and bald eagles roosting in lodgepole pines or soaring over the water in search of fish. Shoals of suckers – native bottom-feeders – crowd the pools beneath the boat; large cutthroat trout are found here, too.

Two miles below the dam, you'll reach **Cattleman's Bridge**, a rickety wooden affair with low clearance and a surprisingly swift current welling between its posts. You'll need to portage it during high water.

Just beyond, the Snake slows at **Oxbow Bend**, a series of slack-water pools that are actually abandoned river meanders. A pause here is sure to turn up something interesting – moose, trumpeter swans, perhaps river otters.

Below the bend, the current picks up again, running deep and clear for two more miles to **Pacific Creek Landing**. Along the way, you pass through territory favored by calving elk in spring and used by the herd as a river crossing during its migration.

As the river bends south beyond Pacific Creek, it emerges from the forest and opens into another terrific view of the Tetons. In about half a mile, the **Buffalo Fork River** flows in from the left and the Snake divides around a series of lightly wooded islands, gravel bars, and sandbars. Keep an eye on the river; snags here are particularly hazardous.

Paddling Jackson Lake

With the Teton Range rising directly from its western shore, 19-mile-long **Jackson Lake** is one of the most dramatic flatwater destinations in the West and a good spot for beginners or families to try kayak touring. There are several busy marinas and a good deal of motorboat traffic on the eastern shore, so your best bet for solitude is to reserve a campsite on the undeveloped western shore or, even better, on one of the islands. Gusty winds and big waves can kick up suddenly, so keep your eye on the weather, and consider signing on with a guide for your first trip.

Early morning is the best time to find calm water and solitude on Jackson Lake.

If you want to avoid motorboats altogether, try canoeing on small, sheltered **Leigh Lake**, where no motors are permitted. A short portage leads to neighboring **Jenny Lake**, making a good day's paddle. If you want to stretch out the trip, reserve a campsite on the lakeshore and spend the night.

The current picks up significantly and remains fast all the way to Deadman's Bar.

The braided channels below the Buffalo Fork continue for about a mile, then tail off at a major wildlife crossing often used in spring by elk cows and calves.

The river passes beneath a high bank on the right, then pulls away and makes a sharp bend that nearly doubles back on itself. The Tetons come back into view and remain there for nearly a mile as the river heads straight for **Grand Teton**, at an elevation of 13,770 feet the tallest peak in the Teton Range. To the right is **Mount Owen**, and in the foreground to the right of Owen is **Teewinot Mountain**. Together they comprise the aptly named **Cathedral Group**.

The river continues as a more or less unified thread for about four miles, passing several branches of **Spread Creek** on the left and leading past sagebrush flats, groves of cottonwoods, and stands of evergreen forest. Ospreys are sometimes seen here diving to the water and carrying off fish. Pronghorn and bison often ford the shallows.

Before long, the river breaks into a two- to three-mile section of braided channels known locally as the **Spread**, a good place to spot pronghorn and coyotes. As the channels reunite, the river heads into a deep gorge and slides through modest rapids.

As you swing west beneath the steep, left-hand wall of the gorge, a jaw-dropping vista of the Cathedral Group and Mount Moran bursts into view. It's a good spot to stop for lunch and much quieter than the bustling landing at Deadman's Bar just a mile below.

Challenging Finish

The run from Deadman's Bar to Moose is the most challenging in the park. The current is faster, the braided channels more complex

and extensive, the snags and logjams more frequent. If you're going to paddle this stretch, it's imperative that you first inquire about river conditions at the visitor center in Moose.

Just below Deadman's Bar, the river slips over another set of mild rapids, bends sharply west, and exits the gorge. For the next three miles or so, the Snake flows as a single stream through what at this point should be a familiar mix of habitats – sagebrush flats, semi-arid benchland, stands of evergreen forest, and groves of cottonwood and aspen. Pronghorn, bison, and elk all frequent the area, and bald eagles roost in the trees.

Before long, the river divides into a series of braided channels, islands, and gravel bars – a veritable maze that

Dusk finds a party of rafters near the end of its run (left).

The snowcapped peaks of the Teton Range (below) dominate the skyline. It's easy to let the scenery distract you from the business of avoiding gravel bars and fallen trees.

stretches almost all the way to Moose and changes with every flood season. Route-finding can be difficult, especially in a section tangled with snags that starts about a mile below **Schwabacher Landing**. This is where you're at the greatest risk of running into trouble.

Just above **Cottonwood Creek**, which flows in from the right, the river pulls itself together again for the last mile to Moose Landing, which you'll find on the right bank, well above the bridge.

TRAVEL TIPS

DETAILS

When to Go

Perhaps the best time to paddle the Snake through Grand Teton National Park is in summer, when water levels are most reliable and the weather is warm. Daytime highs in July and August are around 90°F, and nights are cool. Afternoon thunderstorms are common but brief. Early fall features crisp air, gold aspen leaves, and fewer tourists. High water levels in spring may be hazardous; the Snake River is closed to public entry from December 15 to April 1. Check information on flow rates at river landings and visitor centers, or by calling 800-658-5771.

How to Get There

Jackson Hole Airport is served by several commercial airlines, including American, Delta and United. Car rentals are available at the airport.

Permits

A boat permit is required within Grand Teton National Park; rental canoes should already have permits. Permit stickers for nonmotorized craft cost $10 for the year or $5 for a week and can be purchased at Buffalo Fork and Signal Mountain Ranger Stations, and Colter Bay and Moose Visitor Centers. Entrance fees to the national park may also apply.

INFORMATION

Grand Teton National Park
P.O. Drawer 170, Moose, WY 83012; tel: 307-739-3300.

Jackson Hole Chamber of Commerce
532 North Cache Street, P.O. Box 550, Jackson, WY 83001; tel: 307-733-3316.

CAMPING

Colter Bay Village
Grand Teton Lodge Company, North Highway 89, P.O. Box 250, Moran, WY 83013; tel: 307-543-2811 or 800-628-9988.

This campground and marina complex on Jackson Lake has separate areas for trailers and RVs and tents. Cabins are also available.

Gros Ventre Campground
Grand Teton National Park, P.O. Drawer 170, Moose, WY 83012; tel: 307-739-3300.

The 360 sites at this campground are spread through a grove of aspen and cottonwoods on the bank of the Gros Ventre River with views of the Tetons across the valley. Sites are available on a first-come, first-served basis, and the campground often has space when others are full.

Jenny Lake Campground
Grand Teton National Park, P.O. Drawer 170, Moose, WY 83012; tel: 307-739-3300.

The 49 sites at this popular tents-only campground are usually taken by early morning. The campground adjoins the picturesque lakeshore, with tree-sheltered camping, a small store, and the lake's excursion boat nearby.

Signal Mountain Campground
Grand Teton National Park, P.O. Drawer 170, Moose, WY 83012; tel: 307-739-3300.

This campground north of Jenny Lake has 86 sites and is usually full by about 10 A.M. in summer. It is next to Signal Mountain Lodge and marina, with a camp store and other amenities close by. Sites are generally small and intimate.

LODGING

PRICE GUIDE – double occupancy

$ = up to $49 $$ = $50–$99
$$$ = $100–$149 $$$$ = $150+

Alpine House
285 North Glenwood Street, P.O. Box 20245, Jackson, WY 83001; tel: 307-739-1570 or 800-753-1421.

Two blocks from town square, this timber-frame bed-and-breakfast has seven guest rooms with private balconies, heated floors, down comforters, and antique furniture. $$–$$$

Jackson Lake Lodge
Grand Teton Lodge Company, P.O. Box 240, Moran, WY 83013; tel: 307-543-3100 or 800-628-9988.

Sixty-foot windows grant spectacular views of Jackson Lake and the Tetons. There are 348 guest rooms in cottages around the property and 37 rooms in the lodge. The lodge has a pool and several dining rooms and offers float trips and horseback rides. $$$–$$$$

Jenny Lake Lodge
Grand Teton Lodge Company, P.O. Box 240, Moran, WY 83013; tel: 307-733-4647 or 800-628-9988.

This deluxe resort near the north shore of Jenny Lake consists of 37 log cabins with quilts and handmade furniture. Dinner, breakfast, horseback riding, and bicycling are included in the price. A minimum three-night stay is required. $$$$

Snow King Resort
400 East Snow King Avenue, P.O. Box SKI, Jackson, WY 83001; tel: 800-522-5464.

This is Jackson's classic in-town resort, located at the base of the Snow King ski hill, about 10 blocks from the town square. The full-service hotel has 204 rooms, an airy lobby, pool, sauna, hot tubs, and a restaurant. About 50 condominiums are also available. $$$$

Spur Ranch Cabins

P.O. Box 39, Moose, WY 83012; tel: 307-733-2522.

Twelve log cabins with lodgepole furniture and kitchens are set on the Snake River at Moose. $$$–$$$$

TOURS AND OUTFITTERS

Most outfitters will rent canoes for use only on lakes or the Snake River between Jackson Lake Dam and Pacific Creek. Braided channels and logjams in the lower stretches of the river are hazardous; these sections can be paddled with an outfitter.

Dornan's Adventure Sports

P.O. Box 39, Moose, WY 83012; tel: 307-733-3307.

Dornan's offers canoe rentals near the river.

Leisure Sports

1075 South Highway 89, P.O. Box 11510, Jackson, WY 83001; tel: 307-733-3040.

This in-town shop rents canoes, inflatable kayaks, and rafts for use on the Snake and other waterways. It also rents trailers that can carry up to six boats.

Rendezvous River Sports/ Jackson Hole Kayak School

P.O. Box 9201, Jackson, WY 83001; tel: 800-733-2471.

Canoes and sit-on-top, hardshell, and inflatable kayaks can be rented for solo use on the Snake and other waterways. The affiliated Jackson Hole Kayak School offers two- to four-day kayak courses and can customize instruction or tours.

Snake River Kayak and Canoe School

155 West Gill Street, Jackson, WY 83001; tel: 307-733-3127 or 800-529-2501.

Group clinics and custom instruction cover whitewater and touring, with an emphasis on safety and skill-building. Equipment can be rented for use on the Snake River.

Excursions

Snake River Canyon

Targhee National Forest, c/o Multi-Agency Visitor Information, 532 North Cache Street, Jackson, WY 83001; tel: 307-733-3316.

About 20 minutes south of Jackson, the Snake River ends its quiet drift along the Teton front and turns west, carving through the Snake River Range in a wooded canyon studded with splashy Class III whitewater. Hoback Canyon is a popular half-day raft trip from Jackson and can be tackled by intermediate kayakers. Several raft companies offer trips through the canyon; some do a full-day version that starts in the wildlife-rich Class I-II water upstream.

Island Park

Targhee National Forest, Island Park Ranger District, P.O. Box 220, Island Park, ID 83429; tel: 208-558-7301.

An ancient volcanic crater in the shadow of the Continental Divide, the Island Park region of eastern Idaho is a high-elevation paradise of clear air, wetlands, teeming wildlife, and world-class trout fishing. Paddlers can explore several lakes and streams in the area. Perhaps the best introduction is the gentle five-mile-long Big Springs National Scenic Water Trail on the North Fork of the Henry's Fork. From the put-in at Big Springs to the take-out at Coffeepot Campground, there is plenty of opportunity to spot moose, waterbirds, and other wildlife, and to enjoy some of the best fly-fishing in the West.

Yellowstone Lake

Yellowstone National Park, P.O. Box 168, Yellowstone, WY 82190; tel: 307-344-7381.

Yellowstone Lake is one of the largest high-altitude lakes in the world. Its three southeastern arms, inaccessible by road and open only to nonmotorized vessels, have remarkably clear water, pristine shorelines, and some of the best wildlife viewing in the lower 48 states. Canoeists and kayakers can paddle directly from the busy western shore or shuttle across the lake in a powerboat. A growing number of tour companies offer trips to the area. Late spring and early fall ensure solitude, but be prepared for chilly weather.

Labyrinth and Stillwater Canyons
Utah

CHAPTER **16**

Anticipation hangs in the air at the two put-ins for the journey down Utah's **Green River** through **Labyrinth** and **Stillwater Canyons**. Both **Green River State Park** and the private launch site at **Ruby Ranch**, 20 miles downstream, are nondescript, mud-banked spots. The silt-heavy river rolls sedately past as boaters in shorts and T-shirts grapple with gear for the multiday trip. Backpacks, coolers, dry bags, and water jugs fill every niche in canoes and rafts. A faint urgency hovers over the scene, fueled by expectations of what lies downstream. ◆ Once afloat, it is a long wait, even paddling hard, before the spell of great canyons and powerful currents starts to work its magic. At first the change is subtle, a vague rising of the riverbanks, occasional sections of low sandstone cliffs, coarse sedimentary layers in reds, browns, and yellows casting **Sandstone walls tower** blocky shadows onto the river. The current seems **over a gentle river as it** to speed up, canting downhill, but it is **loops through the canyon** only an illusion created by the upward slope **country of southern Utah.** of the rock. ◆ Then the view becomes increasingly narrow, framed by rising canyon walls. Boats float in and out of shade. Conversation stops, as if marking the transition with a moment of reflection. A raven's shadow races across a cliff. The great river, fed by snowmelt from the far-off Wind River Mountains in Wyoming, murmurs past the gritty points, caresses the water-worn stone. Labyrinth Canyon has begun. ◆ The flatwater float from the town of **Green River** to **Spanish Bottom**, just downstream of the confluence of the Green and Colorado Rivers in **Canyonlands National Park**, winds through 123 miles of stunning Utah desert. Most of the route meanders alongside deeply incised layers of Navajo, Wingate, and

The Green River offers one of the most spectacular multiday canyon trips in the West. The water is particularly calm in Labyrinth and Stillwater Canyons.

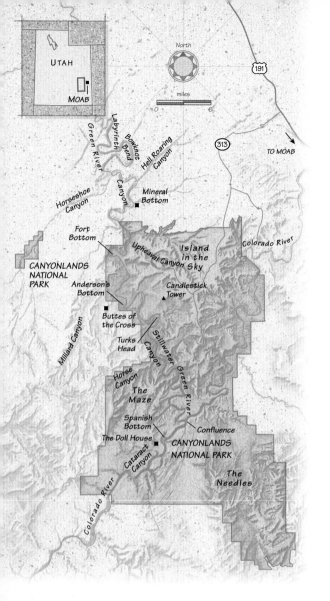

three- to five-day trip. Once past Mineral Bottom, floaters are committed to the entire run, 10 days or more of river life, depending on the amount of time spent hiking and exploring. The longer journey ends at the confluence of the Green and Colorado Rivers, where jet-boats tow paddlers up the Colorado to **Moab**, Utah. Several outfitters in town handle jet-boat shuttles; arrangements must be made in advance of the trip.

Labyrinth and Stillwater Canyons are notable for their lack of turbulence. They are quiet, smooth-water journeys, not the rapid-filled tumult characteristic of other canyons along the Green. Open canoes are appropriate craft for the trip, and paddlers with intermediate skills can easily handle the challenge. In fact, rafts are at a disadvantage in strong upriver winds and may get into trouble running aground on sandbars when the flows drop below 1,200 cubic feet per second.

At high water, from mid-May through June, the Green clips along at a deceptive seven to 10 miles per hour. Currents lap at the cliff walls well into the many tributary canyons, which often provide the most secluded and scenic places to camp. Midsummer is not a particularly friendly period; July and August serve up searing heat and moderate river flows.

By August the river has usually dropped to the point where many sandbar campsites are exposed. The current slows to as little as two miles per hour, and itineraries should be adjusted accordingly. Shallows in the river also become problematic during the late summer. The river at **Millard Canyon** and **Horse Canyon**, along the Stillwater section, is particularly troublesome at low water.

White Rim sandstone. Soaring panels of bedrock rise abruptly out of the flow. Others jut up in cross-bedded layers, ancient sand dunes frozen in stone, which look, from a distance, like bands of sinew and muscle.

There is only one take-out along this route. Boaters can arrange to shuttle off the river on the rough road that descends to **Mineral Bottom** (at mile 68), making it a

September is a lovely, quiet time on the Green, despite the inconvenience of low flows. The number of floaters tapers off dramatically, nights are cool, and daytime temperatures are perfect for hiking.

In the Wake of the One-Armed Man

As is the case along all of the major canyons of the Green and lower Colorado Rivers, the ghost of explorer John Wesley Powell – the first man known to have run these two rivers – is inescapable. For one thing, he is responsible for naming nearly every prominent landform in sight, not to mention a bevy of plant and animal species.

A tributary (left) cascades over a paddler in one of the many side canyons that feed into the Green.

Ancient petroglyphs, like this image of a bighorn sheep (opposite), are found throughout the region.

Sandstone walls (below) about 300 million years old rise above the river's mirror-smooth surface in Labyrinth Canyon.

Powell lost his right arm during the Battle of Shiloh in the American Civil War, but his energy and insatiable curiosity overcame his disability to such a degree that the other members of his expedition stopped taking note. Not only did Powell handle his fair share of the daily work, he managed to keep an exhaustive chronicle of his travels and observations.

Powell was a Renaissance man, versed in geology, meteorology, anthropology, and botany as well as the humanities. After a long day of steering his boat, coping with rapids, and attending to the other duties of leadership, he routinely headed out to

explore the countryside. Many evenings he walked for miles, scaled thousand-foot cliffs for the view, or waded up tributary streams, returning after dark to write in his journal by candlelight while the rest of the crew slumbered.

On July 15, 1869, Powell recorded, "There is an exquisite charm in this beautiful canyon. It gradually grows deeper with every mile; the walls are symmetrically curved and grandly arched, of a beautiful color, and reflected in the quiet waters in many places so as almost to deceive the eye and suggest to the beholder the thought that

he is looking into profound depths… [As] we eat supper, which is spread on the beach, we name this Labyrinth Canyon."

Canyon Rhythms

Modern boaters could do far worse than to follow Powell's example, especially along this section of his route. Short excursions lead into any number of side canyons such as **Horseshoe**, **Hell Roaring**, and **Upheaval**, where oasislike seeps and springs are ringed with maidenhair fern. Desert plants like evening primrose, globemallow, and the ubiquitous prickly-pear cactus thrive, and the rocks are alive with lightning-quick collared lizards. Lucky explorers

Bowknot Bend (above), an entrenched meander, loops to within a quarter mile of itself.

Shallow water (left) is one of the drawbacks of a fall trip, but the payoffs are fewer mosquitoes and better campsites.

Canoeists drift past Dellenbaugh's Butte (right), also known as the Inkwell, upstream of Ruby Ranch.

Sandbars like this one near Upheaval Canyon (below) are ideal campsites.

stumble across ancient granaries, petroglyphs, and other artifacts left behind by the Anasazi, who populated Utah's plateau country before disappearing in about A.D. 1200.

Roughly halfway through Labyrinth Canyon, the Green twists into a nine-mile double loop called **Bowknot Bend**. The second loop meanders back to within a quarter mile of itself, and a short, steep hike up the narrow neck of rock pinched off by the river earns a fetching desert view.

Beyond Bowknot Bend is Mineral Bottom, where floaters who haven't already registered for a Stillwater Canyon permit can sign in. Mineral Bottom is also the main put-in for those going past the **Confluence** into the spectacular rapids of the Colorado's **Cataract Canyon**. During peak season, the place is often crowded with river-scarred rafts, trucks pulling trailers,

and tanned guides rigging their boats.

By this time, three to five days into the trip, the rhythm of river travel begins to take over, camp chores become routine, and the journey unfolds at an easygoing pace. Clocks and calendars are virtually irrelevant. Time is kept by the arc of the sun, the sway of the boat, the flutelike calls of canyon wrens, the chatter of white-throated swifts.

Landmarks drift by, signaling the approach of Stillwater Canyon – the **Buttes of the Cross**, **Queen Anne Bottom**, **Candlestick Tower**, **Turks Head**, and **Fort Bottom**, where outlaw Butch Cassidy is said to have lain low from time to time. Stillwater, true to its name, is even more sedate than Labyrinth. Here, the subtle side of the Green River's personality reveals itself. The water casts a seductive trance, and a halo of stalled time settles like mist, all overhung by walls of White Rim sandstone.

Water Dance

Even as the hushed miles pass, expectation builds for the confluence of two of the West's most powerful rivers. The boat passes through a final bend, and then the mud-red current of the Colorado River comes into view. The two waterways flow together in an awkward dance of currents. The rivers mingle and swirl, jostling the boats like nervous horses before sending them downstream.

"Late in the afternoon our boats make the junction of the [Colorado] and Green [at] the foot of Stillwater Canyon, as we have named it," wrote Powell. "These streams unite in solemn depths, more than 1,200 feet below the general surface of the country ... we look up [the Colorado] and out into the country beyond and obtain glimpses of snow-clad peaks, the summits of a group of mountains known as the Sierra La Sal."

The Colorado feels heady with new volume. At first, the water is two-toned, then grad-

Rock layers (left) in Labyrinth Canyon appear to be flat but are actually part of a broad arch covering much of southeastern Utah.

The Doll House

Boaters with half a day available to explore the area around Spanish Bottom most often head toward the Doll House and adjacent Surprise Valley. From the downstream, or southwest, edge of Spanish Bottom, a trail climbs in steep switchbacks to one of the most striking regions in the Canyonlands.

The Doll House itself is made up of a concentration of prominent sandstone spires – a thicket of eroded pillars, knobs, and columns etched into soft red and white layers. The nearby flats in Surprise Valley provide several vantage points with stunning views upstream to the Confluence and beyond. Across the river lies the **Needles District** of Canyonlands, the **Grabens**, and **Lower Red Lake Canyon**. Off in the distance float high, forested mesas and the snow-peaked La Sal Mountains.

Several small archaeological sites are found in the area, including a nearly intact set of granary storage structures tucked under an overhang in a corner of Surprise Valley. **Beehive Arch** bends high overhead about a mile to the north of the Doll House. More energetic hikes, requiring a day or longer, reach the **Land of Standing Rocks**, the **Fins**, and the edge of the **Maze**, some of the most remote and seldom-visited country in this lonely slickrock wilderness.

The Chocolate Drops (above) are unusual sandstone formations in the Maze district of Canyonlands National Park.

Sea kayaks (below) are increasingly popular on this stretch of the Green River, though canoes afford more space for gear.

ually takes on its new hue, mixed from a pallet of sediments plucked from the earth across Colorado, Utah, and Wyoming. In five quick miles the broad flats at Spanish Bottom, a wide bench made up of centuries of flood sediments, spread away from the high dirt banks. The expanse is vegetated by sagebrush and prickly pear and is large enough for scores of campers. Even so, on some days at the height of rafting season, finding an open spot is a challenge, and the coveted shady sites are snatched up early.

Pity those who schedule their jet-boat pickup to coincide with their arrival at Spanish Bottom. They are whisked upstream before exploring the eroded rock wonderland of **Surprise Valley** and the **Doll House**, only a short hike away. Parties with a day or two to

spare are free to scramble up into the fantastic formations or to stroll downstream and bear witness to the first formidable rapids in Cataract Canyon. Either way, pausing a day or two before returning to civilization leaves time for the images of your journey to settle firmly into the embrace of memory.

TRAVEL TIPS

DETAILS

When to Go

Spring and fall are ideal times to visit this region. Summer can be very hot, with temperatures in the 90s by June. High water covers good campsites in late spring, and mosquitoes may be a problem. Low water exposes the best sandbars for camping in fall, though slower water will mean a longer float or more paddling. Up-canyon winds in any season can slow your progress.

How to Get There

The put-in at Green River is about a two-hour drive south of Salt Lake City, Utah; Moab is about five hours away. The take-out at Mineral Bottom, about halfway through the run, is reachable by road. Paddlers continuing through Stillwater Canyon to Spanish Bottom, where the Green joins the Colorado just upstream of Cataract Canyon, must hire a powerboat to shuttle them up the Colorado River to Moab or pass through the formidable raft-only rapids of Cataract. Shuttle and pickup service can be arranged by outfitters if the service isn't already included in a rental or guide package.

Permits

The Bureau of Land Management in Moab (435-259-6111) issues permits for the Labyrinth Canyon section from Green River to Mineral Bottom. Canyonlands National Park (435-259-7164) issues permits for the Stillwater Canyon section from Mineral Bottom to Spanish Bottom.

INFORMATION

Bureau of Land Management

82 East Dogwood Avenue, Moab, UT 84532; tel: 435-259-6111.

Canyonlands National Park

2282 S.W. Resource Boulevard, Moab, UT 84532; tel: 435-259-7164 or 435-259-4351 (back-country trip planning).

Grand County Travel Council

P.O. Box 550, Moab, UT 84532; tel: 800-635-6622.

CAMPING

Camping is permitted along the river unless otherwise posted; sandbars make excellent spots. All parties must carry portable toilets (available for rent from some outfitters).

Dead Horse State Park Campground

P.O. Box 609, Moab, UT 84532; tel: 435-259-2614 or 800-322-3770.

This popular campground is situated near Island in the Sky about 40 minutes north of Moab. Water, flush toilets, and picnic tables are available at 35 sites and may be reserved in advance.

Green River State Park

P.O. Box 93, Green River, UT 84525; tel: 435-564-3633 or 800-322-3770.

Many boaters use this riverside park just off Interstate 70 as their put-in. The park has hot showers, flush toilets, 42 campsites, and a nine-hole golf course.

Squaw Flat Campground

Canyonlands National Park, 2282 S.W. Resource Boulevard, Moab, UT 84532; tel: 435-259-7164.

This campground, in the Needles district, is about an hour southwest of Moab. It has 26 sites allotted on a first-come, first-served basis and limits groups to 12 people. Picnic tables, grills, and vault toilets are available.

LODGING

PRICE GUIDE – double occupancy

$ = up to $49 $$ = $50–$99

$$$ = $100–$149 $$$$ = $150+

Best Western Greenwell Inn

105 South Main Street, Moab, UT 84532; tel: 435-259-6151 or 800-528-1234.

This downtown motel has 72 rooms, a restaurant, outdoor pool, and hot tub. $$

Best Western River Terrace

880 East Main Street, Green River, UT 84525; tel: 435-564-3401 or 800-528-1234.

This riverside motel has 51 rooms, an outdoor pool, and hot tub. $$

Canyon Country Bed-and-Breakfast

590 North 500 West, Moab, UT 84532; tel: 435-259-5262.

Four of the five rooms at this ranch-style inn have private baths, and all have a patio entrance to the inn's garden. The landscaped yard has a volleyball court, hot tub, and outdoor theater showing old films. $$–$$$

Gonzo Inn

100 West 200 South, Moab, UT 84532; tel: 435-259-2515 or 800-791-4044.

When this stylish in-town lodge describes itself as "a little off Main," it's not referring only to location. The 43 large rooms, including some suites with fireplaces, whirlpool tubs, balconies, and kitchenettes, have a bright, offbeat, "retro" look with a Southwest twist. There is an outdoor pool and hot tub. $$$

Sunflower Hill Bed-and-Breakfast Inn

185 North 300 East, Moab, UT 84532; tel: 435-259-2974 or 800-662-2786.

Pine trees and flower gardens surround this inn, which is a few blocks from the center of town. Eleven guest rooms have private baths and antique beds. Some also have patios or balconies. $$$–$$$$

TOURS AND OUTFITTERS

Jerkwater Canoe Company

P.O. Box 800, Topock, AZ 86436; tel: 520-768-7753 or 800-421-7803.

Weeklong canoe and kayak trips travel Labyrinth Canyon from Green River to Mineral Bottom. Trips include optional transportation from Las Vegas, Nevada, or the company's base in Arizona.

Moki Mac River Expeditions

P.O. Box 71242, Salt Lake City, UT 84171; tel: 801-268-6667 or 800-284-7280.

After a six-day canoe trip through Labyrinth and Stillwater Canyons, guests switch to rafts for the whitewater of Cataract Canyon. Rentals are available for self-guided trips in Labyrinth Canyon, with pickup service at Mineral Bottom.

Red River Canoe Company

702 South Main Street, Moab, UT 84532; tel: 435-259-7722 or 800-753-8216.

This outfitter offers guided tours, canoe rentals, and instruction.

Sherry Griffith Expeditions

P.O. Box 1324, Moab, UT 84532; tel: 435-259-8229 or 800-332-2439.

Green River trips in oar rafts and inflatable kayaks emphasize comfort, natural history, and good food.

Tex's Riverways

P.O. Box 67, Moab, UT 85432; tel: 435-259-5101.

Outfitting is provided for self-guided trips through Labyrinth and Stillwater Canyons. Motorboats shuttle paddlers up the Colorado River from Spanish Bottom to Moab.

Excursions

Desolation and Gray Canyons

Bureau of Land Management, Price River Resource Area, 125 South 600 West, Price, UT 84501; tel: 801-636-3622.

The Green River slices into the 10,000-foot-high Tavaput plateau in eastern Utah, creating a spectacular pair of canyons. Colorful cliffs and rock spires keep all eyes occupied in the calm stretches between Class III rapids. Petroglyphs, abandoned mines, a sunken ferry, and markers commemorating the 1869 Powell expedition remind boaters of the area's rich history. The entire run from Sand Wash to Green River is about 95 miles long. Adventure Bound (800-423-4668) and Moki Mac River Expeditions (800-284-7280) are among the many companies that offer four- to seven-day trips.

San Juan River

Bureau of Land Management, San Juan Resource Area Office, P.O. Box 7, Monticello, UT 84535; tel: 435-587-2201.

Paddlers from all over the country come to the San Juan for its ancient cliff dwellings, towering sandstone walls (the river runs through the looping Goosenecks section), moderate Class II-III whitewater, and unusual "sand waves," which migrate with the river's shifting bottom. Paddlers take about a week to run the entire 84-mile course; shorter trips of three to five days can be made using the access at Mexican Hat, Utah. Adventure Discovery (602-774-1926), High Desert Adventures (800-673-1733), and OARS (800-342-5938) run raft and inflatable-kayak trips.

Westwater Canyon

Bureau of Land Management, River Office, Grand Resource Area, 82 East Dogwood Street, Moab, UT 84532; tel: 435-259-8193.

Long a favorite of kayakers, this 18-mile stretch of the Colorado River has stunning canyon scenery, good hiking, fine play spots, several menacing Class IV rapids, and an infamous eddy called the Room of Doom, where ill-fated rafts have been trapped for hours. Though the run can be done in one day, many boaters take two to enjoy the setting. Several raft companies, including Adventure Bound (800-423-4668) and Holiday Expeditions (800-624-6323), run trips through Westwater.

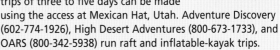

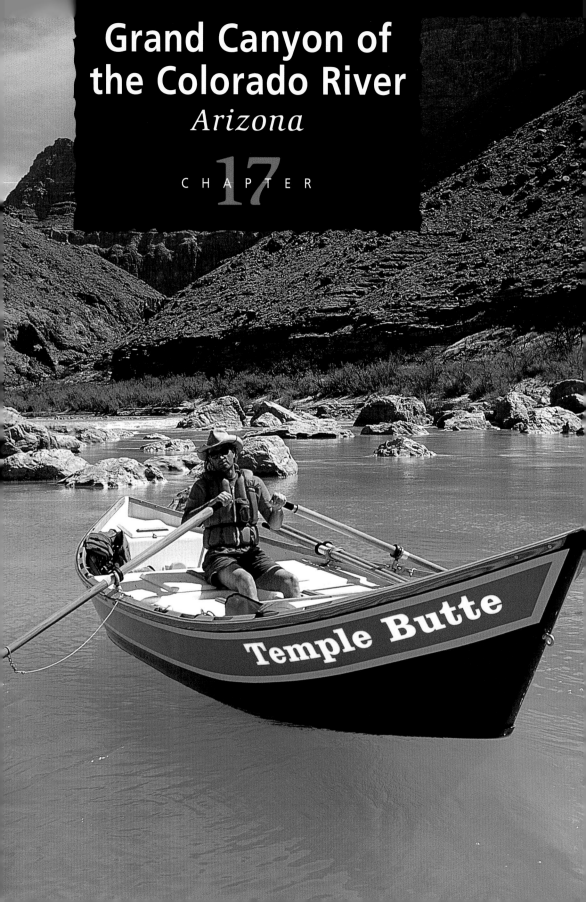

Grand Canyon of the Colorado River

Arizona

CHAPTER 17

On a hot July day, a flotilla of rubber rafts floats down a serene stretch of the Colorado River in the Grand Canyon. A high-pitched buzz echoes off the sun-drenched cliffs. It's a peregrine falcon sounding an intruder alarm as it swoops down to the water, then soars back up into the blue sky. ◆ For boaters, the sight of this majestic raptor is an awesome spectacle, and one of the many reasons that a journey through the canyon is such a singular adventure. Here boaters enter the heart of the Southwest's remaining great wilderness and one of the planet's deepest gorges. They encounter wild creatures, pass in wonder through stunning desert canyons, and ride some of the biggest whitewater in the West. ◆ The Rio Colorado courses wild and free through the million acres of Grand Canyon National Park in northern Arizona. From the launch point at **Lees Ferry**, the only way out in the next 227 miles is by foot on long, steep trails up to the canyon's rims. ◆ Summer is prime season for running the "Grand," and while private individuals with the proper gear and experience are allowed to make the trip, a Park Service permit can take years to obtain. That's why most of the 22,000 people who boat the canyon each year go as paying passengers with outfitters licensed by the Park Service. On these trips, experienced guides row the boats, and the company furnishes all the food and gear. The guides know the river, the best places to hike and camp, and the canyon's stories. It's a tough job – part navigator, part tour guide, part entertainment director. They're up before dawn to make the coffee, they rig and row the boats, and they strum their guitars by starlight.

Journey into the world's most spectacular chasm on the West's mightiest river.

The Colorado is clear blue at Lees Ferry; the water takes on a coffee color farther downstream as tributaries deposit silt into the river.

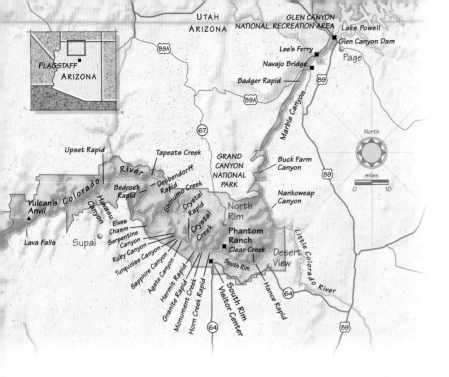

UTAH
ARIZONA

GLEN CANYON
NATIONAL RECREATION AREA

Lake Powell

Glen Canyon Dam

89A

Page

FLAGSTAFF
ARIZONA

Lee's Ferry

Navajo Bridge

Badger Rapid

89

89A

67

GRAND
CANYON
NATIONAL
PARK

Buck Farm
Canyon

89

North

miles

0   10

Upset Rapid

Tapeats Creek

River

Detbendorff
Rapid

Shinumo Creek

Crystal
Rapid

Nankoweap
Canyon

Bedrock
Rapid

Vulcan's
Anvil

Colorado

Havasu
Canyon

Elves
Chasm

Serpentine
Canyon

Crystal
Rapid

Crystal
Creek

North
Rim

Phantom
Ranch

Lava Falls

Supai

Ruby Canyon

Turquoise Canyon

Clear Creek

South Rim

Desert
View

Little Colorado River

Sapphire Canyon

Agate Canyon

Hermit Rapid

Granite Rapid

Monument Creek

Horn Creek Rapid

South Rim
Visitor Center

Hance Rapid

64

64

89

numbing experience. The Grand Canyon is a remote and wild place; emergency help is more than a phone call away. But if you're armed with proper information and take sensible precautions, the trip can be safe and pleasurable for everyone.

Choosing a Vessel

Many companies run both oar-powered and motorized boats. Oar boats are smaller, holding four or five people, and trips usually last two weeks (though partial trips are an option). Motor trips last a week or less, and each boat carries many more passengers. Purists eschew the motors because they disturb the canyon's sublime silence. Others who go by motor swear their journey could not have been more profound; as one riverman put it, you could go down the Colorado in a bathtub and still have a peak experience. Yet another option is dories – elegant, wooden, oar-powered boats that are reminiscent of (though much more river worthy than) the vessels used by such early explorers as John Wesley Powell, who first ran the Colorado in 1869.

Even with seasoned guides, passengers need to know a few rules and risks. The rules are: wear shoes on shore, don't use soap in the water, drink plenty of fluids, never litter, and most important, wear life jackets at all times on the river. Helping in camp and kitchen is welcome but certainly not mandatory. The risks are: boats can flip, and they do once in a great while. Should this happen, the best advice is to keep your feet up and point them downstream. The reason is twofold: first, to ward off rocks with your feet rather than your head and, second, to prevent your feet from getting trapped on the bottom, which can cause you to be dragged under by the current. Get back in the boat if possible; if not, swim to shore and wait for a ride. The water temperature hovers around 50°F, and even a short dip can be a

A river guide (right) negotiates a formidable series of standing waves at Hermit Rapid.

No matter what kind of boat you choose, you're guaranteed a white-knuckle ride. Though most of the Colorado's rapids aren't technical in the sense that they don't require a rapid-fire succession of precise maneuvers, the sheer size of the waves packs a mighty wallop. Unlike other rivers, which are rated on the familiar International Scale of Whitewater Difficulty, the Colorado has its own rating system, 1 being the most tranquil, 10 the hairiest.

A youngster (left) enjoys a sunny morning. Canyon temperatures can exceed 100°F.

The Little Colorado River, a storm-swollen tributary, pours over Grand Falls (below).

Canyon Time

Canyon trips start at Lees Ferry, a desert outpost where a road goes down to the river's edge. It's a busy place on summer days, with several parties rigging at the same time. Tanned, muscled guides lash bags, coolers, and metal ammo cans onto boat frames and laugh and joke with their pals. Then, a big bus or van pulls up, disgorging passengers, many of whom have never met before but who will be sharing perhaps the most intense two weeks of their lives together. It's hard to imagine, standing by the gentle, gurgling water, just what the Colorado has in store for them.

With everything neatly stowed and ready, the passengers buckle on life jackets and climb aboard. The boats push off from shore and bounce through the Paria riffle. Everyone stares up at **Navajo Bridge**, 300 feet overhead, the last bit of civilization they'll see for many, many miles.

Around lunchtime, **Badger Rapid** bellows its presence. Boats slide easily down the shining tongue at the top, and passengers squeal with shock and delight at their baptism in the river's chilly water. The trip continues down through **Marble Canyon**, past canyon walls rising ever higher.

The river routine sets in – eat breakfast, pack boats, travel downriver for a few miles, walk up to an ancient Pueblo granary or stop to view a historic inscription on a boulder, lunch under a shady tamarisk, boat a few more miles, then pull up onto a sandy beach for the night. Change into dry clothes, enjoy social hour and dinner, then hit the sleeping bag under a starry sky.

By the third or fourth day of a trip, the sense of being in and of the earth is palpable. Skin toughens to the sun and dry air, people start to talk more about what they're seeing around them than what the stock market

is doing back home. Wristwatches are shed as canyon time takes over.

Past the scalloped cliffs of the **Desert Palisades**, the stone tower at **Desert View** punctuates the rim skyline. Soon, the aquamarine waters of the **Little Colorado River** interweave with the main Colorado, and the pace quickens. A little farther on, at Mile 77, the canyon walls change from colorful sandstones and limestones to the ominous dark black schist of the **Inner Gorge**. Here is **Hance Rapid**, the first big drop on the river. Its predecessors were only teasers.

Hance is a long jumble of rocks and waves, featuring a nasty hole midway through called the **Mixmaster**. At low water it earns a rating of 10.

As the canyon closes in, boaters gear up for another series of rambunctious rapids including **Sockdolager**, translated as "the knock-out punch." A taste of rustic civilization rears its head briefly at **Phantom Ranch**, where people can sip an ice-cold lemonade, stare at backpackers toiling into camp, and send home a postcard that will be carried out of the canyon on the back of a mule.

This is the point at which an interchange of passengers may occur. Some hike out of the canyon, while others join the trip. They have no idea what's in store for them below Phantom Ranch, because rapids that heretofore inspired awe and fear will soon pale in comparison to those ahead.

Whitewater Quartet

At lunch, the usually garrulous guides get a little serious. Furrowed brows, furtive conversations, gear tied down

Paddling Lake Powell

Set on the Arizona–Utah border in the heart of Glen Canyon National Recreation Area, Lake Powell was created when the Glen Canyon Dam backed up the Colorado River for 186 miles upstream. Here sparkling water reflects a clear turquoise sky, and cliffs of chiseled orange sandstone cut cleanly down to the water's edge. With nearly 2,000 miles of shoreline, the lake offers paddlers a lifetime of exploration in one of the most stunning landscapes in the Southwest.

While most of the lake traffic is given over to throaty motorboats, houseboats, jet skis, and various other toys, sea kayaks are ideal because they can venture into tight slot canyons where motorboats dare not go. Hours and days can be idled away on the still surface of the lake, and where the water ends, a million-acre desert wilderness of sand, rock, and sagebrush begins. Nearly a hundred canyons spill into Lake Powell, winding ribbons of vaulted rock, many with shallow streams and deep pools of cold water.

Sheltered coves and inlets along the lakeshore provide flat ground for camping in this delicate, slickrock environment. Everything must be packed in and packed out. Coyote choruses and skies painted with stars provide nighttime entertainment.

Kayakers can launch at **Wahweap Marina**, a few miles from the town of **Page**, Arizona, or farther uplake at **Hite**, **Halls Crossing**, or **Bullfrog**. A Wahweap put-in means paddling a sprawling fetch of lake, prone to sudden windstorms with accompanying chop and whitecaps. Motorboats also set out big wakes best taken nose-on by small, human-powered craft. Sprayskirts on kayaks are highly recommended.

To reach less populated parts of the lake, such as the **San Juan Arm** or the **Escalante River**, paddlers might beg a ride with a friend who owns a motorboat, or contact marinas for concession-operated shuttles.

Sublime red-rock scenery awaits kayakers in the quiet corners of Lake Powell (below).

a little tighter. Then it's **Horn Creek**, a short, sweet jolt. At lower water levels, when the vicious rocks, or "horns," are showing, this rapid requires a precise entry and one or two strategic oar strokes. A few miles downstream, the roar of **Granite Rapid** drowns out jokes and laughter. Formed by boulders washed in from **Monument Creek**, Granite is a chaotic flume of monstrous waves issuing off the right wall, along with a few crushers coming in from the left, not to mention dreaded **King Edward**, a major eddy at the bottom. A left entry into Granite is desirable, but the river often has other ideas, as all the current piles into the right. Granite's been known to flip a few boats, so everybody's happy to be right side up at the bottom and beyond the clutches of King Edward.

Hermit Rapid awaits – a series of five beautiful, standing waves – approached head on, right down the middle. The fifth wave, the granddaddy of them all, can grab a raft and hold it for a few seconds – though it feels like an eternity – as it decides whether to permit passage or capsize the prisoner.

With adrenaline nearly exhausted, some guides elect to stop on a pleasant little beach for the night before attempting the last of the quartet – infamous **Crystal Rapid**. Crystal – the name is pronounced with reverential dread – deserves its 10-plus rating. Before 1966, Crystal was a mere riffle. But during a storm that winter, a flash flood deposited a mass of boulders in the riverbed, transforming Crystal into one of the two toughest runs on the river. A far-right entry in this rapid is almost mandatory. A faulty start can send a boat into the frightening maw at center-left, which may result in a trip through the strainer known as the **Rock Garden** down below.

Heart of the Earth

Once all the excitement is over, passengers can enjoy the beauty of the Inner Gorge, surrounded by walls of fluted, blue-black

The mouth of Redwall Cavern (left) frames sheer canyon walls and the silhouettes of rafters enjoying a volleyball game.

Crystal Rapid (below) was created by a flash flood in 1966.

feet below the surface. For boaters downstream, that means cold, clear, green water. In the old days, the Rio Colorado was choked thick with mud and silt, but no more. Also, electricity demand now determines water levels on the Colorado, which has caused more stable and predictable levels over the course of the year, though daily fluctuations can be dramatic. In some cases boats are left high and dry on beaches in the morning when the water level drops precipitously during the night.

Vishnu schist gleaming like forged iron. The Vishnu, nearly two billion years old, is the oldest rock in the canyon. All the rock on top, and all the rock since leaving Lees Ferry, is younger. The Grand Canyon lays out in textbook fashion a neat chronology of the Earth's history, one of the most complete records anywhere, from two billion through about 250 million years ago, with only a few gaps.

The rock is old, but the canyon is young. It took the Colorado River only about six million years, and maybe as few as two million, to carve the mile-deep Grand Canyon. It's still trying to cut deeper, but the old, hard, crystalline schist is resisting mightily.

Another major impediment has slowed the work of the river. **Glen Canyon Dam**, 15 miles above Lees Ferry, was completed in 1963. This 710-foot-high, 10-million-ton concrete plug now holds back the waters of the Colorado in **Lake Powell**. The hydroelectric power generated at the dam electrifies cities all over the West. The water that goes through the turbines is pulled out of the lake about 200

Glen Canyon Dam has also been the single most important influence on the river ecosystem in modern times. Native fish and plants, like humpback chubs and willow trees, have given way to introduced trout and tamarisk. Altered though it may be, the river corridor still harbors a wealth of wildlife – bighorn sheep perched on impossibly sheer cliffs, coyotes coming

down to the river to drink, great blue herons standing stock-still on a mudflat, Bell's vireos calling from the thickets, bats fluttering overhead at dusk, collared lizards scampering from boulder to boulder in search of shade, canyon wrens warbling their liquid trill.

While the river remains the focus, each day brings new places and new discoveries. Boaters frequently stop and walk up side canyons, paradises in the desert with year-round flowing streams, pools reflecting canyon colors, waterfalls where hummingbirds hide, and freshwater springs lush with maidenhair ferns and crimson monkeyflowers. The names of these places are legendary among river rats – **Buck Farm**, **Nankoweap**, **Clear Creek**, **Shinumo**, **Elves Chasm**, **Havasu**.

Lava and Beyond

Moving ever downstream, boaters soon come to a stretch of the river below

Crystal Rapid known as the **Jewels**: **Agate**, **Sapphire**, **Turquoise**, **Ruby**, **Serpentine**, **Garnet**. Boats swirl peacefully past the colonnade of **Conquistadore Aisle**, down to Mile 130 and **Bedrock Rapid**, and below it to **Deubendorff**, a long rapid to be run before camping for the night. **Tapeats** and **Deer Creeks** are fine places to linger before facing **Upset Rapid** with its sharp surprises. On to Mile 157 and **Havasu Canyon**, "place of the blue-green waters," home of the Havasupai Indians, where river trips often spend the

Rafters (above) prepare to enter a drop. The canyon's world-famous whitewater actually accounts for only 10 percent of the run.

The blue-green waters of Havasu Creek (right) issue from springs 10 miles upstream.

better part of a day.

Farther on, the rocks assume a new form. Black volcanics fill side canyons and form etched pillars. **Vulcan's Anvil**, a remnant of basalt standing in the middle of the river, is an ominous marker of what lies just ahead.

Lava Falls is yet another Grand Canyon legend, the one the guides have been talking about ever since the trip began. It's a frightful maelstrom of foaming, seething turbulence stretching the width of the river, and it's rated a 10 at all water levels.

After a scouting session that seems to last forever, everyone walks back down the hot, dusty trail to the boats, hushed and sobered. Life jackets are buckled tight, the

A raven (left) alights on a dory; the birds hunt and scavenge throughout the canyon.

Canyon walls (right) record nearly two billion years of the planet's history.

A fearless paddler leaps into the plunge pool at Deer Creek Falls (below).

guides check every loose line, cameras and binoculars are securely stowed. This one's for real, and everyone seems to know it.

Untied, the boats swing into the current. The guide stands up for a better view, searches for the proverbial "bubble line" that marks the entry. "Hang on," he says, and the passengers clutch whatever hand-hold they can find. The boat slips down the tongue. Slam. A wave hits the bow like a two-ton truck. Then the boat drops down into a trough of air and climbs up the front of another wave. In a brief second, people stare over into the gargantuan hole formed by Lava's famous V-wave. The boat just kisses it, and the guide shouts, "Get ready." Another slam of water engulfs boat and passengers. Seconds later, the boatman whoops and orders: "Bail! Bail!" The passengers oblige, tossing bucket after bucket of water back into the Colorado.

Relief. Exultation. Joy. Camp below Lava is always a big celebration. Of course, the trip isn't over. This is only Mile 179.6. There are still another 50 miles to go. The terrain changes again as the canyon widens and the river drops into even more austere desert. Finally, **Diamond Peak** spears the horizon. The trucks wait at the **Diamond Creek** take-out. Boats are unpacked one last time, the fine canyon sand sloshed away. It will be a while, though, before all the sand and all the memories are washed clean. Dreams of diving falcons and the sweet songs of canyon wrens will fill many nights to come. Dreams of the canyon and river may last forever.

TRAVEL TIPS

DETAILS

When to Go

Most trips in the canyon run between April and October. Temperatures on the river can reach 115°F in summer but are much cooler in April, May, September, and October. Flash floods sometimes deter hikes in side canyons during spring; thundershowers are common in August.

How to Get There

The put-in at Lees Ferry is about a two-hour drive north of Flagstaff, Arizona, which is served by several airlines, including Mesa/America West (800-235-9292). Grand Canyon Airport, just south of the park, has limited commercial service.

Permits

The waiting list to obtain a private permit takes about 10 years, but you can bypass the process by signing on with a commercial outfitter. For information about permits, contact the National Park Service, River Permits Office, P.O. Box 129, Grand Canyon, AZ 86023; tel: 520-638-1843.

INFORMATION

Flagstaff Convention and Visitors Bureau

211 West Aspen Avenue, Flagstaff, AZ 86001-5399; tel: 520-779-7611.

Grand Canyon Chamber of Commerce

P.O. Box 3007, Grand Canyon, AZ 86023; tel: 520-638-2901.

Grand Canyon National Park

P.O. Box 129, Grand Canyon, AZ 86023; tel: 520-638-7888.

Grand Canyon Private Boaters Association

P.O. Box 2133, Flagstaff, AZ 86003; tel: 520-214-8676.

CAMPING

Boulder Beach Campground

Lake Mead National Recreation Area, 601 Nevada Highway, Boulder City, NV 89005; tel: 702-293-8907.

This recreation area within driving distance of the take-out offers 10 campgrounds along the shores of Lake Mead and Lake Mohave, downstream of the Hoover Dam.

Jacob Lake Campground

Kaibab National Forest, P.O. Box 248, Fredonia, AZ 86022; tel: 800-283-2267 (reservations) or 520-643-7395.

This campground in Kaibab National Forest, 45 miles west of Lees Ferry, has 53 campsites with tables and fire grills, drinking water, and toilets. Prepare for cool nights at the camp's 7,920-foot elevation.

Lees Ferry Campground

Glen Canyon National Recreation Area, Box 1507, Page, AZ 86040; tel: 520-355-2234.

Fifty-one sites, with flush toilets and drinking water, are available at this campground at the Lees Ferry put-in. Sites are available on a first-come, first-served basis.

LODGING

El Tovar Hotel

AmFac Parks and Resorts, 14001 East Iliff Avenue, Suite 600, Aurora, CO 80014; tel: 303-297-2757.

This hotel along the South Rim is convenient for boaters doing partial canyon trips. The three-story log-and-rock hotel has 78 rooms, a stone fireplace, and a veranda. A concierge assists with adventure plans. $$$–$$$$

Jacob Lake Inn

Highways 89A and 67, Jacob Lake, AZ 86022; tel: 520-643-7232.

At the gateway to the North Rim, about 45 miles west of Lees Ferry, this inn's 35 guest accommodations include basic motel rooms and cabins. A restaurant, gift shop, grocery store, and bakery are on the grounds. $$

Lees Ferry Lodge

HC 67, Box 1, Highway 89A, Marble Canyon, AZ 86036; tel: 520-355-2231.

About eight miles from the put-in, this motel has 11 simple rooms and a restaurant. $$

Marble Canyon Lodge

Highway 89A, Marble Canyon, AZ 86036; tel: 800-726-1789 or 520-355-2225.

Five miles from the put-in, this lodge offers 48 guest rooms, a cottage, and eight apartment-style units that sleep six to eight people. $$–$$$

TOURS AND OUTFITTERS

At least 15 outfitters are licensed to take passengers through the Grand Canyon. Most offer partial trips, which either end or begin at Phantom Ranch, a strenuous seven-mile hike from the South Rim. Trips take anywhere from eight to 19 days, depending on the number of layovers and the amount of time devoted to side hikes. A few outfitters provide support for kayakers who want to bypass the waiting list for private permits. For a complete list of outfitters, contact Grand Canyon National Park.

Arizona Raft Adventures, Inc.

4050-F East Huntington Drive, Flagstaff, AZ 86004, tel: 800-786-7238 or 520-526-8200.

Outfitted raft adventures last up to six days. Along the way,

stops are made for sightseeing, hiking, and swimming.

Canyon Explorations

P.O. Box 310, Flagstaff, AZ 86002; tel: 800-654-0723 or 520-774-4559.

Guided trips through the Grand Canyon include daily hikes up side canyons, interpretive talks, and camping. Trips last one to two weeks.

Grand Canyon Dories

P.O. Box 216, Altaville, CA 95221; tel: 800-346-6277 or 209-736-0805.

Multiday excursions aboard dories specialize in side hikes to Matkatamiba Canyon, Deer Creek Falls, Elves Chasm, and Havasu Creek. A stop is made at the Little Colorado for a dip in its famous swimming hole.

High Sonoran Adventures

10628 North 97th Street, Scottsdale, AZ 85620; tel: 602-614-3331.

Customized whitewater rafting, biking, and hiking trips explore the Grand Canyon and a number of national forests.

Moki Mac River Expeditions

P.O. Box 21242, Salt Lake City, UT 84121; tel: 800-284-7280 or 801-268-6667.

Trips through the Grand Canyon last from six to 14 days. Inflatable kayaks are available. The outfitter also offers expeditions through Westwater and Cataract Canyons.

Outdoors Unlimited

6900 Townsend Winona Road, Flagstaff, AZ 86004; tel: 800-637-7238 or 520-526-4546.

The lower, upper, or entire Grand Canyon can be covered on five- to 15-day trips. Passengers hike side canyons and take short excursions to Native American ruins and remote grottoes.

Excursions

Colorado River, Glen Canyon Dam to Lees Ferry

Glen Canyon National Recreation Area, Box 1507, Page, AZ 86040; tel: 520-355-2234.

The 13-mile-long stretch of the Colorado River above Lees Ferry is a sampler of the landscapes to come, especially if you are short of the time required to do a full Grand Canyon run. Tawny cliffs tower up to 1,400 feet above the river, and the placid water is perfect for canoeing. There's great trout fishing, too. Wilderness River Tours (800-992-8022) runs raft trips through the canyon. Solo paddlers can rent canoes in Page and arrange for a motorboat to shuttle them back to town at the end of their trip.

Gila River

Gila Box Riparian National Conservation Area, 711 14th Avenue, Safford, AZ 85546; tel: 520-348-4400.

The Gila River offers paddlers solitude, scenery, and a glimpse of desert wildlife. Bird-watching is particularly good in spring, when migrating neotropical songbirds pass through the region. The 23-mile run from old Safford bridge to Dry Canyon is a popular overnight trip, although it can be completed in a single day during periods of higher flows.

Verde River

Tonto National Forest, Camp Verde Ranger District, P.O. Box 670, Camp Verde, AZ 86322; tel: 520-567-1108.

Arizona's only federally designated wild and scenic river lives up to its name. Verdant stands of cottonwoods, sycamores, and willows flourish in the river corridor in the high Sonoran Desert, about halfway between Flagstaff and Phoenix. A three- to five-day paddling trip passes through the Mazatzal Wilderness, with fine mountain and desert views, and opportunities to explore archaeological sites and multicolored cliffs and canyons. Fallen trees and shallow rock gardens create hazards; the Verde River is navigated most safely in inflatable kayaks or rafts.

Monterey Bay
California

CHAPTER 18

The titanic geologic forces that formed the ragged edge of North America are still hard at work. About midway along the 1,264-mile California coast, the **Santa Lucia Mountains** tumble down to the sea, causing the **Monterey Peninsula** to bulge into the Pacific. Where land ends, the seafloor falls steeply away into a vast submarine canyon more than 8,400 feet deep. Cold, nutrient-rich water wells up from the trough, forming the first link in a food chain that sustains an extravagant variety of life from tiny plankton and dense kelp beds to migrating whales. ◆ When Spanish explorer Sebastian Vizcaino sailed north from Mexico in 1603 to map the California coast, he was particularly taken with Monterey: "Among the ports of greater consideration which I discovered was one in 37 degrees of latitude which I called Monterey ... I found it sheltered from all winds, while on the coast there are pines from which masts of any desired size can be obtained." The Spanish made Monterey their capital in California and wasted no time making their mark on the place. Missions and ranchos were quickly established, Indians were forcibly converted, and the last of the fearsome coastal grizzly bears was lassoed by *vaqueros* and dragged into Monterey to fight bulls at a fiesta. ◆ Sadly, much of the wilderness that the Spanish discovered has gone the way of the grizzlies. Most of what remains lies offshore and is encompassed by **Monterey Bay National Marine Sanctuary**, the country's largest. Modern-day sea kayakers can explore this bountiful marine environment by utilizing boats and skills passed down to them by early coastal hunters. In an ironic twist of history,

A sea kayak is your ticket to a coastal wilderness teeming with life.

A team of kayakers prepares for a sunset paddle. "Surf landing" is an essential skill to acquire before tackling the open ocean.

classes and natural-history tours, and lots of good advice.

A short paddle across the harbor takes you past **Municipal Wharf #2**, where commercial fishing boats may be unloading their catch or preparing nets for their next trip out to sea. Stay alert and out of the way of moving boats. Motorized vessels are supposed to yield to sail and paddle craft, but harbor traffic is heavy and visibility sometimes poor.

You will probably hear the wildlife before you see it, as a large herd of California sea lions has taken up residence on the wooden piers of the wharf and along the **Coast Guard Jetty** beyond. The din of their more or less continual family squabbling is audible from a great distance. Sanctuary rules require visitors to stay at least 50 feet away from wildlife, although this may prove impossible when sea lions start popping up all around you. Resist the temptation to paddle too close to

the last Native people to paddle these waters were Aleutian Islanders, who were brought here from Alaska by Russian fur traders to hunt sea otters.

Seals at Play

The most sensible place to launch into Monterey Bay is just west of the harbor at the beach directly in front of Monterey Bay Kayaks. The shop offers boat and equipment rentals, nautical charts, a full schedule of

them, even though their antics may seem like an invitation to draw near.

Turn left at the end of the Coast Guard Jetty, an especially popular hangout for gangs of adolescent sea lions, who may follow playfully behind. For such inquisitive creatures, they seem unnaturally camera-shy, diving beneath the surface the moment you turn to snap a picture – or perhaps that's part of their game.

You're moving into somewhat more exposed water here, so keep your eyes open. If no waves that look big enough to break over you are rolling in, continue paddling fairly close to shore into patches of kelp where sea otters are often found. An effective way to observe these beautiful animals without intruding is to paddle your kayak upwind and off a little to the side. Then lay your paddle across your lap and let the breeze blow you silently past. You may see them floating on their backs, cracking abalone, crabs, or other shellfish on rocks that they balance on their bellies, or perhaps napping at the surface with strands of kelp draped across their bodies to anchor themselves in place.

Continue paddling along the shore past **San Carlos** and **MacAbee Beaches** and colorful **Cannery Row**. Thousands of tons of sardines were processed here until over-fishing caused the sardine population to collapse in the early 1950s. Now the canneries and their infamous aroma have faded away, and the old buildings are filled with restaurants and shops and hordes of tourists. Just beyond, at the site of the Hovden Cannery immortalized by author John Steinbeck, is the **Monterey Bay Aquarium**, a state-of-the-art facility that recreates the bay's marine environment in giant glass-fronted tanks.

Farther on is the **Hopkins Marine Station Research Area**, where kayaks are not allowed to land. Then, like a scene out of Homer's classic tale, storm-battered rocks rise up out of the sea at historic **Point Cabrillo**. You can almost hear the sirens calling, and for good reason. Big swells often charge in from the open ocean and crash in the shallows. Conditions can get hairy in little more than a blink of the eye, especially in the afternoon when the wind comes up. Unless you have a good weather sense, all the right gear, and ample experience paddling in

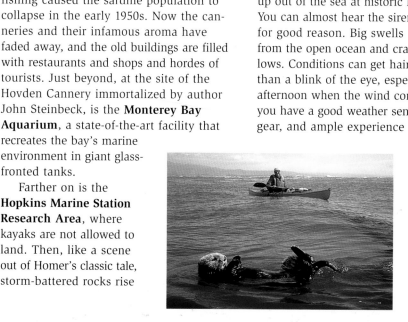

Surf kayaking (opposite, top) requires skills akin to those employed by whitewater paddlers.

A sandy cove on the Monterey coast (opposite, bottom) is a good resting place, but only at low tide.

Kayakers (left) should give sea otters a wide berth.

Big Surf, Big Sur

The sea caves (right) at Big Sur are intriguing but often battered by powerful waves. Limited access along the rugged coast (below) makes point-to-point paddling exceptionally exposed. Visitors should seek the aid of a local guide.

Dusk silhouettes paddlers in a tandem kayak (bottom).

It's been said that **Big Sur** is more a state of mind than a geographical location, a place where nature reigns and people merely gaze in wonder. Here the turquoise sea batters sea caves and arches; ragged headlands shelter coves where sea lions and otters have dwelled undisturbed for centuries; streams cascade down seaside cliffs; and lush redwood canyons remain much as they were when Esalen Indians hunted and gathered on their bristled shoulders.

The terrain is so rugged that a road wasn't completed until 1937. Now motorized tourists whisk through Big Sur on Highway 1, but they catch only glimpses of the spectacular landscape and wildlife that surround them. To savor the area, one must walk, climb, or, best of all, paddle a sea kayak.

Unfortunately, relatively safe and easy access to the sea in Big Sur is limited to a very few protected inlets and beaches. Some sites are on private or park property, where launching and landing are discouraged. While kayaking from state beaches like **Garrapata**, **Pfeiffer**, and **Sand Dollar** is permitted, paddling through the minefield of jagged rocks and unpredictable surf along this exposed coast can be extremely dangerous. Only sea kayakers with solid rock-garden and surf-zone skills should attempt it, and even they should plan carefully, heed the advice of paddlers who know the area, and keep a sharp eye on changing weather and surf conditions. Big Sur is a challenge, but the rewards, like the risks, are extreme.

rough water, this is the point at which you should turn around and head back.

Sheltered Coves

When winter storms lash the California coast, big swells crash like thunder upon **Point Lobos**, sculpting the rocky headlands just south of Monterey as they have for countless centuries. A weathered forest of Monterey cypress trees clings to the cliffs above the sea like stately sentinels. In summer, poison oak sprouts bright warning colors and hillsides blaze with apricot blossoms of sticky monkeyflowers.

It's a short ride down the coast from Monterey to Point Lobos State Reserve, just off

Highway 1, where the paddling is a good deal more challenging. Pass through the ranger station and turn right to **Whaler's Cove**, the only place in the reserve where kayakers are allowed to launch or land.

While you're there, you may want to investigate the historic whaler's cottage, which now houses artifacts from a late-19th-century whaling station and an interesting collection of abalone shells, some of which were collected by Japanese divers in the early 1900s.

Before you launch, take a few minutes to hike out to **Cannery Point** at the mouth of the cove to survey conditions. If ocean swells are running, locate where they're breaking so you can avoid those areas when you're out on the water. Take note of wind speed and direction, and how rough the water looks farther out to sea.

Monterey Bay (left) offers sea kayakers a blend of marine ecology and colorful human history.

California sea lions (below) laze on the rocky coast and occasionally approach kayakers for a fleeting game of hide-and-seek.

It's a short portage down to the beach from the parking lot. Launching is easy in the calm, protected cove. Even here, you're likely to spot sea otters at play in the kelp beds and fat harbor seals hauled out on the rocks, basking contentedly in the sun. Paddle out of the cove and turn left along the rocky, convoluted shore, being careful to stay in water deep enough to avoid breaking waves.

The first main inlet you pass is **Bluefish Cove**, where a great blue heron or snowy egret may be perched on a drift log, its head cocked toward the water. Beneath the surface, Bluefish contains the reserve's richest marine life in a maze of undersea canyons. Gray whales pass this way on their biannual migrations north and south, swift pods of dolphins sometimes flash by in pursuit of prey, and roving herds of California sea lions honk and bark and frolic in the water, raising noses and flippers into the air. In summer, immature males hang around the reserve, and by fall adult males begin to arrive from breeding grounds farther south.

Only four kayakers at a time are permitted at Point Lobos. If you find that the quota has already been filled, consider launching at **Monastery Beach** about a mile up the highway. Keep in mind that

this beach is much more exposed to the open sea than Whaler's Cove. Wise paddlers know when to bide their time: if the shore break looks too formidable, wait for better conditions.

A Bounty of Wildlife

Conditions are entirely different at **Elkhorn Slough**, a seven-mile-long estuary that cuts inland at the midpoint of the bay. Although there is no breaking surf to worry about, prudent kayakers will plan their trip to coincide with the tides. Currents run up the slough during a rising, or flood, tide, and back toward the sea when the tide ebbs. You should also try to avoid having to beat your way against the brisk onshore winds that often come up in the afternoon. If you do run into strong headwinds, paddling close to shore may give you some protection.

Wildlife is abundant here, and first-timers would do well to sign on with a guided tour led by a naturalist. Paddlers going solo can launch their kayaks at **Moss Landing** or drive up the eastern side of the slough and put in at **Kirby Park**. It is crucial that kayakers not disturb the animals, which means staying far enough away to avoid altering their behavior. Harbor seals and sea otters come to the estuary to rest and warm themselves in the sun after their rigorous existence on the coast, and a great variety of birds nests in the surrounding salt marsh. The mudflats are host to a large summer roosting population of brown pelicans, and shorebirds arrive in winter by the thousands. Marbled godwits, sandpipers, dowitchers, and curlews scurry about, probing the mud with beaks of various shapes and sizes. Terns glide back and forth, while great egrets fly from water's edge to their rookery in a grove of Monterey pines. In June, you might glimpse leopard sharks or bat rays coming into the shallows and tidal creeks to bear their young.

In short, those who love to paddle where

wildlife abounds but yearn for a more protected environment where they can take pictures or merely observe birds and animals at leisure will find that kayaking in Elkhorn Slough delivers just about everything they are looking for.

Sea otters (above) crack shell-fish on rocks that they balance on their bellies.

Sit-on-top kayaks (top) are increasingly popular with California surf paddlers; wet suits are essential.

Elkhorn Slough (opposite, top) is the second-largest coastal wetland in California.

The Tsunami Rangers (opposite, bottom), a group of expert paddlers based in Northern California, take on heavy surf.

Sea Otters

The most charismatic animal along the Monterey coast is the sea otter, an undeniably charming mustelid with fluffy fur and a Kewpie doll face. About 2,000 otters inhabit California waters, and virtually all are found along the central coast. It's highly unlikely that any extended Monterey trip won't include at least a few sightings.

Sea otters were almost extirpated by Russian fur traders in the 19th century. By 1900, it was assumed they were extinct, but a remnant colony was found near Bixby Creek on the Big Sur coast in 1938 and immediately was afforded full protection. Since then, they have made an impressive, if halting, recovery. In the past few years, their numbers have undergone a gradual decline, a worrisome situation some scientists attribute to disease or food shortages caused by warm-water phenomena such as El Niño.

Sea otters play a critical role in the ecology of the kelp forest, because they are voracious predators of sea urchins, which in turn are insatiable consumers of kelp. In the absence of otters, the urchin population explodes, and its habitat is virtually denuded.

Cute as otters are, they should be given a wide berth. They're not dangerous, but they are easily disturbed. Unlike seals and whales, otters have no underlying layer of blubber. Instead, they rely on their dense fur to insulate them from the cold waters of the Pacific. To maintain their core body heat, they must eat constantly, stopping only to sleep, mate, and minister to their pups. If their behavior is in any way disrupted, they can lose critical energy reserves, a situation that could ultimately prove fatal. – *Glen Martin*

TRAVEL TIPS

DETAILS

When to Go

Weather is mild year-round, though storms, chill winds, and rough seas are common from November to February. The ocean is calmer in summer, and foggy mornings give way to temperatures in the 70s and 80s.

How to Get There

Major airlines serve San Francisco, Los Angeles, San Jose, and Oakland International Airports. Commuter airlines fly into Monterey Peninsula Airport. Greyhound Lines (800-231-2222) provides service between San Francisco and Monterey. Amtrak's Coast Starlight train (800-872-7245) stops at Salinas on its way from Los Angeles to Seattle.

Getting Around

Car rentals are available at the airports. A car is essential for travel in the Monterey Bay area and between parks. A good site to launch into Monterey Bay is just west of the harbor. There are also several good possibilities for launching kayaks at the north end of the Big Sur Coast, including the mouth of the Big Sur River and Mill Creek.

Permits

Permits are required to launch a boat from a California state park. For information, contact the California State Parks Store, P.O. Box 942896, Sacramento, CA 94296; tel: 916-653-4000.

INFORMATION

Monterey Bay National Marine Sanctuary

299 Foam Street, Monterey, CA 93923; tel: 831-647-4201.

Monterey County Travel and Tourism Alliance

137 Crossroads Boulevard, Carmel, CA 93923; tel: 831-626-1424.

Monterey County Visitors and Convention Bureau

380 Alvarado Street, Box 1770, Monterey, CA 93942-1770; tel: 831-649-1770.

Monterey Peninsula Chamber of Commerce

380 Alvarado Street, Monterey, CA 93940; tel: 831-648-5360.

Point Lobos State Reserve

Route 1, Box 62, Carmel, CA 93923; tel: 831-624-4909.

CAMPING

Andrew Molera State Park

Big Sur Station #1, Big Sur, CA 93920; tel: 831-624-9507.

The popular campsites at this large coastal park 21 miles south of Carmel may be reached only on foot or by bicycle. You can take a one-mile stroll to the beach or ask the rangers for the best places to spot marine wildlife like sea otters. Water, chemical toilets, and picnic tables are available; no reservations are accepted.

Laguna Seca Recreation Area

Monterey County Parks, P.O. Box 5279, Salinas, CA 93915; tel: 831-755-4899.

The park has 185 RV and tent sites. There are showers, restrooms, and RV hookups.

Pfeiffer–Big Sur State Park

Big Sur Station #1, Big Sur, CA 93920; tel: 831-667-2315 or 800-444-7275 (reservations).

This park, 26 miles south of Carmel, has more than 200 campsites set amid redwoods, conifers, oaks, and seaside meadows. The park is laced with hiking trails and contains the highest waterfall on this part of the coast.

Santa Cruz/Monterey Bay KOA

1186 San Andreas Road, Watsonville, CA 95076; tel: 800-562-7701.

This privately owned campground has 250 RV sites, 15 tent sites, and 50 cabins with electricity. Full hookups are available.

LODGING

PRICE GUIDE – double occupancy

$ = up to $49	$$ = $50–$99
$$$ = $100–$149	$$$$ = $150+

Big Sur Lodge

Pfeiffer–Big Sur State Park, P.O. Box 190, Big Sur, CA 93920; tel: 831-667-3100 or 800-424-4787.

Set in an ancient grove of redwoods and oaks in a scenic coastal park, this lodge was originally built as a homestead about a century ago. Each of the 61 cottages sleeps up to six people, and many have fireplaces and/or kitchens. There is a restaurant, gift shop, pool, and general store, and access to the park's network of hiking trails. $$–$$$$

Deetjen's Big Sur Inn

Highway One, Big Sur, CA 93920; tel: 831-667-2377.

Built in the 1930s by Norwegian immigrants, this inn, set near a ravine thick with redwoods, has a rustic, Scandinavian flavor, with hand-hewn doors and stone fireplaces. Twenty rooms are simply furnished, with shared or private baths; some have fireplaces. A restaurant is on the premises. $$–$$$$

Lighthouse Lodge and Suites

1150 and 1249 Lighthouse Avenue, Pacific Grove, CA 93950; tel: 831-655-2111 or 800-858-1249.

The lodge is nestled among pine trees one block from Point Pinos Lighthouse. Sixty guest rooms have private baths. Thirty-five suites have king-sized beds, fireplaces, kitchenettes, and

Jacuzzis. A swimming pool is on the premises. $$$–$$$$

Monterey Hotel

406 Alvarado Street, Monterey, CA 93940; tel: 800-727-0960.

Victorian touches in this downtown hotel include oak paneling, ornate fireplaces, marble floors, and antique furnishings. The hotel's 45 rooms have private baths; suites have sunken baths and fireplaces. $$$–$$$$

Ventana Inn and Spa

Highway One, Big Sur, CA 93920; tel: 800-628-6500 or 831-667-2331.

Ventana's 60 guest rooms have fireplaces, private terraces, and ocean or mountain views; some have hot tubs. The inn, on 240 acres, offers pools, saunas, and spa services. Rates include breakfast and afternoon wine and cheese. $$$$

TOURS AND OUTFITTERS

ESKAPE Sea Kayaking

415 Windsor Street, Suite B, Santa Cruz, CA 95062; tel: 831-427-2297.

Guided trips and instruction are provided for paddlers of every skill level. Tours are offered throughout the West Coast, including Monterey Bay.

Kayak Connection

2370 Highway One, Moss Landing, CA 95039; tel: 831-724-5692.

This outfitter offers a variety of tours, including guided trips into Elkhorn Slough and tours for bird-watchers and children. Instruction and kayak rentals are also available.

Monterey Bay Kayaks

693 Del Monte Avenue, Monterey, CA 93940; tel: 800-649-5357.

Set on the beach near Monterey Harbor, this shop offers sales, rentals, and instruction. Guided tours of Monterey Bay and Elkhorn Slough range from three to six hours and emphasize natural history.

Excursions

Angel Island State Park

Angel Island Association, P.O. Box 866, Tiburon, CA 94920; tel: 415-435-3522 or 415-435-1915.

A short ferry ride from San Francisco brings you to one of the nation's great urban getaways: 740-acre Angel Island in San Francisco Bay. The island has a colorful past. It was used as an immigration station in the early 1900s and a missile base in the 1950s and 60s. These days it's devoted to hikers, history buffs, paddlers, and anyone else looking for a quick escape from the city. Sea kayaking is a popular way to explore the forests, meadows, and beaches along the shore. Sea Trek (415-488-1000) offers guided sea-kayaking tours.

Channel Islands

Channel Islands National Park, 1901 Spinnaker Drive, Ventura, CA 93001; tel: 805-658-5730.

Sea kayakers head to the "Galapagos of California" for the blue water, dramatic sea caves, and abundant wildlife. Island Packers (805-642-1393) ferries kayakers and their gear to the islands. Camping is permitted on all of the islands within the park but is perhaps best on Santa Cruz, where a pebble beach makes a convenient spot for launching and landing. Seas are often rough; helmets and wet suits are essential. Guides are a must for novices and will make the trip safer and more interesting for paddlers at all skill levels.

Half Moon Bay

Miramar Beach Kayak Club, 1 Mirada Road, Half Moon Bay, CA 94019; tel: 650-726-2748.

A complex reef system in the far north of the bay creates a wide range of conditions in a fairly compact area. Calm water inside the reef is host to a large kelp bed populated by sea otters and harbor seals. In big-swell conditions or at high tide, small waves rebound from several directions at once, inspiring rapid development of surf-zone skills. Only seasoned paddlers should attempt the rough waters outside the reef, especially around the surf break to the north.

South Fork of the American River
California

CHAPTER 19

t doesn't have to look pretty, just so we get down the river." So says river guide Claire Norton as she and the four novice paddlers aboard her raft speed toward **360 Rapid** on the **South Fork of the American River**. She calls for the left-side paddlers to make forward strokes and the right side to backpaddle, sending the boat into the dizzying spins that give the rapid its nickname.   ◆   Though famous among paddlers as a whitewater destination, the South Fork is better known to the world at large for spawning one of the most turbulent episodes in U.S. history. On January 24, 1848, James Marshall scooped gold ore from the race at nearby **Sutter's Mill**, triggering the gold rush that lured tens of thousands of forty-niners to this and other streams in the Sierra Nevada. Droves of people still flock to the South Fork each year to reflect on this defining moment in California's history or to swirl gold pans in the shallows with hopes of tapping more of the mother lode.

Whether beginners or experts, lovers of whitewater find what they crave on California's river of gold.

Then there are those drawn to the river itself, who seek nothing more than the thrill of whitewater.   ◆   Known as an ideal beginner's run that can still surprise experienced boaters, the South Fork sports about a dozen Class II and Class III rapids, providing ample splashes and an occasional spill. The river draws day-trippers from the Bay Area and Sacramento as well as tourists from Southern California and beyond – about 90,000 people every year. Some have already tried the mostly flatwater section farther downstream along the wild and scenic **American River Parkway** and seek an added surge of excitement. Though seasoned paddlers soon graduate to more challenging and less crowded waterways such as the North or Middle

Satan's Cesspool is one of the biggest drops on the South Fork, the busiest river in California and a favorite of play boaters.

Forks of the American or the Tuolumne River, the South Fork offers an attractive blend of history, scenery, and fun. It's also a favorite with play, or rodeo, boaters, who spend hours perfecting acrobatic moves: end-over-end flips, cartwheels, and nose-stand pirouettes. You'll see kayaks spinning, twirling, and being tossed completely out of the water.

A river guide (left) briefs his charges on safety and paddling techniques.

Great surfing (below) keeps kayakers lined up at well-known play spots.

Troublemaker Rapid (opposite) lives up to its name. Guides use rescue ropes and pulleys to dislodge a raft.

Wild Thing

The South Fork is a textbook pool-drop river, with a string of rapids separated by calm, flat stretches. The upper reach begins at **Chili Bar** and covers eight miles of technically taxing, boulder-strewn rapids. The lower run, through the **Gorge**, extends for 13 miles from a put-in at **Camp Lotus** to **Salmon Falls Bridge** on **Folsom Reservoir**. Many of the 50 or so commercial outfitters who operate on the South Fork between April and October offer the option of boating either portion as a one-day trip or combining them over two days. Hardy or indecisive paddlers can opt to make the entire run –

all 21 miles – in a single, long day. Solo boaters who want more control of their course can bring a hard-shell kayak or rent an inflatable "funyak" for an even more exhilarating encounter with the power of fast-moving water.

Twenty years before Marshall's momentous discovery, explorer Jedediah Smith dubbed the South Fork the "Wild River." But dams have shackled the South Fork's natural flow, and while the surroundings are pretty, the river is hardly pristine. **Chili Bar Dam**, just upstream from the most popular put-in spot, regulates the release of water to downstream boaters, so the river

and the rapids change constantly. **Folsom Dam**, the South Fork's largest, forms an immense lake at the end of the Gorge; the journey ends with either a long slog of paddling to the take-out point or a tow by a powerboat.

Aside from kingfishers, mergansers, and other feathered inhabitants, the most active wildlife on the South Fork are the weekend revelers, who can make finding solitude afloat as elusive as nuggets of gold. A multicolored parade of rafts and kayaks floats downriver, clogging narrow channels at the head of some rapids. Splash fights with paddles and long-range water guns impart a party atmosphere along placid sections. Come in May for bigger water and fewer people, or try a weekday in summer to avoid peak crowds.

Rapid Fire

Pines and oaks cloak the steep canyon walls at the Chili Bar put-in. Here and there, outcroppings of pink-and-gray Coloma granite break through the tawny slopes or jut into the river, giving spectators and fellow paddlers a platform on which to observe the proceedings.

The first rapid is **Meatgrinder**, a quarter-mile-long rock garden that at low water seems pretty tame for its name, though the ride at high water is long and bumpy with several intimidating holes and waves. Less than a mile downstream, the river enters the next rapid, **Racehorse Bend**, which curls like a horseshoe around a sandbar and sends rafts hugging the sheer wall on the right. It's followed in short order by **Maya**, a Class II riffle in low water but a formidable obstacle with gaping holes during heavy flows. **Triple Threat** features a trio of widely spaced rapids. The first, called **African Queen**, is a long, steady patch of riffles, the aquatic equivalent of a washboard road. A good-sized hole that marks the second threat sends an invigorating wave crashing across the bow.

More than halfway into the upper run comes the aptly named **Troublemaker**, where photographers perch on riverside rocks and spectators line up lawn chairs to watch the action. River guide Norton outlines three options for getting through without mishap. The current tugs the raft across the

The paddle toss (left) is the unofficial *coup de grâce* of a well-done "ender."

Stretches of calm water (below) and an official "quiet zone" mellow the action.

river, but furious backpaddling allows it to catch a hairpin right turn and then slide past a massive pointed rock that juts from the middle of the rapid like a gunsight. "We did Plan A," Claire exclaims. "That's awesome. I never get to do Plan A." All paddles rise and clack for a midboat high-five.

A bit farther downstream, the river passes by **Marshall Gold Discovery State Park** with its replica of Sutter's historic mill. The floating dredges of modern-day prospectors moored along the river serve as reminders that the gold rush lingers. Camp Lotus, a favorite overnight stop for paddlers

less than two miles downstream, marks the end of the run's first half.

The Gorge Run

Just beyond Camp Lotus, kayakers are sometimes seen gracefully sliding in and out of a standing wave, a practice known as surfing, at a rapid named **Barking Dog** for a now-deceased pet who used to greet passing boats loudly. Sunny summer days invite paddlers to take the plunge at **Swimmers' Rapid**, where guides encourage their passengers to slip into the river. Bobbing like corks through gentle waves, swimmers in proper position – facing forward with feet pointing downstream, knees slightly bent, and arms extended like rudders – are slapped with facefuls of chilly water and may get submerged briefly and recirculated like a load of laundry before being hauled back aboard at the next eddy.

The river canyon narrows in the long, flat stretch leading toward the Gorge. Grassy hills are replaced by lush forest. The lone "Lollipop Tree" on a distant hilltop appears, then vanishes around a bend and reappears,

Gold Rush Days

Gold pans like this one (right) made a few men rich while thousands went empty-handed.

Marshall Gold Discovery State Historic Park (below) has a mining museum and a replica of Sutter's Mill.

Coloma, California, hasn't changed much in the last 150 years. It's a small town on the banks of the South Fork in the foothills of the Sierra Nevada. Even today, Coloma looks too pretty, too gentle, to be a place where so much boisterous and brawling history was made.

It started on the morning of January 24, 1848. Early that morning, a carpenter named John Marshall was inspecting the sawmill he had constructed for John Sutter, a Swiss immigrant who had amassed vast land holdings in Northern California. He saw something glint in the millrace. "I reached my hand down and picked it up," he recalled later. "It made my heart thump, for I was certain it was gold."

Eureka! The gold rush had begun. Marshall and his employer Sutter tried to keep the discovery secret, but that proved futile. Within a year, gold-seeking forty-niners by the thousands were braving trails across the frontier or the perilous voyage around Cape Horn. They seemed to come from everywhere – eastern cities and midwestern farms, England and Ireland and China and Chile. "It was the only population of the kind that the world has ever seen," Mark Twain wrote in *Roughing It*, "and it is not likely that the world will ever see its like again."

Historians estimate that in the 50 years following the strike, some 125 million ounces of gold ($50 billion worth in present dollars) were pulled from the oak-studded foothills. Still, far more miners failed than succeeded. Neither Marshall nor Sutter profited from the discovery. Marshall was booted off his mining claim and ended his days a blacksmith. Sutter fared worse: his lands were stolen by squatters, and he died penniless. Likewise, many forty-niners went home broke.

signaling the approach of the Gorge, 15 miles downstream from Chili Bar. Just above the first rapid, **Fowler's Rock**, are riverside remnants of camps settled by Chinese miners who followed the forty-niners and gathered gold dust from the gravel. But there's no time for nostalgia as a sharp ledge looms, dropping the raft into a big wave that threatens to dash it against the rapid's namesake – a muddy green boulder that obstructs the river's left side.

A pair of small rapids lead up to **Lost Hat**, a dropoff and short wave train that runs straight into what is the biggest and certainly the best-named rapid in the Gorge, **Satan's Cesspool**. Another spot for photographers and spectators, Satan's features a boiling midstream hole where two walls of water clash. Once safely through, a boat slides into **Son of Satan's**, which, like most sequels, pales beside the original.

The Gorge run concludes with a few more fun rapids. **Lower Haystack Canyon** throws up a steady set of buffeting waves, like a Colorado River rapid shrunk to Lilliputian scale. At the sharp left turn in **Bouncing Rock**, the raft seems drawn toward the rocks on river right. "Forward paddle," Norton shouts. "A little harder."

Their loss was the nation's gain. The gold rush started by Marshall and Sutter and thousands of other argonauts helped to wrest California from Mexico. After a brief stint as an independent republic, California became the country's 31st state.

The rocks advance closer. "A lot harder!" The boat squeaks past unscathed. Around the next bend comes the final trio of rapids: **Ambulance Driver**, **Hospital Bar**, and **Recovery Room**. Then you're out of the Gorge and safely through what was once, even before the rise of the Sierra Nevada, the maw of a massive, extinct volcano – something to ponder at the end of a day spent on California's river of gold.

DETAILS

When to Go

The South Fork is runnable all year, thanks to dam-controlled flows and a moderate climate. Peak flows are in May and June. Most outfitters offer trips from April through October. Midday temperatures average 80°F from June through October and 69°F from November through May.

How to Get There

The South Fork's whitewater runs are about 35 miles east of Sacramento via Highway 50. The put-in for the most popular stretch is at Chili Bar, about four miles north of Placerville, along State Route 93. Coloma, eight miles downstream of Chili Bar, serves as a center for whitewater enthusiasts. Georgetown, another community with tourist services, is about 15 miles northwest of Placerville on Route 193.

Permits

User registration tags are required for private boaters and can be obtained at the river store at Chili Bar.

INFORMATION

Bureau of Land Management

63 Natoma Street, Folsom, CA 95630; tel: 916-985-4474.

El Dorado County Parks and Recreation

3000 Fairlane Court, Suite 1, Placerville, CA 95667; tel: 530-621-5864 (weekdays) or 530-621-6616 (weekends).

CAMPING

In addition to the camping listed here, many outfitters provide private camping for their clients on two-day river trips.

Camp Lotus

P.O. Box 578, Lotus, CA 95651; tel: 530-622-8672.

This boat-in campground is set between the Chili Bar and Gorge runs and is a convenient stopping place for paddlers on a two-day trip. It has hot showers, a store with paddling equipment, a deli, and cafe.

Coloma Resort

6921 Mount Murphy Road, P.O. Box 516, Coloma, CA 95613; tel: 530-621-2267 or 800-238-2298.

Just across from Sutter's Mill, this private campground has hot showers, a swimming pool, climbing wall, general store, and other amenities.

Folsom Lake State Recreation Area

7806 Folsom–Auburn Road, Folsom, CA 95630-1797; tel: 916-988-0205 or 800-444-7275 (reservations).

This busy state park on 12,000-acre Folsom Reservoir, about halfway between Sacramento and Placerville, has 170 campsites, biking and hiking trails, boating, and horseback riding.

LODGING

PRICE GUIDE – double occupancy

$ = up to $49 $$ = $50–$99
$$$ = $100–$149 $$$$ = $150+

American River Inn

Main and Orleans Streets, Box 43, Georgetown, CA 95634; tel: 530-333-4499 or 800-245-6566.

Once a gold-rush boardinghouse, this inn has 18 rooms (12 with private baths) and seven suites featuring down comforters and featherbeds. A few rooms have fireplaces and private balconies. Wine and hors d'oeuvres are served in the parlor, and the grounds feature redwood trees, formal landscaping, and an outdoor hot tub. $$–$$$

Chichester–McKee House

800 Spring Street, Placerville, CA 95667; tel: 530-626-1882 or 800-831-4008.

This 1892 Victorian house has fireplaces, stained glass, and mahogany woodwork. The three guest rooms have private half-baths. $$

Coloma Country Inn

345 High Street, P.O. Box 502, Coloma, CA 95613; tel: 530-622-6919.

Five garden acres surround this 1852 home, half a block from the river and within walking distance of Sutter's Mill. There are seven guest rooms, three with private baths. $$–$$$$

Delta King River Boat Hotel

1000 Front Street, Sacramento, CA 95816; tel: 916-444-5464 or 800-825-5464.

The Delta King sternwheeler once ferried passengers between Sacramento and San Francisco. Now docked for good in Old Sacramento, it has been converted into a hotel, with a restaurant, lounge, and promenade deck. The 44 updated staterooms have private baths. $$$

Shadowridge Ranch and Lodge

Fort Jim Road, Placerville, CA 95667; tel: 530-295-1000 or 800-644-3498.

The guest room and two cabins at this lodge feature hand-hewn beams, stone hearths, and antique furnishings. Room rates include full breakfast, wine and hors d'oeuvres in the afternoon, and fresh-baked cookies at bedtime. $$$–$$$$

TOURS AND OUTFITTERS

American River Recreation

P.O. Box 465, Lotus, CA 95651; tel: 530-622-6802 or 800-333-7238.

The company offers guided one- and two-day raft trips on the South Fork and nearby branches of the American River.

Beyond Limits Adventures

P.O. Box 215, Riverbank, CA 95367; tel: 800-234-7238.

This outfitter guides one- and two-day trips on the South Fork and nearby waters and has a private campground in Coloma.

California Canoe and Kayak

Nimbus Winery, 12401 Folsom Boulevard, Suite 205, Rancho Cordova, CA 95742; tel: 916-353-1880 or 800-366-9804.

This paddling school and outfitter runs a "rapid immersion" five-day kayaking course, specialized clinics, and paddling tours.

Chili Bar Outdoor Center

P.O. Box 554, Coloma, CA 95613; tel: 530-621-1236 or 800-356-2262.

One- and two-day raft trips are available. Clients can stay in a riverside campground in Coloma.

Current Adventures

1800 Twitchell Road, Placerville, CA 95667; tel: 916-642-9755 or 888-452-9254.

River guides lead paddling trips and classes for both children and adults.

Gold Rush Whitewater Rafting

P.O. Box 1070, Lotus, CA 95651; tel: 800-900-7238.

Guided one- and two-day raft trips on the South Fork and nearby branches of the American River are available.

Mariah Wilderness Expeditions

P.O. Box 248, Point Richmond, CA 94807; tel: 510-233-2303 or 800-462-7424.

Raft instruction includes intensive guide training. Mariah also runs women-only trips and other river tours in the western states.

Tributaries Whitewater Tours

20480 Woodbury Drive, Grass Valley, CA 95949; tel: 530-346-6812 or 800-672-3846.

Raft and inflatable-kayak trips are available on the South Fork.

Excursions

East Fork of the Carson River

Toiyabe National Forest, Carson Ranger District, 1536 South Carson Street, Carson City, NV 89701; tel: 775-882-2766.

The charms of this sunny, Sierra river are manifold: mountain views, great camping, moderate Class II rapids, and natural hot springs that bubble up at a soothing 104°F. The only problem is arriving when there's enough water to float on, usually only in May and June. The 20-mile section from Hangman's Bridge to Diversion Dam is a favorite; just upstream, the one-day trip from Cave Creek has Class III whitewater.

Mono Lake

Caldera Kayaks, Crowley Lake Marina, Mammoth Lakes, CA 93546; tel: 760-935-4952.

Mono Lake offers the closest thing to a moonscape that a paddler may ever experience. A maze of ghostly limestone towers known as tufa rises above the surface, the product of the lake's unusual alkaline chemistry. Fish can't tolerate the water's high mineral and salt content, but brine shrimp thrive, attracting flocks of migratory birds. Summer, the most popular paddling season, can also be the stormiest. For the ultimate Mono Lake experience, try a full-moon paddle among the glowing white formations.

Tuolumne River

Stanislaus National Forest, Groveland Ranger District, 24545 Highway 120, Groveland, CA 95321; tel: 209-962-7825.

The Tuolumne River tumbles out of the High Sierra through a canyon scattered with the ruins of abandoned gold mines. The run is divided into two parts: the upper, Class V, experts-only section, and the lower, Class IV-V section, which is considered to be the most difficult commercially run whitewater in California. Most outfitters take two or three days to savor the beauty of the wilderness setting and tackle the rapids carefully.

Rogue River

Oregon

CHAPTER **20**

How can a river named **Rogue** have such an agreeable personality? Though it dishes out plenty of whitewater excitement, the Rogue's craggy banks are sweetened by the blossoms of wild azaleas. Its evergreen forests open to sun-dappled meadows and golden sandbars. Otters caper in velvety rapport; killdeer and water ouzels parade along gravel bars; and steelhead trout flash like strands of silver in its emerald pools. The place is as amenable as it is dramatic. ◆ The explanation for the Rogue's unusual charm is simple. After tumbling from the mile-high southern Oregon Cascades into pastoral softness around **Grants Pass**, the river awakens for one last brawny task: to cut its way straight through the Coast Range to the Pacific Ocean. The result is a canyon blessed with the low-elevation lushness of a coastal ecosystem but the whitewater and rugged setting of a mountain stream, not to mention a community of wildlife that rivals Noah's.

Right from the put-in, the Rogue displays its character: rambunctious one minute, placid the next, and steeped in the colorful history of the Old West.

◆ Already rich in history, the **Rogue River Canyon** became known to Americans everywhere through the writing of famed author Zane Grey. Then, in 1968, the isolated, 34-mile stretch from **Grave Creek Landing** to **Foster Bar** became one of the eight original wild and scenic rivers designated by Congress, providing even more enticement for the thousands of rafters and kayakers who now vie for permits to run its Class III and IV rapids. ◆ The three- or four-day trip begins where the road ends, not far from the hamlet of **Galice**, Oregon. The usual launch-site chaos prevails, with dry bags, oars, driftboats, rafts, coolers, and kayaks strewn around like an oversized yard sale. Sometimes a contingent from a kayak

Stair Creek Falls spills into the Rogue at Mile 22. The creek's cool waters are a good place to spot salmon.

a rare opportunity to run a remote river with all the amenities. Black Bar Lodge, a 1930s log ranch house surrounded by flower beds and an inviting lawn, is nine miles from the put-in. Marial Lodge at Mile 20 is the last vestige of a mining town where 250 people once received mail. Paradise Lodge, around Mile 24, is the biggest operation on the river and attracts tourists motoring upstream as well as river runners heading down. Half Moon Bar Lodge is just below Paradise; Clay Hill is around Mile 30; and Illahee Lodge is less than a mile from the take-out at Foster Bar.

Whether loaded with full camping gear or packing only a credit card and toothbrush, everyone gets an immediate taste of the canyon's roguish character. Class III **Grave Creek Falls**, a few yards from the launch, provides a welcome transition from the bustle of the put-in to the rhythm of a multiday wilderness trip. After Grave Creek, the cars disappear from view, and all eyes turn downstream.

school arrives, ready to combine four days of whitewater instruction with one of the West's finest multiday river trips. Other groups are led by commercial outfitters, professional fishing guides, or self-guided rafters and kayakers.

And some people look as if they just don't have enough gear. Where are their tents, sleeping bags, cooking equipment? The answer reveals one of the Rogue's most attractive features: the best lodge-to-lodge wilderness paddling in the western United States.

Six lodges – the legacy of mining, ranching, and trapping camps – offer

Down the "Fish Ladder"

Within two miles, paddlers begin to hear a gut-tightening roar coming from downstream. An unmistakable mist rises from the river, and idle conversation peters out. Dead ahead lies **Rainie Falls**. "In one clean, quick leap the Rogue plunges 15 vertical feet over a ledge," writes Roderick Nash in *The Big Drops*.

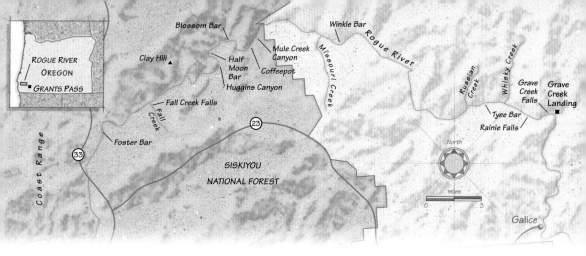

"At the bottom is a frightening spectacle: a chaos of white, churning water that on first glance appears destined to swallow and hold any boat exposed to it."

Lest a first-timer panic, only a few experts actually run Rainie Falls. Everyone else lines or bumps boats down the rocky "fish ladder" along the right bank or runs the narrow dory chute in midriver. But Rainie still leaves an indelible impression on the mind of anyone who has contemplated it firsthand.

After Rainie, the Rogue "regains its composure," as Nash says, at least temporarily. If the afternoon is hot, a dip in the clear river feels great after the hard work of lining around Rainie. The valley grows deeper, and low cliffs frame the river channel. Daggers of sunlight glint off the water ahead and colors intensify as afternoon shadows lengthen. Unless you're staying at Black Bar Lodge, camp

will be at the mouth of one of the clear creeks like **Whisky**, **Russian**, or **Missouri**.

Rogue place names, along with the many abandoned cabins, graves, and mines on its banks, remind visitors of the canyon's history. **Tyee Bar**, site of the next significant rapid, was once the workplace for hundreds of Chinese miners who took an estimated $5 million worth of gold from the area. A 19th-century cabin stands a few yards up Whisky Creek, and many more lie in ruins in meadows along the river.

"This Is My Country"

The demise of the region's Native Americans is perhaps the most poignant of the stories. Takelma Indians, whom European arrivals called the Rogues, lived on the river's

A breakneck run through Mule Creek Canyon (right) ends in a quiet pool.

Solitude Bar (left) makes a sunny campsite. A placer mine operated here around 1900.

The dory chute (opposite, top) at Rainie Falls is an exhilarating alternative to lining.

The Dean of Whitewater

One name above all others is associated with running the Rogue River. Glen Wooldridge, the "dean of whitewater," presided over the river for more than half a century starting in 1915, when he made his first run at age 19. Two years later he began guiding, negotiating the river in his oar- or motor-equipped boats countless times through his 80s.

Among Wooldridge's most famous and permanent contributions was his "clean-up" of Rogue rapids. Impatient with the lining and portaging necessary at many boulder-choked sections, he arrived at an effective, if dramatic, solution: dynamite. Wooldridge described his methodology, which featured weighted bags of powder, to writer Florence Arman in *The Rogue, A River to Run.* "While the fellow in the bow of the boat would be lighting his fuses, we would get in as close as possible. Run our boat right up to the rock. Then he would drop the bundle of dynamite right above the rock, where there'd be no current. Then we'd get the hell out of there fast."

Blossom Bar, completely unrunnable until then, presented the ultimate challenge and took several years before it remained open. No one ever got hurt, but at least one resident complained of boulders raining into his yard.

By 1947 the way was clear, and Wooldridge became the first to motor *up* the Rogue from the Pacific Ocean all the way to Grants Pass. He remains a legendary character – with an unusually tangible legacy.

Glen Wooldridge, third from right (above), devoted much of his life to the Rogue. "Move a rock anywhere," said a friend, "and I'm sure he'd notice."

Bailing (below) turns into a good-natured water fight.

Kayakers (opposite) pick their way through a stretch of whitewater.

sun-dappled "bars" such as **Winkle**, **Blossom**, and **Half Moon**. They flourished until a tide of trappers and gold miners began creeping upstream from the Pacific, and inevitable conflicts broke out. By the 1850s, hostilities had escalated into a series of battles called the Rogue River Wars.

In May 1856, a Rogue chieftain named John led his people in a final attempt to remain in their beloved canyon. He refused to leave for a reservation in northern Oregon, telling U.S. military authorities, "This is

my country; I was in it when those large trees were very small, not higher than my head. My heart is sick with fighting, but I want to live in my country." On May 27, he and his warriors held the troops at bay during the daylong Battle of Big Bend, just downstream of the take-out at Foster Bar. The Indians were eventually overwhelmed when Army reinforcements arrived. Chief John was the last to surrender.

In the big pool at Mile 15, boaters pull out to make a pilgrimage to the neat little cabin at Winkle Bar. In 1926, Zane Grey, a onetime semiprofessional baseball player turned popular Western writer, bought this place. An ardent angler, Grey fell in love with the Rogue for its beauty as well as its splendid steelheads. He returned often until his death in 1939 and immortalized the river in *Rogue River Feud.*

Attention soon turns back to whitewater as **Mule Creek Canyon** approaches at Mile 21 just past Marial Lodge. A stark, dramatic cleft several hundred yards long, Mule Creek is not so much a rapid as a funnel where turbulence churns so unpredictably that one spot is called the **Coffeepot**. River guides are careful not to get their boats wedged sideways between Mule Creek's narrow walls.

The trip is more than half over at this point, and by now everyone has a wildlife story – of a she-bear and her cub spotted along the bank, a deer swimming across the river right in front of a raft. One lucky boater caught a rare glimpse of a mountain lion as it lapped a drink from the river, and *everyone* heard those coyotes last night. Blue and ruffed grouse roam the surrounding forests, and wild turkeys have been seen. And the otters! No creature ever seemed to be having so much fun.

The Pinball Machine at Blossom Bar

A few short miles downstream of Mule Creek Canyon, all boaters wordlessly pull in to the right bank to scout ahead. A line of boulders guards what appears to be the end of the river. This is Blossom Bar, the most challenging rapid run on the trip; indeed, Blossom Bar was unrunnable until legendary river guide Glen Wooldridge literally blew it apart with dynamite to make a clear passage. Even so, the rapid resembles a pinball machine. Enter far left. Pull *hard* right. Cross fingers, clear nasty rock. Reverse direction and head left. Do a few more quick maneuvers, then exhale. And cheer.

Blossom Bar is the last big rapid. Just downstream, Paradise Lodge, the busiest on the river, slips by high on the right bank. Big, shallow-draft powerboats loaded with tourists pass by on their way upstream to Paradise for the lodge's famous fried-chicken lunch buffet.

It's still another 12 miles to the take-out, and though the spell of wilderness has faded

ever so slightly, the Rogue's charm has not. There is **Huggins Canyon**, steep-walled and dramatic like Mule Creek. **Fall Creek Falls** spills into the river down a series of mossy ledges. Staircases lead up the dark banks to the four other lodges, and steelhead fishermen nod to passing paddlers between casts.

All too soon the incongruous sight of sun glaring off parked cars heralds the Foster Bar take-out. When everything is packed for the trip home, the visitor returns to the river's edge for one last look. A friend's words to Keven, the fictitious hero of Zane Grey's *Rogue River Feud*, sum up the inescapable conclusion: "Who would ever tire of the music and the beauty of a running river? Especially the Rogue! It's the best in the world, Kev."

TRAVEL TIPS

DETAILS

When to Go

Mid-May to mid-September are the most popular times to float the Rogue, when days are warm and generally sunny with cool evenings. Daytime temperatures in July and August reach the upper 80s, with overnight lows around 52°F. Temperatures in September range from 84° to 45°F, and in May from 44° to 73°F.

How to Get There

The Rogue flows roughly east to west about 60 miles north of the Oregon–California border. Grants Pass is about a one-hour drive east of the Graves Creek put-in. Jackson County Airport, 22 miles south of Grants Pass in Medford, is served by Horizon Airlines (800-547-9308); car rentals are available. Many outfitters will arrange transportation from Grants Pass. The take-out is about 40 miles from the Pacific Ocean at Foster Bar, a few miles from the village of Agness.

Permits

Permits, granted by lottery, are required for private boaters between May 15 and October 15. For information about applying, write or phone Tioga Resources, P.O. Box 5149, Roseburg, OR 97470; tel: 541-672-4168. Occasional cancellations make permits available within nine days of a launch date. Most paddlers bypass the process by signing on with an outfitter.

INFORMATION

Bureau of Land Management

Medford District, Rogue River Office/Rand Visitor Center, 14355 Galice Road, Merlin, OR 97533; tel: 541-479-3735.

Grants Pass Visitor Information Center

P.O. Box 1787, Grants Pass, OR 97526; tel: 800-547-5927.

CAMPING

Open camping along the river is permitted; the Bureau of Land Management maintains outhouses at 31 sites and can provide a list of their locations. Paddlers must bring self-contained toilet systems.

Alameda Park Campground

Josephine County Parks, 125 Ringuette Street, Grants Pass, OR 97527; tel: 541-474-5285.

About 25 wooded campsites with flush toilets, air for rafts, and a boat launch are available on a first-come, first-served basis about four miles east of the put-in at Grave Creek.

Griffin Park Campground

Josephine County Parks, 125 Ringuette Street, Grants Pass, OR 97527; tel: 541-474-5285.

Twenty developed sites, flush toilets, showers, and a boat launch are on the Rogue about seven miles west of Grants Pass.

Illahee Campground

Siskiyou National Forest, Gold Beach Ranger District, 1225 South Ellensburg Street, Box 7, Gold Beach, OR 97444; tel: 531-247-6651.

This campground near the take-out has 14 sites with drinking water and pit toilets.

Indian Mary Campground

Josephine County Parks, 125 Ringuette Street, Grants Pass, OR 97527; tel: 541-474-5285.

Flush toilets, air for rafts, a playground, and boat launch are available at this riverside campground 12 miles east of the put-in at Grave Creek.

LODGING

Lodge-to-lodge trips can be arranged with the following riverside inns. Rates include three meals a day.

Black Bar Lodge

P.O. Box 510, Merlin, OR 97532; tel: 541-479-6507.

Reservations at this woodsy inn are essential. Situated at Mile 10, it's the only lodge on this stretch of the river. $$–$$$

Clay Hill

06373 Rogue River, Agness, OR 94406; tel: 800-228-3198.

A favorite of fishermen and hikers, Clay Hill, at Mile 29, has a river view and room for 20 guests. $$–$$$

Half Moon Bar

P.O. Box 455, Gold Beach, OR 97444; tel: 541-247-6968.

Hidden from the river by the wooded edge of a large, sunny bar, Half Moon, at Mile 24.5, accommodates 36 guests. $$–$$$

Illahee Lodge

33709 Agness-Illahe Road, Agness, OR 97406; tel: 541-247-6111.

Illahee is one mile upstream of the Foster Bar take-out; it accommodates 26 guests. $$–$$

Marial Lodge

P.O. Box 1395, Grants Pass, OR 97526; tel: 541-474-2057.

Located in a former mining settlement at Mile 20, Marial sits high on a riverbank just above Mule Creek Canyon and has room for 34 people. $$–$$$

Paradise Bar Lodge

P.O. Box 456, Gold Beach, OR 97444; tel: 541-247-6022 or 800-525-2161.

This lodge at Mile 24 accommodates up to 30 guests in several cabins and guest rooms. $$–$$$

TOURS AND OUTFITTERS

Echo River Trips

6529 Telegraph Avenue, Oakland, CA 94609; tel: 510-652-1600 or 800-652-3246.

Lodge-to-lodge and camping trips are available on the Rogue and other western rivers. Theme tours include wine and whitewater, hiking and rafting, and a kids' trip.

Orange Torpedo Trips

P.O. Box 1111, Grants Pass, OR 97528; tel: 541-479-5061.

Guided trips use one-person inflatable kayaks well-suited to beginning paddlers. Space in a raft can also be arranged. The trips can be done with lodge-to-lodge or camping stops.

Rogue River Raft Trips

8500 Galice Road, Merlin, OR 97532; tel: 541-476-3825 or 800-826-1963.

Lodge-to-lodge or camping trips are offered, along with one-day excursions on other sections of the Rogue. Some trips are designed especially for fishing.

Sundance Kayak School

14894 Galice Road, Merlin, OR 97532; tel: 541-479-8508.

Seven- and nine-day beginner kayaking courses start with lodge-based instruction and end with a raft-supported four-day trip down the Rogue.

Whitewater Warehouse

625 Northwest Starker Avenue, Corvallis, OR 97330; tel: 541-758-3150 or 800-214-0579.

Lodge-to-lodge or camping trips use rafts and inflatable kayaks. Theme trips include wildflowers, hiking, women-only, hardshell kayaking instruction, and fishing.

Excursions

Klamath River

Klamath National Forest, 1312 Fairlane Road, Yreka, CA 96097; tel: 530-842-6131.

The Klamath runs for about 100 miles from the confluence of Scott River to the town of Weitchpec, a fine one-week trip in a forested valley known for wildlife and the ruins of old mining towns. Novice and intermediate kayakers and experienced canoeists will enjoy the first 35 miles to Happy Camp, where the whitewater becomes much more challenging. Below Weitchpec, the Klamath joins the Trinity River and regains its composure. From here to the ocean it's a big river with a moderate Class I-II gradient.

Lower Columbia River Estuary

Skamokawa Paddle Center, 1391 West State Route 4, Skamokawa, WA 98647; tel: 360-795-8300 or 888-920-2777.

The lower Columbia River, a few miles from the Pacific Ocean, is a misty, time-forgotten world of mazelike channels, marshes, islands, and sitka-spruce swamps that has changed little since Lewis and Clark reached the Pacific in 1805. Wildlife refuges protect habitat for white-tailed deer, harbor seals, Caspian terns, bald eagles, and great numbers of waterfowl. The Skamokawa Paddle Center offers guided kayak tours in association with both the Nature Conservancy and Audubon Society.

North Umpqua River

Umpqua National Forest, 2900 N.W. Stewart Parkway, P.O. Box 1008, Roseburg, OR 97470; tel: 531-672-6601.

Clear water, a lush canyon, and a medley of Class II-IV whitewater make the North Umpqua a favorite destination for regional paddlers. Route 138, winding along the river toward Crater Lake, provides excellent access, and several riverside campgrounds serve as fine base camps for a week or more of one-day trips. When your arms need a break, hike to a hot spring; explore the beautiful forests, peaks, and lakes; or simply relax in camp under towering pine trees.

San Juan Islands
Washington

CHAPTER 21

Wildlife biologists have yet to report on the rapidly evolving breed of Mensa raccoons on **Jones Island**, but kayakers are certainly acquainted with them. On summer evenings, when paddlers are settled into camp, several pairs of phosphorescent eyes reconnoiter the site from the forest perimeter. When the kayakers finally zip themselves into their tents, the eyes wait patiently for another hour or two, then converge on the camp and begin disassembling the kayaks in search of nocturnal snacks. They disconnect bungee cords, open hatches, ransack drybags. If nothing edible turns up, the raccoons unzip tents and stalk right in, demanding tribute. ◆ In the morning, surveying the chaos and retrieving oddments of camp gear, the kayakers exchange incredulous speculation. "It's a wonder they don't just carry the boats down to the beach and paddle away," says one. Replies another, "They're just having trouble figuring out which side of the paddle is the power face. So far." ◆ At 79 acres, Jones is one of the smaller islands in the San Juan archipelago, a scattering of amoeba-shaped emeralds in the straits between the Washington mainland and Vancouver Island. The islands number either 172 or 743 or some figure in between, depending on one's definition of "island." Many are just rocks that break the surface at low tide, providing sun decks for harbor seals and sea lions. The big islands, **San Juan**, **Orcas**, and **Lopez**, are booming tourist destinations, bursting with boutiques and bed-and-breakfasts as bewildered old-timers watch their peace and quiet sail into history.

Sheltered bays are ideal for beginners, while experienced paddlers embrace the challenges of the open sea.

Puget Sound laps at the bows of two handmade kayaks. Though surf is generally moderate around the San Juans, currents can be powerful and complex.

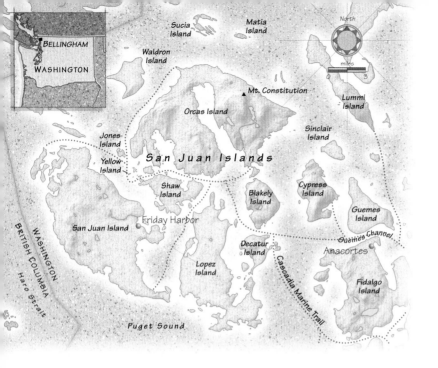

evergreen landscape."

Kayakers should take these descriptions with a grain of sea salt. San Juan weather can pivot on cosmic whim, suddenly funneling arctic gales between islands or blossoming with fog. Any wise mariner is wary here, but a kayaker will have every sense and seafaring instinct (and a waterproof weather radio) tuned in.

The islands form one of the most popular sea-kayaking destinations in the world but are also one of the most complicated. A San Juan current atlas looks like one of those cartoons of opposing armies clotting the sky with volleys of curving arrows. Currents of two to four knots are common, and there are so many backcurrents, eddies, tide rips, and general watery commotion that it could be a colossal washing machine. A calm day in a wide passage will find the sea as smooth as a velvet bedspread, but paddle out of the lee of a protective island, and suddenly a breeze

Currents and Climate

Climate forms part of the San Juans' allure, something that can't be said of many destinations in the Pacific Northwest. A glance at a map shows why. The islands huddle in the rain shadow of the Olympics and Vancouver Island Range, so a year's rainfall averages a little more than half of Seattle's 39 inches. Locals cleverly call it the "banana belt." Writer and photographer Joel Rogers describes it as "a Mediterranean experience in an

blowing into an opposing current will boil up three-foot breakers. The water is always frigid – 55° to 60°F in *August* – and summer boat traffic resembles swarming bees. A kayaker who can thread the San Juans can confidently paddle inland waters anywhere on the planet.

Yet, amazingly, there is plenty of opportunity for the beginner. At least a dozen outfitters on San Juan, Orcas, and Lopez take newbies out on three-hour or even three-day guided excursions to view marine life and explore sheltered bays. Legions of avid kayakers got themselves hooked in the San Juans, passing a sign in one of the villages that reads, "Kayak Adventure Tours/No Experience Required."

Whales and Wildflowers

Most excursions into the San Juans begin one way or another in **Anacortes**, a pretty waterfront town 80 miles north of Seattle. Launching from Anacortes, it's a quick two-mile paddle to **Guemes Island** across **Guemes Channel**, which has an unfortunate habit of becoming a carnival of speeding boats, all much bigger than a kayak, on summer weekends. Many more paddlers take their boats aboard the ferry at Anacortes for a ride to Lopez, Orcas, Shaw, or San Juan Island and launch from there. Unfortunately, the Washington State Ferry system is overwhelmed with summer tourist traffic, and three- to five-hour waits at the terminal are becoming routine. Practical tips: catch the earliest ferry, or at least avoid weekends. And bring a kayak cart for portaging, since the ferry system prohibits launching from its docks.

Once on the water, the tumult usually evaporates. The sheer visual variety in paddling among the San Juans is hard to match;

Halibut steaks (left) finish the day on a tasty note; groceries are available in several waterside towns.

Guided kayak trips (opposite) range from an hour to a few days or longer.

Pebble beaches (below) are found throughout the islands and are often convenient launching and landing sites.

the seascape has everything but icebergs. The islands themselves form a gallery of amusingly zoomorphic shapes, from long, curving whales' backs to steep dromedary humps. Some of the small islands are claimed by a single cabin, leading to speculation about the inhabitants' lives. The water itself is lovely, the color ever-changing; depending on meteorological whim it can range from sapphire blue to antique jade.

What's in this water, however, may be the most fascinating attraction. Salmon migrating to spawning grounds in Washington and British Columbia have to pass through the San Juans, drawing a fascinating variety of predators. Most notable is the orca. Kayakers have the best seats on the sea during peak orca season, May through July. Orcas have never been known to show aggression toward kayaks, but when one of these five-ton monsters suddenly breaches nearby, it can be as dangerous as it is spectacular. To make matters worse, hundreds of boats may be buzzing around, jockeying for a view.

Recreational destinations on the islands are as varied as the

A flutist (left) serenades the dolphins from a beach on Patos Island. The kayaks are a traditional Aleutian design.

A kelp stalk (right) doubles as a makeshift horn.

rentals available.

But if it seems, well, just too bourgeois to tug a kayak onto a beach and then dress up (not down) for dinner, the San Juans still offer serenity and solitude. The kayaker's most accommodating friend is the **Cascadia Marine Trail**, a network of beach campsites begun in 1993 and still expanding, stretching from the southern fingertip of Puget Sound through the San Juans. For a small fee, campers arriving by muscle- or sail-powered boats may spend the night on any of about three dozen beaches, some in state parks and others on uninhabited islands. One of the most convenient features of the Marine Trail – of vital interest to kayakers, whose plans can be scattered to the winds by an unexpected turn in the weather – is that nobody is ever turned away from a campsite because it's full. Late arrivals just squeeze in.

islands themselves. Sybarites who crave a lavish dinner, hot shower, and warm bed instead of a nightly battle of wits with raccoons can plot a route through the San Juans that calls at an inn or resort every night. The villages on the larger islands – particularly San Juan's **Friday Harbor** – offer all the amenities of civilization, from Native art galleries and quirky bookstores to ethnic restaurants. For land transportation, there are bicycle, moped, and even car

No camping is allowed on **Yellow Island**, a 10-acre preserve owned by the Nature Conservancy since 1980, but it's a popular stop in summer because of its stunning display of 150 species of wildflowers, the best in the San Juans. A short trail curls around the island, and Nature Conservancy monitors are vigilant about insisting that visitors who stay on it leave no trace.

ominous volcanic cone of Mount Baker, and the distant reaches of the Cascade Mountains in British Columbia. Other trails connect with four alpine lakes and a chain of waterfalls along aptly named **Cascade Creek**.

But the San Juan experience is more a matter of unplanned encounters than awesome spectacles such as Mount Constitution. It might be the sight of a bald eagle launching itself from a snag, or an American dipper, a wren-sized bird that strolls underwater in creeks, pecking at insects and small fish. It could be a human encounter – a kayaker pausing for a moment's conversation beside a millionaire's yacht anchored off Friday Harbor, the two mariners trading small tales about their vastly different worlds. Or a simple evening at one of the coveted west-facing campsites, the dying sun torching the water into an outrage of orange and red. It doesn't get much better than this, nor does it need to.

Orcas Island, at the opposite end of the recreational spectrum, offers enough natural sights and entertainment to occupy a visiting kayaker for several days. Orcas' 56 square miles encompass a lot of varied geography, some of it fairly rugged. Hiking to the 2,407-foot summit of **Mount Constitution**, the highest peak in the San Juans, is not a great idea on the same day as the 15-mile paddle from Friday Harbor. But on a clear day this summit is arguably the crown jewel of the entire state park system. The view gathers in Lummi, Sucia, and Matia Islands, the city of Bellingham, the

Orcas (below), the largest members of the dolphin family, are often spotted around the San Juans.

Neither Killers nor Whales

For the love of Ishmael, let us now scuttle the term "killer whale." The orca is neither. It has no interest in killing humans, and it is a dolphin, not a whale.

It is a *colossal* dolphin, however – up to five tons and 30 feet – and this, along with its gregarious nature, athletic behavior, and smart "tuxedo" colors, is making it the quarry of hundreds of "whale-watching" tours in the San Juans. Some marine biologists worry that the attention is becoming too intense and that the "watching" now equals harassment.

There's no harassing at the **Whale Museum** in Friday Harbor, a small nonprofit educational museum a 10-minute walk from the ferry on San Juan Island. Its centerpiece is the skeleton of L8, a 20-foot male orca who died of unknown causes and washed up on Vancouver Island in 1977. Even in death, L8 seems both awesomely graceful and powerful. His spine, thick as a fire hose, curves like an ocean swell; his rib cage could be a phone booth.

This is a worthwhile stop for all ages. Adults can contemplate whale exploitation – their oil illuminated the pre-electric world – while kids ponder the contrast between pickled human and fin-whale brains; the latter is three times our size. Everyone can listen to recorded arias of orcas and humpback, beluga, and sperm whales and wonder at their meaning.

The Whale Museum subtly suggests new definitions of intelligence and raises the bar. The orcas – giant dolphins, remember – glide over and challenge us to follow.

DETAILS

When to Go

The San Juan Islands are a year-round destination: the climate is moderate, with highs in the 80s in summer and only occasionally below freezing in winter. Summer is most popular; expect ferries, campgrounds, and accommodations to be crowded. Spring and early summer are a good time to see resident orca whales, though they can be spotted year-round. Fall and winter are quiet, but paddling is excellent in protected areas if you're properly equipped with cold-weather gear. Tides and winds can be hazardous in any season but are particularly strong in winter.

How to Get There

Ferries and small planes serve the San Juans. Washington State Ferries (800-843-3779) depart from Anacortes, 70 miles north of Seattle, several times a day. The ferry takes one to two hours depending on schedules and your destination. Kenmore Air (800-543-9595) offers seaplane transportation directly from Seattle's Lake Union to various points in the San Juans such as Eastsound and Friday Harbor. Harbor Airlines (800-359-3220) operates from Seattle–Tacoma International Airport, and West Isle Air flies from Seattle's Boeing field (800-874-4434). Airporter Shuttle (800-235-5247) provides ground transportation from Seattle–Tacoma International Airport to the Anacortes ferry terminal.

Permits

No permits are required, but some boat-in campsites are reserved for members of the Washington Water Trails Association; stickers for one-time use are available from the group.

INFORMATION

San Juan Information Center
P.O. Box 2809, Friday Harbor, WA 98250; tel: 360-378-8887.

San Juan Islands Visitor Information Center
P.O. Box 65, Lopez Island, WA 98261; tel: 360-468-3663.

Washington Water Trails Association
4649 Sunnyside Avenue North, Room 305, Seattle, WA 98103; tel: 206-545-9161.

CAMPING

San Juan County Park
San Juan County Parks, P.O. Box 86, Lopez, WA 98261; tel: 360-378-2992.

This park, on the west side of San Juan Island, is a popular staging area for kayakers. The campground has 12 fairly cramped sites with flush toilets, a boat launch, and some of the best whale-watching in the islands.

South Beach
San Juan County Parks, P.O. Box 86, Lopez, WA 98261; tel: 360-468-2580.

South Beach is on Shaw Island, the least touristy of the islands serviced by state ferries. Shaw has no lodging or restaurants, but it offers a 12-site waterfront campground and excellent opportunities for protected and open-water kayaking trips.

Spencer Spit State Park
521-A Bakerview Road, Lopez, WA 98261; tel: 360-468-2251.

The campground at this state park makes a good base for exploring the island by sea kayak. There are 45 sites, pit toilets, and convenient shoreline access.

LODGING

Doe Bay Village Resort and Retreat
Star Route 86, Olga, WA 98279; tel: 360-376-2291 or 360-376-4755.

This resort on Orcas Island offers cottages, platform tents, and a dormitory-style hostel, and is a good base for exploring nearby islands and wildlife sanctuaries. Shearwater Adventures (see Tours and Outfitters) runs guided trips. $–$$$

Duffy House Bed-and-Breakfast
76 Pear Point Road, Friday Harbor, WA 98250; tel: 360-378-5604 or 800-972-2089.

This inn, just a few minutes from Friday Harbor on San Juan Island, offers five bedrooms with private baths. Paddlers can pull up their boats on the inn's private beach. $$–$$$

MacKaye Harbor Inn
949 MacKaye Harbor Road, Lopez Island, WA 98261; tel: 360-468-2253.

This waterfront bed-and-breakfast has five guest rooms, three with private baths. The inn's beach provides good access; kayak rentals are available. $$–$$$$

Roche Harbor Resort
P.O. Box 4001, Roche Harbor, WA 98250; tel: 360-378-2155 or 800-451-8910.

This harbor resort on San Juan Island has more than 50 units, many of them one- to three-bedroom condominiums with fireplaces and decks. Kayak tours depart from the dock. $$–$$$$

Spring Bay Inn
P.O. Box 97, Olga, WA 98279; tel: 360-376-5531.

A daily two-hour kayak tour is included in the room rate at this bed-and-breakfast in a wooded corner of Orcas Island. Five guest rooms have private baths with clawfoot tubs, fireplaces, and featherbeds. $$$$

West Beach Resort
Route 1, Box 510, Eastsound, WA 98245; tel: 360-376-2240 or 877-937-8224.

This Orcas Island resort has beachfront cabins, excellent kayak access, and kayak tours. $$–$$$

TOURS AND OUTFITTERS

Adventure Associates
P.O. Box 16304, Seattle, WA 98116; tel: 206-932-8352 or 888-532-8352.

Multiday, weekend, and women-only trips are available.

Crystal Seas Kayaking
P.O. Box 3135, Friday Harbor, WA 98250; tel: 360-378-7899.

This outfitter leads half- to three-day trips in the San Juans.

Eddyline Kayaks
1344 Ashten Road, Burlington, WA 98233; tel: 360-757-2300.

Sunset, half- and full-day guided trips are available. A waterfront shop sells and rents equipment.

Elakah! Sea Otter Expeditions
P.O. Box 4092, Bellingham, WA 98227; tel: 360-734-7270.

One- to five-day guided tours are available as well as clinics and women's trips.

San Juan Safaris
P.O. Box 2749, Friday Harbor, WA 98250; tel: 360-378-2155 or 800-451-8910.

Half- and full-day trips depart from Roche Harbor.

Shearwater Adventures
P.O. Box 787, Eastsound, WA 98245; tel: 360-376-4699.

This outfitter provides guides, equipment, and camp cookery.

Excursions

Lake Union

Northwest Outdoor Center, 2100 Westlake Avenue North, Seattle, WA 98109; tel: 206-281-9694 or 800-683-0637.

Lake Union, just north of downtown Seattle, offers a distinctly urban paddling experience. The lake is a hub of activity: seaplanes buzz in and out, houseboats crowd the waterfront, kites fly from the grassy knoll at Gas Works Park, and sailboats scud across the surface. This may be one of the few places where sea kayakers can stop for a lakeside espresso or perhaps a lunch of salmon and chips. Hourly kayak rentals and some tours are available at the Northwest Outdoor Center.

Ross Lake

North Cascades National Park, Ross Lake National Recreation Area, 2105 State Route 20, Sedro Woolley, WA 98284; tel: 360-856-5700.

Deep, green, fjordlike Ross Lake stretches 21 miles into the alpine splendor of the North Cascades, surrounded by dense forests and snowcapped peaks. Boat-in campsites are scattered on various islands and along the lakeshore. Some are at trailheads leading to peaks like Desolation, where literary icon and one-time fire-watcher Jack Kerouac once ruminated for a summer. Help with logistics and one-way trips is provided by Ross Lake Resort (206-386-4437). Check lake levels before you go; big drawdowns can result in long hikes up muddy banks to some campsites.

Skykomish River

Mount Baker–Snoqualmie National Forest, 21905 64th Avenue West, Mountlake Terrace, WA 98043; tel: 425-775-9702.

Snowmelt fattens the Skykomish as it races out of the Cascade Range at Stevens Pass, tumbling through rounded boulders at Class IV Boulder Drop and other scenic cataracts. Like most streams in western Washington, the "Sky" is frigid, and few paddlers venture onto it without wet suits or dry suits. Several outfitters, including Seattle-based Orion Expeditions (800-553-7466), run guided raft trips on a 10-mile stretch between Index and Big Eddy.

Glacier Bay National Park

Alaska

The 50-mile flight from Bartlett Cove to Muir Inlet traverses the length of **Glacier Bay**, from the spruce and hemlock rain forest at the mouth of the lower bay to the barren glaciated mountains of the upper reaches. Below, the lovely jade and turquoise waters are peppered with icebergs and rich with a summer bounty of plankton, shrimp, and fish. ◆ The pilot points out to his two passengers a shadowy pod of killer whales, five in all, a family group, swimming into a long cove on the morning tide. Birds in their untold thousands are everywhere – parrotlike puffins, broad-winged gulls, red-necked phalaropes. After an hour of sightseeing, the pilot spirals down to a little-known fjord and taxies to a sandy beach. ◆ An hour later the adventurers from the Lower 48 launch their two-seat collapsible kayak into a wilderness unlike anything they had **Kayakers encounter whales,** ever seen or would ever see again. On that first **eagles, and countless** day of paddling, they would observe many **seabirds in the fjords and coves** things – an immense blue iceberg covered **of an icebound wilderness.** with young harbor seals, a humpback whale's barnacled tail fluke as the great leviathan dove to feed on the bottom, a bald eagle with a fresh-caught salmon thrashing in its talons. But nothing would give them a greater sense of solitude than their campsite on a wild, nameless headland. All around lay granite boulders the size of automobiles, each one as round and smooth as an enormous egg. Hundreds of arctic terns and kittiwakes clustered and swirled over the water. Far up the bay, a glacier thundered as it calved a huge slab of ice. And then, for the first time ever, they saw a river otter. Black-eyed and curious, the otter poked its rounded face up through the water just below a rock ledge. It looked at them for a long,

Small chunks of ice known as "bergie bits" gently bump a sea kayak cruising through Johns Hopkins Inlet in the West Arm of Glacier Bay.

The Beardslee Islands (left) are composed of rubble washed into place by melting glaciers.

Icebergs (opposite) are alluring but unpredictable; they have a tendency to roll suddenly as ice melts or calves off.

for sea kayakers: a 65-mile-long saltwater bay with a dozen major fjords, 12 tidewater glaciers, and an extraordinary abundance of wildlife. The park is served by the small gateway community of **Gustavus** at the mouth of the bay and can be reached by boat and plane. The town offers all the normal services, including a store, lodges, cabins, and inns. Kayak rentals and guided kayak tours are also available. Kayakers are required to check in for the latest information at park headquarters at **Bartlett Cove**, about 10 miles west of the Gustavus airport via shuttle bus or taxi. The season at Glacier Bay runs from mid-May through mid-September. In the early season, icebergs are generally more numerous and the tidewater glaciers are more difficult to approach. Summer at Glacier Bay is usually cool and cloudy, with intermittent periods of sunshine. September is often rainy.

friendly moment and then, without a sound, vanished back into the pristine water that was its home, and theirs, for the next week.

Choices and Attractions

Situated about 60 miles northwest of Juneau, the capital of Alaska, Glacier Bay is the only national park that includes a long and deep arm of the sea. First designated a monument in 1925, Glacier Bay was later given national park and preserve status as part of the Alaska National Interest Lands Conservation Act in 1980. The park is nearly 3.3 million acres in size, which makes it more than four times larger than the state of Rhode Island.

Glacier Bay has three chief attractions

Glaciers are the architects of **Glacier Bay National Park**. They have quarried and shaped the landscape, ground the native rock, and freighted enormous boulders across long distances. They have carved out valleys filled with seawater, given birth to powerful fresh-water rivers, and deposited what are now extensive ridges of gravel, sand, and boulders. Today the massive glaciers of the region are in rapid retreat, having moved back more than 50 miles since they were discovered nearly two centuries ago, opening a vast new territory to animal and plant recolonization. Some scientists theorize that this is a result of global warming; others speculate that it may be part of cyclical climate change. What this dynamic state of affairs means for sea kayakers is that, first, the park is visually spectacular (many who have traveled widely in Alaska believe Glacier Bay is the most beautiful park in the state), and second, there are extensive flatwater bays and coves formed by the glaciers that are perfect for paddlers.

Sea kayakers have three choices: to remain in the vicinity of **Bartlett Cove** and the **Beardslee Islands** near the visitor center; to take a tour boat 43 miles to the north, be dropped off, and then explore one of the two major arms of the bay (**Muir Inlet** and the **West Arm**); or to be transported into the upper bay by floatplane. Some visitors choose to combine two of the three, exploring, for example, the heavily forested lower bay for a few days and then traveling by boat or plane to the more austere, glaciated upper bay for a different sort of experience.

The first alternative is the easiest and least expensive. The choices include a leisurely trip three miles up the timbered seacoast to the mouth of the **Bartlett River**, a popular spot

during the midsummer salmon fishing season; a 20-mile tour around **Lester Island** to **Secret Bay** on the east side of **Young Island**; or a more extensive paddling journey north to the Beardslee Islands and **Beartrack Cove**, about 15 miles north of Bartlett Cove. Views of the snow-covered **Fairweather Range** in this part of the park, including 15,300-foot **Mount Fairweather**, are quite impressive.

Exploring the Arms

The upper bay is probably the most popular destination for sea kayakers. Those who choose this option will have their equipment and kayaks transported on one of the park's daily tour boats (reservations well in advance are recommended). Those with hard-shelled

The knobby flukes of a humpback whale (right) slip beneath the surface.

kayaks must go by boat and not by plane. The park boat drops kayakers off at pre-designated locations in the upper bay; most are set ashore at one spot and then picked up at another. Kayakers in the right arm of the upper bay can venture past **Muir Point** (where naturalist John Muir built his cabin more than a century ago) to explore beautiful **Adams Inlet**, **Wachusett Inlet**, and the head of Muir Inlet, with its enormous fronting glacier. The left arm of the upper bay leads to majestic **Queen Inlet**, **Rendu Inlet**, **Reid Inlet**, **Tarr Inlet**, and **Johns Hopkins Inlet**. This is a much more extensive region than the right arm. Those who choose to travel by floatplane will have wider access to these same areas (but will pay proportionally for the freedom, an amount that can equal the round-trip airfare to Juneau from many locations in the Lower 48 states).

Kayakers in Glacier Bay can expect to see a variety of wildlife both on and off the water. Marine mammals are frequently observed by kayakers during the summer months. These include three species of whale (humpback, orca, and minke), sea lions, harbor seals, porpoises, and sea otters. The cliffs and shores of Glacier Bay provide rookeries for countless seabirds each summer, including puffins and guillemots, black oystercatchers, common murres, and cormorants. Eagles, ravens, and crows are commonly seen along the shores, as are black and brown bears, wolves, and moose. Kayakers often spot mountain goats

Bear Essentials

Most people who visit Glacier Bay consider a bear sighting to be one of the highlights of their trip. Bears symbolize the wildness and beauty of the north country. Both brown and black bears are common in the park and can be seen virtually anywhere – from avalanche chutes just below the glaciers to the dense inland forests and wide-open beaches. Bears are also capable of swimming anywhere that kayaks can go.

A few commonsense rules apply when it comes to traveling in bear country. First, remember that bears are most aggressive when they are surprised; always make your presence known when hiking through bear country by singing, talking loudly, or tying a bell to your day pack. Whenever possible, travel in a group of three or more. Avoid thick brush and hiking at dusk and dawn. Second, keep in mind that bears are always hungry. Food is fairly difficult for bears to obtain in the Alaskan wilderness. From the time they leave their winter dens in the early spring to the first snowflakes of autumn, they are preoccupied with putting on enough fat to survive the next big sleep. Cook and store food several hundred yards from your tent, and store all food away from your camp. Keep fish and fishing equipment and anything smelling of fish far from your sleeping area. Third, if a bear approaches you, wave your arms and jump up and down so that the animal can identify you as human. Talk in a normal but strong voice. Never make the potentially fatal error of establishing eye contact with the bear. If attacked, curl up in a ball with your hands behind your neck. Many people carry pepper spray as a defense. Such sprays can be effective at a range of about five yards. If you carry a spray can, keep it on a shoulder or belt holster, and know how to use it.

Sighting a bear cub (left) should serve as a warning sign: a protective mother may be nearby.

Calm water (opposite, top) makes for easy paddling, though storms can kick up suddenly in any season.

Bald eagles (right) are sometimes seen plucking fish from the water.

feeding on lush wildflowers in the high country. Some kayakers carry fishing equipment, as fresh salmon can considerably enhance the camping cuisine, but be alert for bears wanting their share. The many tidepools of Glacier Bay are always a delight for kayakers to explore; the colorful sea stars, anemones, sea urchins, crabs, and other fauna seem almost tropical in their profusion.

Like most wilderness parks in Alaska, Glacier Bay presents a unique set of local conditions for kayakers to deal with. The bay experiences some of the highest tide fluctuations in Alaska (up to 25 feet); kayakers camping on the beach, or on rocks above the water, should carefully secure kayaks and other equipment in safe locations. Similarly, kayakers need to be wary both of the icebergs, which are unstable and may shift or even turn completely over without warning, and of the tidewater glaciers, which can calve off huge chunks of ice at any time. Park officials recommend staying at least half a mile from the front of a glacier. Both breaching whales and heedless cruise ships pose additional hazards and should be avoided. Another constant concern in this cold, rainy part of the world is hypothermia. Seawater temperatures rarely exceed 35°F. Finally, black and brown bears are common in Glacier Bay. Anyone exploring the park, either on water or on foot, should pay close attention to the bear briefing given by park rangers at the visitor center.

Because of the often soggy, buggy conditions in Glacier Bay, sea kayakers should carry as much of the following equipment as they can: traditional backcountry rain gear (poncho and rain pants); knee-high rubber hiking boots (available at stores in Juneau); bug spray, head nets, and cotton gloves (for the mosquitoes that gather in the coves). Some kayakers also take along portable two-way radios, as rangers constantly monitor several frequencies.

In the end, paddlers will find that

Glacier Bay National Park offers some of the best saltwater kayaking in the United States, if not the world. Few other locations present kayaking enthusiasts with such a wonderful combination of great paddling, exceptional scenery, and amazing wildlife. Here water folk will find cloud-draped peaks and rain-drenched forests, salt water as clear as glass and sculpted icebergs that glow with inner light, timbered coves as quiet as museum galleries, and sprawling glaciers washed in brilliant sunshine. Here are whales and seals, otters and salmon, puffins and eagles, marmots and moose. Here is a place to see the world as it was when glaciers ruled and canoes and kayaks were the best means of transportation. If there is an earthly paradise for kayakers, it may just be Glacier Bay.

TRAVEL TIPS

DETAILS

When to Go

The paddling season at Glacier Bay runs from mid-May through mid-September, though the park is open year-round. In the early season, icebergs are more numerous and tidewater glaciers are harder to get close to. Summer is usually cool and cloudy, with intermittent periods of sunshine. Average temperatures in July range from 48° to 63°F.

How to Get There

Commercial airlines serve Juneau International Airport, 70 miles from Glacier Bay. The park may be reached only by charter boat and plane. Scheduled air service is available from Juneau to Gustavus; buses and taxis run the 10 miles between Gustavus and the park entrance. Contact the park office for a list of transportation services.

Getting Around

Kayak rentals and guide services are available in Gustavus. The park's tour boat departs from Glacier Bay Lodge and offers drop-off and pickup service for kayakers and hikers. Air taxis will transport boaters and hikers to remote parts of the park.

Permits

Boating permits are required from June 1 through August 31 and are available at the Visitor Information Station in Bartlett Cove.

INFORMATION

Alaska Public Lands Information Center

605 West 4th Avenue, Suite 105, Anchorage, AK 99501; tel: 907-271-2737; or 3031 Tongass Avenue, Ketchikan, AK 99901; tel: 907-228-6220.

Glacier Bay National Park

P.O. Box 140, Gustavus, AK 99826-0140; tel: 907-697-2230.

Gustavus Visitor Association

P.O. Box 167, Gustavus, AK 99826; tel: 907-697-2475.

CAMPING

Primitive campsites at Bartlett Cove are available on a first-come, first-served basis. Backcountry camping is permitted elsewhere in the park. Campers must attend a free orientation at the Visitor Information Station and check out a bear-resistant food canister.

LODGING

PRICE GUIDE – double occupancy

$ = up to $49 $$ = $50–$99
$$$ = $100–$149 $$$$ = $150+

Annie Mae Lodge

Grandpa's Farm Road, P.O. Box 80, Gustavus, AK 99826; tel: 800-478-2346 or 907-697-2346.

This two-story log lodge, about four miles from Gustavus Airport, has wraparound porches and spectacular views of the rain forest, mountains, and Icy Strait. Eleven guest rooms offer private or shared baths. Two- to five-day packages include breakfast, packed lunches, and fresh seafood dinners served in the dining room. Also included are whale watching, sea kayaking, flightseeing, and hiking. Free ground transportation is provided. $$$$

Bear Track Inn

P.O. Box 255, Gustavus, AK 99826; tel: 888-697-2284 or 907-697-3017.

This log lodge has 14 rooms with private baths and two queen-sized beds. The lobby has a walk-around fireplace, over-stuffed suede couches, and moose-antler chandeliers. Packages include gourmet meals, ferry transportation from Juneau, and ground transportation. Guests choose from activities such as whale watching, sea kayaking, and airplane tours. Open February 15 to October 1. $$$$

Glacier Bay Lodge

Glacier Bay Park Concessions, 520 Pike Street, Suite 1400, Seattle, WA 98101; tel: 800-451-5952 or 206-626-7110.

The park's only lodge is in Bartlett Cove. Men's and women's dormitories provide more than 50 rooms, each with three bunk beds. Guests share bath and shower facilities. Breakfast, lunch, and dinner are served. Boat tours depart from a dock below the lodge; drop-off services are available for campers and kayakers. Open May 15 to September 10. $

Gustavus Inn

P.O. Box 60, Gustavus, AK 99826 (May to September) or 7920 Outlook, Prairie Village, KS 66208 (October to April); tel: 800-649-5220 or 907-697-2254.

This cedar-sided inn overlooks Icy Strait about eight miles from the park. Thirteen rooms have private baths, a queen-sized bed, and one twin bed. Three daily meals are included. Boat tours, fishing charters, and sea kayaking are available. Open May 15 to September 15. $$$

Whalesong Lodge

P.O Box 389, Gustavus, AK 99826; tel: 800-628-0912.

Accommodations range from guest rooms with private baths to condominiums. Arrangements can be made for overnight tours, private day charters, guided kayaking trips, and whale-watching excursions. $$–$$$

TOURS AND OUTFITTERS

Alaska Discovery Wilderness Adventures

5449 Shaune Drive, Juneau, AK

99801; tel: 800-586-1911
or 907-697-2411.

Guides, equipment, and instruction are available for sea kayaking, rafting, canoeing, and camping adventures. The company also runs a bed-and-breakfast in Gustavus.

Glacier Bay Sea Kayaks

P.O. Box 26, Gustavus, AK 99826; tel: 907-697-2257.

The park concession offers sea-kayak rentals, outfitting, orientation, and instruction, and can arrange drop-off and pickup service on the park tour boat.

Northgate Tours and Cruises

P.O. Box 20613, Juneau, AK 99802; tel: 888-463-5321 or 907-463-5321.

Three- to five-night adventure cruises aboard the 86-passenger *Wilderness Discoverer* explore Glacier Bay and the Inside Passage. Passengers sleep on board and spend days sea kayaking or hiking.

Spirit Walker Expeditions

P.O. Box 240, Gustavus, AK 99826; tel: 907-697-2266.

Guided sea-kayaking and camping expeditions to destinations throughout the Inside Passage range from a half-day to a week or longer.

Excursions

Kenai Fjords National Park

P.O. Box 1727, Seward, AK 99664-1727; tel: 907-224-3175.

A dramatic seascape of deep fjords, calving glaciers, rocky islands, and abundant wildlife puts Kenai Fjords at the top of any paddler's wish list. The park, accessible by boat or plane from the town of Seward, provides exceptional opportunities for accomplished sea kayakers. Less experienced paddlers can reserve a back-country cabin in one of the spectacular fjords and explore the protected waters nearby. Several outfitters, including Sunny Cove Sea Kayaking (907-345-5339), offer guided trips.

Misty Fiords National Monument

Ketchikan Visitors Bureau, 131 Front Street, Ketchikan, AK 99901; tel: 800-770-3300.

Sea kayak through protected waterways out of Ketchikan along the Inside Passage, where mist hangs moodily over glacier-carved fjords. Leisurely, scenic paddles meander around wooded islets and into coves fringed by coastal rain forest. Otters are a common sight, and if your timing is right, you may even spot a whale or two. You can make this trip as easy or difficult as you like, depending on whether you go out for a day, a week, or longer. Novices should seek the aid of an outfitter. Southeast Sea Kayaks (800-287-1607) offers kayak rentals and a variety of tours.

Prince William Sound

Chugach National Forest, 3301 C Street, Suite 300, Anchorage, AK 99503; tel: 907-271-2500.

Prince William Sound is a sea kayaker's dream. Paddlers can spend weeks exploring its long fjords, hidden coves, and hundreds of islands. Icebergs crackle, glaciers creep to the sea, waterfalls cascade down exposed mountainsides. Wildlife, including sea otters, sea lions, bald eagles, and seabird colonies, is plentiful. Shuttles to the remote corners of the sound can be arranged out of Whittier, Valdez, and Cordova. Or contact one of the many outfitters in the region such as Wilderness Alaska (907-345-3567) or the Prince William Sound Kayak Center (907-472-2452) for guided trips.

Noatak River
Alaska

CHAPTER **23**

Around the bend comes a single canoe, drifting with the current. On all sides, blue-gray mountains rise – pyramids and spires cast in light so pure that the landscape seems a painted backdrop. But the two travelers aren't staring out at the scenery; they're looking down into the river. Six feet beneath the keel of their craft, a mosaic of polished stones flows past; Arctic grayling dart away like birds, startled by the sudden shadow overhead. The water seems a translucent atmosphere, something you should be able to breathe. Above the river, the looming mountains cradle the valley in their great, silent hands. ◆ The Noatak is one of the world's great river trips. From its source in the shadow of cloud-capped **Mount Igikpak**, highest peak in the western **Brooks Range**, it flows 400 miles, draining the heart of northwest Alaska. Along its meandering course west to the **Chukchi Sea**, the river slides through a panorama of Arctic terrain:

A companionable river meanders through the Arctic, offering tundra views, excellent fishing, and encounters with wildlife.

steep-sided headwaters, huge sweeps of rolling tundra, canyons, a spruce-dotted floodplain, and a marshy delta. The scenery isn't the most breath-taking in the state; fish and wildlife are often less abundant than in areas far to the south; and the few, relatively gentle rapids will leave a whitewater enthusiast disappointed. But if a long river trip through an unspoiled, hauntingly beautiful landscape is what you seek, the Noatak is without equal. Virtually the entire valley is part of either Gates of the Arctic National Park or Noatak National Preserve, and the watershed is designated by the United Nations as an International Biosphere Reserve. Each summer, several hundred wilderness travelers raft, canoe, or hike through the area.

The Noatak flows for hundreds of miles through some of the most pristine wilderness in North America. Paddlers must be completely self-sufficient.

River Seasons

The sprawling scale of the Noatak valley is difficult to grasp. Imagine paddling from Washington, D.C., to Boston, and the idea begins to sink in. Now imagine encountering only one small, roadless settlement (the Eskimo village of Noatak, population 350) in all that distance, two thirds of the way down-stream. And that's just the main river. Dozens of tributaries, each with its own wild valley, stretch off into a seemingly infinite sea of

ragged peaks – over seven million acres in all.

To get to the Noatak, charter a float plane out of **Bettles** or **Ambler**, two small bush communities that are connected by regular passenger flights to Fairbanks. It's best to make arrangements at least two months in advance; these small flying services are in high demand during the fleeting Arctic summer. **Kotzebue**, on the Chukchi Sea, is another place to hire an air charter.

The river is usually clear of ice from early June through mid-September. Planning a trip at either end of the season has its appeal – the sometimes huge clouds of mosquitoes are thinner, wildlife is on the move, and there is far less human activity. On the other hand, the normally clear river is often clouded with runoff just after the ice breaks up, and fall weather can be unstable. Without a doubt, the best overall time for a Noatak float trip is mid-July through August. The weather is usually at its best in July – warm days, the water low and clear – but the chance to see autumn colors and the annual caribou migration make mid- to late August a tempting choice. There is no one perfect time. Each month has its drawbacks and rewards, and the Arctic is fickle. If you have a great deal of flexibility, call ahead to your chosen air charter service to check on conditions, and plan accordingly. Whatever weather pattern has set in is likely to remain for at least the next week or two, even for an entire season. Of course, seeing the Noatak in the rain is better than not seeing it at all.

Wildlife Watching

As with most rivers, the headwaters of the Noatak are the wildest and most alluring. Ask to be dropped off as far upriver as possible, and plan to linger a few days. The most common drop-off point is one of several lakes between **Angayu** and **Anorat Creeks** (the river itself is too shallow for safe landing). The dark, craggy mountain slopes on the north side of the river invite exploratory day hikes or ambitious circuits and summits. White Dall sheep are common in this stretch. Red fox and grizzlies forage along the banks, and the patient or lucky observer has an excellent chance of spotting a lone musk-ox bull or members of the several wolf packs that patrol the upper valley. Here, as elsewhere along the Noatak, evenings and early mornings are by far the best chance to view most animals (caribou, who are active through the day, are an exception). Find a good vantage point and spend an hour or two with binoculars every day if wildlife viewing is your goal.

The upper river meanders through mountain walls for the next 50 miles, collecting a dozen creeks and several major tributaries, including the **Kugrak**, **Igning**, and **Imelyak Rivers**, all rising into the vertical, seldom-visited canyon country along the Noatak–Kobuk divide. To the south, the limestone crags of the **Schwatka Mountains** glow as the sun circles the horizon, dipping but never setting.

Under normal conditions, the upper river's current is brisk, spiked with Class II riffles, especially around **Douglas Creek**. Strong eddy lines require constant caution, even in smooth sections. If it's a dry year, you may end up dragging over the shallower

A paddler (right) takes a break to get her bearings. Knowing how to use a compass and topo map are essential skills for any wilderness trip.

Grizzly tracks (opposite) and scat are often found along the river.

runs. There's one power-ful, short drop near Okak bend, where the river piles into a rock wall and makes a sharp turn left. The strong eddy there is easily skirted by hugging the bar on the inside.

Around the **Cutler River**, the character of the Noatak changes as the river spills across a wide tundra basin. The Schwatkas, once so near, fade back and are swallowed in a rolling sea of land. To the south and west, the rounded **Baird Mountains** rim the horizon. If there is one place to sense the vastness of Noatak country, this is it. Sleep late and paddle through the bright Arctic evenings to avoid headwinds and to enjoy the magical light.

Canyons and Channels

Below the confluence of the **Nimiuktuk River**, the mountains close in again, forming the **Grand Canyon of the Noatak** – hardly a canyon in the classic sense, but scenic all the same. The river murmurs through deep green pools where big grayling and sea-run Dolly Varden char lurk. Tiny spinners and flies work best for the for-mer; char prefer a slow, deep presentation, within inches of the bottom. Flourescent orange Pixee spoons or maribou streamers are the lures of choice.

The Noatak pours on, gathered into a single channel. One by one, small tributaries add to the river's flow. A dozen miles or so below the **Nakolik River**, the first stunted white spruce appear on the south bank. Soon the river enters the short but quite spectacular **Noatak Canyon**, marked by overhanging bluffs of dark, quartz-swirled rock. This is a fine spot for a mountain hike before the river spills onto its floodplain. Keep an eye out for Dall sheep on the rocks above. From late August through September, expect to meet Inupiat caribou hunters in outboard skiffs.

At the lower mouth of the canyon, the **Kugururok River** pours in from the north. Bands of spruce forest become common.

Grayling (top) is an Arctic treat. Most pad-dlers use camp stoves, as wood is scarce.

A portage trail (left) leads from a floatplane drop-off on Lake Matcharak to the river.

Fifteen miles downstream, the **Kelly River** is a famous late-summer hot spot for big Dollies, chum salmon, and grayling, and there is a National Park Service ranger station just upstream on the north side.

The next 30 miles to Noatak village are marked by a mile-wide maze of braided channels where thousands of salmon spawn in late summer. Bear tracks and torn fish carcasses litter the gravel along shallow riffles. Though the local grizzlies are generally shy, you may glimpse one if you're quiet.

Keep track of your progress and favor the right as you approach Noatak village. The cluster of cabins and prefabricated buildings, perched on a high bluff, is visible for more than a mile. Landing aircraft and the rumble of the town's diesel generators add further cues. Still, it's possible to miss your turn and end up lining back upstream. This Inupiat settlement is the most common place to take out. Several passenger flights a day connect to Kotzebue, 60 miles away, on the shores of the Chukchi Sea.

If you choose to float the remaining portion of the river, keep in mind that this means making the seven-mile crossing of **Hotham Inlet** from the Noatak delta's mouth to Kotzebue. Irregular sandbars, currents, and wind make this an option for strong, experienced paddlers only. Calm early mornings are your best bet.

Otherwise, the lower river is a fine float – quick runs through the many braided channels below Noatak village, and then a

slower pace as the river deepens, pooling through the green Ingichuk hills. This last bit of rolling high ground, complete with its own brief canyon, the **Lower Noatak**, is a faint echo of that lonely, ragged headwater country, now hundreds of miles upstream. As you glimpse the delta ahead, it's hard not to feel regret, to wish you had stayed longer at places you hurried past. But there could never be enough days or years for this journey. The Noatak is a river and a place beyond time.

The northern lights (above) illuminate the night sky in fall.

Caribou (left) migrate hundreds of miles between summer and winter feeding grounds.

TRAVEL TIPS

DETAILS

When to Go

The Noatak River usually thaws by early June and freezes by late September. Summer is short, cool, and sunny, with nearly 24 hours of daylight in June. Be prepared for high winds and sudden weather changes. Winter is long and harsh, with long periods of sub-zero temperatures. The region receives only about one hour of daylight by December 1.

How to Get There

Reaching the area is neither easy nor inexpensive. Many visitors take a scheduled flight from Anchorage or Fairbanks to Kotzebue and then arrange for a bush plane to drop them off near the river. Flight services include: Arctic Wings (907-373-3475), Ambler Air Service (907-445-2121), Bettles Air Service (907-692-5111), Brooks Range Aviation (907-692-5444), Northwestern Aviation (907-442-3525), and Wright Air Service (907-474-0502).

Getting Around

There are no roads or rail service. Summer visitors travel through the region by boat or plane or on foot.

Permits

No fee or permit is required for float trips on the Noatak.

INFORMATION

Alaska Public Lands Center

605 West 4th Avenue, Suite 105, Anchorage, AK 99501; tel: 907-271-2737; 3031 Tongass Avenue,

Ketchikan, AK 99901; tel: 907-228-6220; or 250 Cushman Street, Suite 1A, Fairbanks, AK 99701; tel: 907-456-0527.

Gates of the Arctic National Park and Preserve

201 First Avenue, Dogon Building, Fairbanks, AK 99701; tel: 907-456-0281.

Noatak National Preserve

P.O. Box 1029, Kotzebue, AK 99752; tel: 907-442-3890.

CAMPING

There are no restrictions on backcountry hiking or camping, but travelers should be respectful of Native camps and villages. There are no developed campgrounds or facilities. Supplies at nearby villages are limited and costly. Visitors must be properly equipped, experienced in wilderness travel, and completely self-sufficient.

LODGING

PRICE GUIDE – double occupancy

$ = up to $49 $$ = $50–$99

$$$ = $100–$149 $$$$ = $150+

Bettles Lodge

P.O. Box 27, Bettles, AK 99726; tel: 907-692-5111 or 800-770-5111.

This year-round, fly-in establishment is a popular jumping-off point for travelers on their way to the Noatak. The lodge includes a restaurant, gift shop, and tavern. Six rooms in the main lodge share two central bathrooms; eight rooms in the Aurora Lodge have private baths, some with Jacuzzis. Dogsledding, float trips, backpacking, fishing, and winter adventures are available, as are air charters. $$$–$$$$

Kobuk River Lodge

P.O. Box 30, Ambler, AK 99786; tel: 907-445-2166.

On the banks of the Kobuk

River, this lodge has two rooms with a pair of twin beds, one room with a double bed, and two cabins that sleep up to three people each. Guests share bath and shower facilities. Kitchenettes are available in the cabins, which overlook the river. Prices include three meals a day. A general store is on the premises, and guided or unguided river tours and backpacking trips can be arranged. $$$–$$$$

Nullagvik Hotel

P.O. Box 336; Kotzebue, AK 99752; tel: 907-442-3331.

This hotel on Kotzebue Sound has 80 guest rooms, each with a private bath and two twin beds. A restaurant has views of the sound and, in summer, the midnight sun. The hotel's gift shop sells arts and crafts made by Inupiat Eskimos, who live in and around Kotzebue. Open year-round. $$$–$$$$

Westmark Fairbanks Hotel

813 Noble Street, Fairbanks, AK 99701; tel: 907-456-7722.

This hotel offers 248 rooms, including 11 two-room suites, all with private baths. Amenities include a 24-hour business center, a gift shop, and passes and shuttles to nearby fitness centers. $$–$$$$

TOURS AND OUTFITTERS

Alaska Discovery

5449 Shaune Drive #4; Juneau, AK 99801; tel: 800-586-1911 or 907-780-6226.

Ten-day raft trips traverse the Noatak River in Gates of the Arctic National Park.

Alaska Wildtrek Adventures

P.O. Box 1741, Homer, AK 99603; tel: 907-235-6463.

Guides lead canoe and raft trips down the Noatak and other area rivers, often blending one or more day hikes into the itinerary. Customized trips for groups or families can be arranged, and help with lodging reservations is available.

Arctic Wild

P.O. Box 80562,
Fairbanks, AK 99708;
tel: 907-479-8203.

River rafting, hiking, backpacking, photography, and wildlife viewing are featured on trips through the Arctic and the Brooks Range.

Bettles Lodge

P.O. Box 27, Bettles, AK
99726; tel: 907-692-5111
or 800-770-5111.

This lodge specializes in hiking, backpacking, fishing, river trips, and winter adventures. Experienced guides plan and outfit customized trips, and arrange transportation.

Equinox Wilderness Expeditions

618 West 14th Avenue,
Anchorage, AK 99501;
tel: 907-274-9087.

Expert guides and naturalists lead seven- to 14-day trips down the Noatak and other Alaskan rivers.

Mountains and Rivers

P.O. Box 874254, Wasilla, AK
99687; tel: 907-373-5221.

Guides lead eight- to 10-day canoeing and rafting trips down the Noatak; groups are kept small to minimize impact on the environment. Custom trips can also be arranged.

Excursions

Kobuk River

Northwest Alaska Areas, National Park Service, P.O. Box 1029, Kotzebue, AK 99752; tel: 907-442-3760.

The Kobuk flows about 350 miles out of the southern Brooks Range to Hotham Inlet on the Chukchi Sea. Along the way, it meanders through dense spruce-and-balsam forest, Arctic tundra, limestone canyons, and the sprawling Kobuk Sand Dunes. The river is gentle for most of its run, though two sections of Class II-IV whitewater make for some tense moments. Both should be lined or portaged. Encounters with an assortment of Arctic wildlife, including musk oxen, grizzlies, moose, foxes, and wolves, are possible. Lucky travelers may see hundreds, perhaps thousands, of migrating caribou.

Nenana River

Alaska Public Lands Information Center, 250 Cushman Street, Suite 1A, Fairbanks, AK 99701; tel: 907-456-0527.

Expect big, powerful water, exploding waves, and giant holes on this brawny glacial stream just outside of Denali National Park. You can go easy or make it tough, depending on which stretch you choose. There are three, each eight to 10 miles long, ranked Class II-IV. Take time on the mellow sections between the rapids to admire some of Alaska's most spectacular scenery. Novices should hire a guide or go with a rafting-trip operator such as McKinley Raft Tours (907-683-2392) or Alaska Raft Adventures (907-276-7234).

Yukon-Charley Rivers National Preserve

P.O. Box 74718, Fairbanks, AK 99707; tel: 907-456-0593 or 907-547-2233 (field office).

Most float trips on the Yukon River run from Eagle to Circle, a 160-mile paddle that takes five to 10 days, depending on the number of stops. Swift but smooth and free of rapids, the Yukon falls only a little more than 200 feet over this distance, passing through a mixed forest of spruce, birch, poplar, and willow. The trip is livelier on the Charley River, one of the Yukon's main tributaries, which flows out of tundra uplands into forested valleys and muskeg. Much of the river is Class III, with Class IV sections, depending on rain and snowmelt. The 203-mile trip is for experienced paddlers planning to spend seven to 10 days on the river.

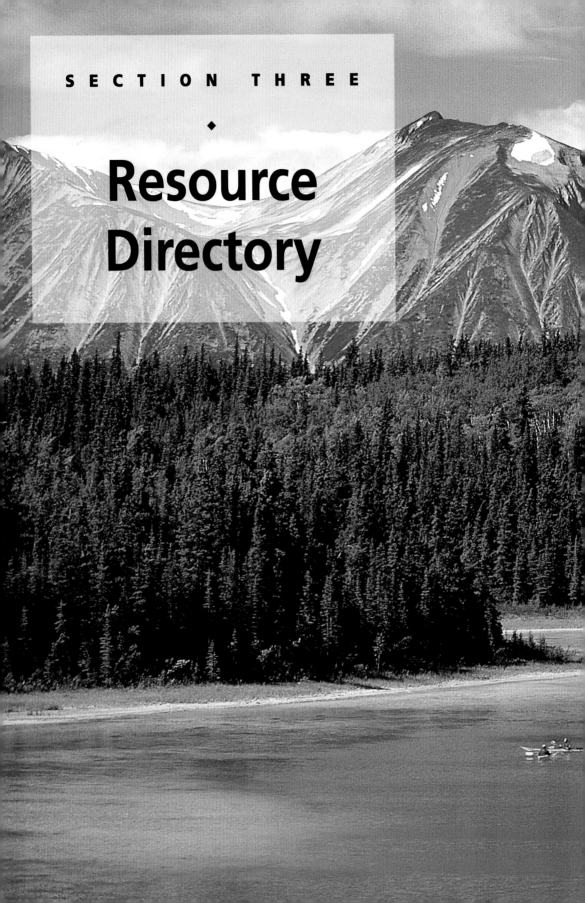

FURTHER READING

Regional Guidebooks

A regional guidebook that supplies information on boating routes, hazards, campsites, water levels, permits, and outfitters is essential for any paddling adventure. The following volumes provide detailed information on many of the regions covered in this book.

East

Adirondack Canoe Waters: North Flow, by Paul Jamieson and Donald Morris (Adirondack Mountain Club, 1988).

Apostle Islands: A Guide to Apostle Islands National Lakeshore, Wisconsin, by the National Park Service Staff (National Park Service, 1988).

The Boundary Waters Canoe Area: The Western Region, by Robert Beymer (Wilderness Press, 1993).

The Boundary Waters Canoe Area: The Eastern Region, by Robert Beymer (Wilderness Press, 1991).

Canoeing the Delaware River, by Gary Letcher (Rutgers University Press, 1997).

Canoeing the Jersey Pine Barrens, by Robert Parnes, Fran Braley, and Al Braley (Globe Pequot Press, 1999).

Carolina Whitewater: A Canoeist's Guide to the Western Carolinas, by Bob Benner and David Benner (Menasha Ridge Press, 1997).

Fun on Flatwater: An Introduction to Adirondack Canoeing, by Barbara McMartin (North Country Books, 1995).

Guide to Sea Kayaking the Western Great Lakes: The Best Trips on Lakes Superior and Michigan, by Don Dimond and William Newman (Globe Pequot Press, 1999).

A Paddler's Guide to Southern Georgia: A Canoeing and Kayaking Guide to the Streams of the Western Piedmont, Coastal Plain, Georgia Coast, and Okefenokee, by Bob Sehlinger and Don Otey (Menasha Ridge Press, 1994).

Paddling Minnesota, by Greg Breining (Falcon Publishing, 1999).

Paddling Okefenokee National Wildlife Refuge, by David O'Neill, Elizabeth Domingue, and Elizabeth Stone O'Neill (Falcon Publishing, 1999).

Playboating the Nantahala River: An Entry Level Guide, by Kelly Fisher (Milestone Press, 1998).

A Pocket Guide to Paddling the Waters of Mount Desert Island, by Earl Brechlin (Down East Books, 1996).

Quiet Water Canoe Guide: New York, by John Hayes (Appalachian Mountain Club Books, 1996).

The Sea Kayaker's Guide to Mount Desert Island, by Jennifer Alisa Paigen (Down East Books, 1997).

Sea Kayaking Along the Mid-Atlantic Coast: Coastal Paddling Adventures from New York to Chesapeake Bay, by Tasmin Venn (Appalachian Mountain Club, 1994).

Sea Kayaking in the Florida Keys, by Bruce Wachob (Pineapple Press, 1997).

Sea Kayaking the Carolinas, by James Bannon and Morrison Giffen (Out There Press, 1997).

Southeastern Whitewater: Fifty of the Best River Trips from Alabama to West Virginia, by Monte Smith (Pahsimeroi Press, 1995).

West

Adventure Kayaking Trips from Big Sur to San Diego, by Robert Mohle (Wilderness Press, 1998).

Adventure Kayaking Trips in Glacier Bay, by Don Skillman (Wilderness Press, 1998).

The Alaska River Guide, by Karen Jettmar (Alaska Northwest Books, 1998).

Belknap's Revised Waterproof Canyonlands River Guide, by Bill and Buzz Belknap (Westwater Books, 1991).

The Big Drops: Ten Legendary Rapids of the American West, by Roderick Nash (Johnson Books, 1989).

California Whitewater: A Guide to the River, by Jim Cassady and Fryar Calhoun (North Fork Press, 1990).

Floating and Recreation on Montana Rivers, by Curt Thompson (Falcon Publishing, 1993).

Glacier Bay National Park: Backcountry Guide to the Glaciers and Beyond, by Jim DuFresne (Mountaineers Press, 1987).

Grand Canyon River Guide, by Buzz Belknap (Westwater Books, 1990).

Guide to Sea Kayaking Central and Northern California, by Roger Schumann and Jan Shriner (Globe Pequot Press, 1999).

Guide to Sea Kayaking in Southeast Alaska: The Best Trips and Tours from Misty

Fiords to Glacier Bay, by Jim Howard (Globe Pequot Press, 1999).

A Guide to Three Rivers: The Stanislaus, Tuolumne, and South Fork of the American, by John Cassidy (Friends of the River Books, 1981).

Handbook to the Middle Fork Salmon River, by Quinn's Staff (Frank Amato Publications, 1993).

Handbook to the Rogue River Canyon, by James M. Quinn, James W. Quinn, and James King (Educational Adventures, 1979).

Idaho, the Whitewater State, by Grant Amaral and Doug Ammons (Watershed Books, 1990).

Idaho Whitewater, by Greg Moore (Class VI, 1989).

Kayaking Puget Sound, the San Juans, and Gulf Islands, by Randel Washburne (Mountaineers Press, 1999).

Kayak Routes of the Pacific Northwest Coast, by Peter McGee (Mountaineers Press, 1999).

Montana's Wild and Scenic Upper Missouri River, by Chan Bigs and Glen Monahan (Northwest Interpretive Association, 1997).

Paddling Yellowstone and Grand Teton National Parks, by Don Nelson (Falcon Publishing, 1999).

Passage of Discovery: The American Rivers Guide to the Missouri River of Lewis and Clark, by Daniel B. Botkin (Penguin Putnam, 1999).

River Guide to Canyonlands National Park and Vicinity, by Michael R. Kelsey (Kelsey Publishing, 1991).

A River Runner's Guide to the History of the Grand Canyon, by Kim Crumbo (Johnson Books, 1994).

River Runners' Guide to Utah and Adjacent Areas, by Gary C. Nichols (University of Utah Press, 1989).

The Rogue River Guide, by Kevin Keith Tice (Mountain N Air Books, 1995).

Sea Kayaking Northern California, by Demece Garepis and Steph Dutton (McGraw-Hill, 1998).

Verde River Recreation Guide, by Jim Slingluff (Golden West, 1990).

Watertrail: The Hidden Path through Puget Sound, by Joel Rogers (Sasquatch Books, 1998).

Western Whitewater: From the Rockies to the Pacific, by Jim Cassady, Bill Cross, and Fryar Calhoun (North Fork Press, 1994).

Instruction

A good instructional book should provide you with nuts-and-bolts information on technique, safety, and gear. Start with a general book and work your way up to more specialized titles as you get more experience under your belt.

Canoeing and Camping: Beyond the Basics, by Cliff Jacobson (Globe Pequot Press, 1992).

Canoeing Basics for Lakes and Rivers, by the American Canoe Association (Menasha Ridge Press, 1996).

Canoeing: The Complete Guide to Equipment and Technique, by David Harrison (Stackpole Books, 1996).

The Complete Book of Sea Kayaking, by Derek Hutchinson (Globe Pequot Press, 1995).

The Complete Inflatable Kayaker, by Jeff Bennett (Ragged Mountain Press, 1995).

Complete Sea Kayak Touring, by Jonathan Hanson (McGraw-Hill, 1998).

The Complete Whitewater Rafter, by Jeff Bennett (McGraw-Hill 1996).

The Complete Wilderness Paddler, by James West Davidson and John Rugge (Vintage Books, 1983).

Cradle to Canoe: Camping and Canoeing with Children, by Rolf Kraiker and Debra Kraiker (Boston Mills Press, 1999).

The Coastal Kayaker's Manual: The Complete Guide to Skills, Gear, and Sea Sense, by Randel Washburne (Globe Pequot Press, 1998)

Derek Hutchinson's Expedition Kayaking, by Derek C. Hutchinson (Globe Pequot Press, 1999).

The Essential Sea Kayaker, by David Seidman (McGraw-Hill, 1997).

The Essential Whitewater Kayaker: A Complete Course, by Jeff Bennett (Ragged Mountain Press, 1999).

Expedition Sea Kayaking on Sea and Open Water, by Derek Hutchinson (Globe Pequot Press, 1995).

Kayak: The Animated Manual of Intermediate and Advanced Whitewater Technique, by William Nealy (Menasha Ridge Press, 1988).

Kayak Cookery, by Linda Daniel (Menasha Ridge Press, 1997).

Kayaking Made Easy: A Manual for Beginners with Tips for the Experienced, by Dennis O. Stuhaug (Globe Pequot Press, 1998).

Kayaking: Whitewater and Touring Basics, by Steven M. Krauzer (W. W. Norton & Company, 1995).

Kayak Touring and Camping, by Cecil Kuhne (Stackpole Books, 1999).

Kids in the Wild, by Cindy Ross and Todd Gladfelter (Mountaineers Press, 1995).

Outdoor Adventures with Kids, by Mary Mapes McConnell (Taylor Publishing, 1996).

Sea Kayaking: A Manual for Long Distance Touring, by John Dowd (University of Washington Press, 1997).

Three Days on a River in a Red Canoe, by Vera Williams (Greenwillow Books/William Morrow & Co., 1981).

Whitewater Paddling: Strokes and Concepts, by Eric Jackson (Stackpole Books, 1999).

Whitewater Rescue Manual, by Charlie Walbridge and Wayne Sundmacher, Sr. (Ragged Mountain Press, 1995).

The Whitewater Sourcebook: A Directory of Information on American Whitewater Rivers, by Richard Penny (Menasha Ridge Press, 1997).

Magazines

Paddle sports magazines are among the best sources of up-to-date information in the paddling world. You'll find tips for gear and skill building, equipment reviews, destination ideas, and advertisements for outfitters, equipment, schools, and more.

Magazines are a bargain, too, when you consider how much information you can get in just one issue.

Canoe & Kayak
P.O. Box 3146, Kirkland, WA 98083; tel: 800-692-2663; www.canoekayak.com.

Canoe & Kayak also publishes several informative annuals: *Beginner's Guide, Whitewater Paddling,* and *Kayak Touring.*

Sea Kayaker
P.O. Box 17170, Seattle, WA 98107; tel: 206-789-9536; www.seakayakermag.com.

Paddler
P.O. Box 7775450, Steamboat Springs, CO 80477; tel: 970-879-1450; www.paddler-magazine.com.

Kanawa
P.O. Box 398, Merrickville, ON K0G 1N0, Canada; tel: 613-269-2910; www.crca.ca.

River
P.O. Box 1068, Bozeman, MT 59771; tel: 406-582-5440; www.rivermag.com.

PADDLING SCHOOLS

While any good tour operator will make sure that you master minimal skills, many aspects of paddling are best learned at a paddling school, where the focus is on developing technique and confidence. The schools listed below employ instructors trained by the American Canoe Association (ACA). Most offer scheduled courses of one to five days, customized instruction, and lodging. For a more extensive list of schools and courses, check the advertisements in one of the paddling magazines listed above, or contact the ACA (7432 Alban Station Boulevard, Suite B232, Springfield, VA 22150; tel: 703-451-0141; www.aca-paddler.org).

East

Adventure Quest
P.O. Box 184, Woodstock, VT 05091; tel: 802-484-3939; www.adventurequest.org.

Adventure Quest specializes in youth whitewater development programs and has started offering adult instruction as well. The associated Academy at Adventure Quest is a full-time academic and training program for serious young competitors; a number of the nation's top whitewater slalom and rodeo team members are students or graduates.

Bear Paw Inn Outdoor Education Center
N3494 Highway 55, White Lake, WI 54491; tel: 715-882-3502.

The center offers instruction in whitewater paddling and other adventure sports. Three-day kayak and canoe courses for novice through advanced paddlers are taught on the Wolf River in northern Wisconsin. The center also offers a "week of rivers" program and sea kayaking on Lake Superior.

Madawaska Kanu Centre
P.O. Box 635, Barry's Bay, ON K0J 1B0, Canada; tel: 613-756-3620 (summer), 613-594-5268 (winter); www.owl-mkc.ca.

This is an established whitewater training center for kayakers and canoeists ranging from beginner to advanced. Many of the instructors are nationally ranked paddlers. Slalom training is included.

Maine Island Kayak Co.
70 Luther Street, Peaks Island, ME 04108; tel: 800-796-2373; www.maineislandkayak.com.

MIKCO offers sea-kayaking instruction on the scenic Maine coast. The courses range from introductory day clinics to instructor training; specialized classes are available in such subjects as Greenland-style paddling, rescue skills, and how to handle breaking waves and rocky landings. Except for overnight camping, MIKCO students must arrange their own accommodations.

Nantahala Outdoor Center
13077 Highway 19 West, Bryson City, NC 28713; tel: 888-662-1662; www.noc.com.

Nestled in the Smoky Mountains, NOC is one of the nation's top whitewater schools, and has branched into sea kayaking in recent years. Classes and clinics are offered for paddlers at virtually every level of skill, with a wide range of options for beginners as well as specialized instruction in slalom and play boating.

RiverRun Paddling Centre
P.O. Box 179, Beachburg, ON K0J 1C0, Canada; tel: 800-267-8504; www.riverrunners.com.

RiverRun offers up to five whitewater canoe or kayak courses on the Ottawa River and surrounding streams.

Riversport School of Paddling
P.O. Box 95, Confluence, PA 15424; tel: 800-216-6991; www.shol.com/kayak.

On the banks of the Yough-iogheny River, Riversport teaches whitewater kayak and canoe skills using its campground and paddlesports shop as a base.

Saco Bound Northern Waters School
P.O. Box 119-C, Center Conway, NH 03813; tel: 603-447-2177; www.sacobound.com.

This school in the White Mountains focuses on beginning and intermediate whitewater kayak and canoe classes on the Androscoggin River. The school operates out of a campground and recreation center.

Zoar Outdoor Paddling School
Mohawk Trail, Charlemont, MA 01399; tel: 800-532-7483; www.zoaroutdoor.com.

Zoar Outdoor, in western Massachusetts, takes advantage of the dam-released Deerfield River, which features whitewater runs ranging from Class I to Class IV. The focus is on technical skills and a range of instructional offerings including canoeing.

West

California Canoe and Kayak
Jack London Square, 409 Water Street, Oakland, CA 94607; tel: 510-893-7833 (Oakland), 916-353-1880 (Sacramento), 650-728-1803 (Half Moon Bay); www.calkayak.com.

With three locations, California Canoe and Kayak offers a variety of instructional options, including whitewater paddling on the South Fork of the American and Trinity Rivers, and sea kayaking in Half Moon and San Francisco Bays.

Jackson Hole Kayak School/Rendezvous River Sports
1035 West Broadway, P.O. Box 9201, Jackson, WY 83001; tel: 800-733-2471; www.jhkayakschool.com.

The school teaches whitewater kayaking at all skill levels on rivers in the scenic Jackson Hole area. It also offers introductory sea-kayaking tours and classes on Yellowstone and Shoshone Lakes. Students arrange their own accommodations or camping in the area.

Northwest Outdoor Center
2100 Westlake Avenue North, Seattle, WA 98109; tel: 206-281-9694 or 800-683-0637; www.nwoc.com.

The center runs five-day "total immersion" sea-kayaking courses, three-day whale-watching tours in spring, and whitewater programs like the "week of rivers" camping course.

Otter Bar Kayak School
P.O. Box 210, Forks of Salmon, CA 96031; tel: 530-462-4772; www.otterbar.com.

For the pampered paddler, Otter Bar in Northern California features excellent whitewater instruction in a mountain resort atmosphere. There's a lodge with hardwood floors and skylights, a sauna, hot tub, gourmet food, and even a masseuse.

Rocky Mountain Outdoor Center
10281 Highway 50, Howard, CO 81233; tel: 800-255-5784; www.rmoc.com.

Well-known instructors teach whitewater kayaking and canoeing on various stretches of Colorado's Arkansas River. Students range from beginners to experts.

Shearwater Adventures and Sea School
P.O. Box 787, Eastsound, WA 98245; tel: 360-376-4699; www.pacificrim.net.

Shearwater operates in the San Juan Islands and offers several intensive sea-kayaking courses and a regular schedule of tours. Classes range from one day to a five-day kayak camp.

Sundance Kayak School
14894 Galice Road, Merlin, OR 97532; tel: 541-479-8508; www.sundance-kayak.com.

Sundance features a seven-day beginner's course that starts with lodge-based instruction at the school's Rogue River facility and concludes with a four-day trip.

WEBSITES

The following websites are merely a starting point. There are countless sites with information on paddling destinations, equipment, tours, outfitters, and more; many have links to related sites.

www.aca-paddler.org

The website of the American Canoe Association has links, club and class listings, and the latest news on paddling.

www.awa.org

American Whitewater, the nation's leading nonprofit whitewater advocacy group, works on access and safety issues and develops the white-water safety code in use around the country.

www.amrivers.org

American Rivers is a nonprofit conservation organization dedicated to preserving and improving the quality of rivers, fisheries, and river-related recreation in the United States. The site includes links and conservation news.

www.wcha.org

The Wooden Canoe Heritage Association is a nonprofit group dedicated to the history and preservation of traditional North American canoes.

water.usgs.gov/public/realtime.html

This invaluable website maintained by the U.S. Geological Survey provides up-to-date water-level information on rivers throughout the United States.

www.gorp.com/gorp/activity/paddle.htm

Gorp (Great Outdoor Recreation Pages) has something for everyone, including lots of links and articles for all types of paddlers.

PADDLING CLUBS

Nothing matches a paddling club for camaraderie, instruction, safety, and a lifetime of paddling adventures. Some clubs specialize in one kind of paddling such as whitewater, sea kayaking, or racing, while others provide a base for all types. Most clubs are open to new members and inexpensive to join. This list is not exhaustive; if you don't see a club near your home, contact the nearest paddle-sports retailer or search the web. Because most clubs are run by volunteers out of their homes, they do not list telephone numbers.

Alabama
Gunwale Grabbers; 4 Bent Rail Lane, Pelham, AL 35124.

Birmingham Canoe Club, P.O. Box 951, Birmingham, AL 35201.

Alaska
Knik Canoers and Kayakers, Inc., P.O. Box 242861, Anchorage, AK 99524.

Juneau Kayak Club, P.O. Box 0218865, Juneau, AK 99802.

Arizona
Desert Paddling Association, 620 East 19th Street, Suite 110, Tucson, AZ 85719.

Prescott Paddle America Club, P.O. Box 12098, Prescott, AZ 86304.

Southern Arizona Paddlers Club, P.O. Box 41927, Tucson, AZ 85717

Arkansas
Arkansas Canoe Club, P.O. Box 1843, Little Rock, AR 72203.

California
Bay Area Sea Kayakers, 229 Courtright Road, San Rafael, CA 94901.

California National Canoe and Kayak Club, P.O. Box 1686, Clovis, CA 93613.

Marin Canoe Club, 810 Idylberry Road, San Rafael, CA 94903.

Nevada County Paddlers Unlimited, 22b Commercial Street #137, Nevada City, CA 95959.

Santa Cruz Kayak Club, P.O. Box 7228, Santa Cruz, CA 95061.

Sequoia Paddling Club, P.O. Box 1164, Windsor, CA 95492.

Western Sea Kayakers, P.O. Box 59436, San Jose, CA 95159.

Colorado
Colorado Whitewater Association, 2 Silver Cloud, Boulder, CO 80302.

Durango Whitewater, P.O. Box 3626, Durango, CO 81302.

Rocky Mountain Sea Kayak Club, P.O. Box 100643, Denver, CO 80210.

Connecticut
Connecticut Canoe Racing Association, 153 Chester Street, East Hartford, CT 06108.

Conn-yak, 64 St. Francis Woods, Madison, CT 06443.

Florida
Emerald Coast Paddlers, P.O. Box 2424, Fort Walton Beach, FL 32549.

Florida Canoe and Kayak Association, P.O. Box 20892, West Palm Beach, FL 33416.

Las Olas Outrigger Canoe Club, 408 N.W. Second Avenue, Fort Lauderdale, FL 33301.

West Florida Canoe Club, P.O. Box 17203, Pensacola, FL 32522.

Georgia
Atlanta Whitewater Club, P.O. Box 33, Clarkston, GA 30021.

Georgia Canoeing Association, P.O. Box 7023, Atlanta, GA 30357.

Hawaii
Hawaii Canoe/Kayak Team, 333 Awini Way, Honolulu, HI 96825.

Hui Nalu Canoe Club, 3373 Campbell Avenue, Honolulu, HI 96815.

Maui Kayak Club, 5211D Kupele Street, Lahaina, HI 96761.

Idaho
Idaho River Sports Canoe Club, 1521 North 13th Street, Boise, ID 83702.

Illinois
Chicago Area Sea Kayaker Association, 26W354 Burdette, Coral Stream, IL 60188.

Chicago Whitewater Association, 473 North LaLonde, Lombard, IL 60148.

Illinois Paddling Council, 1911 Main Street, Spring Grove, IL 60081.

Prairie State Canoeists, 570 Trotter Drive, Coal City, IL 60416.

Indiana
Hoosier Canoe Club, 12330 East 131st Street, Noblesville, IN 46060.

Ohio Valley Whitewater Club, 219 South Welworth, Evansville, IN 47714.

Wildcat Canoe Club, P.O. Box 6232, Kokomo, IN 46904.

Iowa
Midwest River Expeditions, P.O. Box 3408, Dubuque, IA 52004.

Kansas
Kansas Canoe Association, 801 West 25th Street, Hutchinson, KS 67502.

Kentucky
Elkhorn Paddlers, 931 South Preston Street, Louisville, KY 40203.

Viking Canoe Club, P.O. Box 32263, Louisville, KY 40203.

Louisiana
Bayou Chapter Ozark Society, P.O. Box 4693, Shreveport, LA 71134.

Maine
Penobscot Paddle and Chowder Co., 1115 North Main Street, Brewer, ME 04412.

Maine Canoe/Kayak Racing Organization, R.F.D. 2, Box 268, Orrington, ME 04474.

Maryland
Blue Ridge Voyageurs, 13102 Brahams Terrace, Silver Spring, MD 20904.

Canoe Cruisers Association, P.O. Box 15747, Chevy Chase, MD 20825.

Greater Baltimore Canoe Club, P.O. Box 1841, Ellicott City, MD 21401.

Monacacy Canoe Club, P.O. Box 1083, Frederick, MD 21702.

Massachusetts
Appalachian Mountain Club, 5 Joy Street, Boston, MA 02108.

Boston Sea Kayak Club, 15 Waldron Court, Marblehead, MA 01945.

Westfield River Canoe Club, Inc., Ingell Road, Chester, MA 01011.

Martha's Vineyard Oar and Paddle, P.O. Box 840, West Tisbury, MA 01810.

Michigan
Great Lakes Paddlers, 713 Carver, Ypsilanti, MI 48198.

Great Lakes Sea Kayaking Club, 3721 Shallow Brook, Bloomfield Hills, MI 48302.

Lansing Oar and Paddle Club, P.O. Box 26254, Lansing, MI 48909.

West Michigan Coastal Kayakers Association, P.O. Box 557, Jenison, MI 49429.

Minnesota
Cascaders, P.O. Box 580061, Minneapolis, MN 55458.

Minnesota Canoe Association, P.O. Box 13567, Dinkytown Station, Minneapolis, MN 55414.

Twin Cities Sea Kayaking Association, P.O. Box 581792, Minneapolis, MN 55458.

Missouri
Missouri Whitewater Association, P.O. Box 3000, St. Louis, MO 63130.

Ozark Mountain Paddlers, 1445 South Forrest Heights, Springfield, MO 65809.

Montana
Beartooth Paddlers Society, P.O. Box 20432, Billings, MT 59104.

Flathead Whitewater Association, Inc., P.O. Box 114, Whitefish, MT 59937.

Nebraska
Fontendle Forest Association, 14323 Edith Marie Avenue, Omaha, NE 68112.

New Jersey
Garden State Canoe Club, 142 Church Road, Millington, NJ 07946.

Hackensack River Canoe Club, P.O. Box 369, Bogota, NJ 07603.

Hunterdon County Canoe Club, c/o Hunterdon County Parks, 1020 Route 31, Lebanon, NJ 08833.

Kayak and Canoe Club, Five Trail West, Kinnelon, NJ 07405.

New Mexico
Adobe Whitewater Club, P.O. Box 3835, Albuquerque, NM 87112.

New York
Adirondack Paddlers, P.O. Box 653, Saranac Lake, NY 12983.

Metropolitan Association of Sea Kayakers, 195 Prince Street, Basement, New York, NY 10012.

Metropolitan Canoe and Kayak Club, P.O. Box 021868, Brooklyn, NY 11202.

Empire Canoe Club, P.O. Box 452, Salisbury Mills, NY 12577.

Zoar Valley Paddling Club, 1196 Cain Road, Angola, NY 14006.

North Carolina
Carolina Canoe Club, 432 Gum Branch Road, Charlotte, NC 28214.

Western Carolina Paddlers, 7 Garden Terrace, Asheville, NC 28804.

Ohio
Dayton Canoe Club, Inc., 1020 Riverside Drive, Dayton, OH 45405.

Keel Haulers Canoe Club, 1649 Allen Drive, Westlake, OH 44145.

Oregon
Lower Columbia Canoe Club, 17005 N.W. Meadowgrass Drive, Beaverton, OR 97006.

Oregon Kayak and Canoe Club, P.O. Box 692, Portland, OR 97207.

Southern Oregon Paddlers, P.O. Box 2111, Bandon, OR 97411.

Willamette Kayak and Canoe Club, P.O. Box 1062, Corvallis, OR 97339.

Pennsylvania
Lehigh Valley Canoe Club, P.O. Box 4353, Bethlehem, PA 18018.

Philadelphia Canoe Club, 4900 Ridge Avenue, Philadelphia, PA 19128.

Western Pennsylvania Paddle Sport Association, 110 Thornwood Lane, Slippery Rock, PA 16057.

Wildwater Boating Club, 118 East South Hills Avenue, State College, PA 16801.

Rhode Island
Rhode Island Canoe Association, 70 Scott Street, Pawtucket, RI 02860.

South Carolina
Foothills Paddling Club, P.O. Box 6331, Greenville, SC 29606.

Low Country Paddlers, P.O. Box 13242, Charleston, SC 29422.

Tennessee
East Tennessee Whitewater Club, P.O. Box 5774, Oak Ridge, TN 37830.

Tennessee Scenic Rivers Association, P.O. Box 159041, Nashville, TN 37215-9041.

Tennessee Valley Canoe Club, P.O. Box 11125, Chattanooga, TN 37401.

Texas
Austin Paddling Club, P.O. Box 1421, Austin, TX 78761.

Hill Country Paddlers, P.O. Box 2301, Kerrville, TX 78029; tel: 210-895-2359 or 210-896-2211.

Houston Canoe Club, P.O. Box 925516, Houston, TX 77292.

North Texas River Runners, P.O. Box 1152, Arlington, TX 76004.

Utah
Utah Whitewater Club, P.O. Box 520183, Salt Lake City, UT 84152.

Vermont
Vermont Paddlers Club, 11 Discovery Road, Essex Junction, VT 05452.

Virginia
Canoe Cruisers Association, 6306 17th Street, North Arlington, VA 22205.

Coastal Canoeists, P.O. Box 566, Richmond, VA 23218.

Mid-Atlantic Paddlers Association, P.O. Box 1346, Gloucester Point, VA 23062.

Washington
Paddle Trails Canoe Club, P.O. Box 24932, Seattle, WA 98124.

Spokane Canoe and Kayak Club, P.O. Box 819, Spokane, WA 99210.

Washington Kayak Club, P.O. Box 24264, Seattle, WA 98124.

Washington Recreational River Runners, P.O. Box 25048, Seattle, WA 98125.

West Virginia
Mason Dixon Canoe Cruisers, Route 1, Box 169-31, Falling Waters, WV 25419.

West Virginia Wildwater Association, P.O. Box 8413, South Charleston, WV 25303.

Wisconsin
Wolf River Paddling Club, P.O. Box 5212, Madison WI 53705.

Wausau Kayak/Canoe Corp., 1803 Stewart Avenue, Wausau, WI 54401.

Wyoming
Jackson Hole Paddlers Club, P.O. Box 9201, Jackson, WY 83001.

PHOTO AND ILLUSTRATION CREDITS

Daniel H. Bailey 32, 119M

Craig Blacklock/Larry Ulrich Stock Photography 96, 99T, 107B

Tom Bol/Alaska Stock Images 201M

Matt Bradley 53T

Dugald Bremner 14-15, 27T, 154T, 159T, 159B

Arvilla Brewer 83B, 84T

Skip Brown 79B, 82, 124T

Carr Clifton 48

Paige L. Christie 76T, 80, 83T, 84B

W. Perry Conway/Tom Stack & Associates 199B

Dagger, Inc. 28TL, 28BL

Michael DeYoung/Alaska Stock Images 8L, 41B, 202, 205, 206B

John Drew/Imageartist 175T

David Edwards 155T, 157

John Elk III 29TR, 169T, 174B

Patrick J. Endres/Alaska Stock Images 210-211

Patrick J. Endres/Wide Angle Productions 52B, 204, 207T, 209B

Jeff Foott/Jeff Foott Productions 45B, 66, 68T, 132, 133, 167B

John K. Gates 75T, 75B

Henry Georgi 25T, 27B, 33B, 35B, 40T, 46B, 47T, 63B, 101, 143T, 144, 174T

Steve Gilroy/Ken Graham Agency 201B

Thomas Hallstein/Outsight 178, 185T, 185B

Dunbar Hardy 119T, 135T

Bill Hatcher 10-11, 151B, 152, 155B

Kim Heacox/Ken Graham Agency 194

Joe Mac Hudspeth, Jr. 92ML

Nick Jans/Alaska Stock Images 207B

David Job/Ken Graham Agency 196

Byron Jorjorian 93B

Josephine County Historical Society 182T

James W. Kay 130, 134T, 137T, 145B, 197

Wolfgang Kaehler 134-135B

Layne Kennedy 9B, 99T, 100B, 107T, 108T, 108B, 123T, 124B, 125T, 126B

Thomas Kitchin/Tom Stack & Associates 36, 191B

Kitchin & Hurst/Tom Stack & Associates 88

Bill Lea 95T

John and Ann Mahan 103T, 104, 106, 109, 111M

Stephen Matera 186, 193B

Buddy Mays/Travel Stock 164M

Gary McGuffin 22, 38B, 39T, back cover (bottom)

Montana Historical Society 117

Clark James Mishler/Alaska Stock Images 209M

Arthur Morris/Birds as Art 90L

Mark Newman/Folio 198T

Mark Newman/Tom Stack & Associates 198B

Richard T. Nowitz 79M

Tim Palmer 72, 76B, 141T, 143B, 170

Laurence Parent 77

Michael Powers 2-3, 25B, 26T, 28BR, 33T, 38T, 45T, 154B, 156T, 160, 162T, 162B, 163, 164T, 164B, 165T, 165B, 166T, 166B, 167T, 169M, 169B, 172T, 172B, 173, 177B, 182B, 190

Larry Prosor 1, 16, 24B, 34, 42, 120, 123B, 125B, 126T, 177M, 193M

Paul Rezendes 56, 58-59B, 67, 69T, 87T, 92MR, 92B, 92T

Larry Rice 35T, 40B, 41T, 53B, 93T, 95M, 95B, 103M, 103B, 111T, 114, 115B, 116B, 147M

Joel W. Rogers 5B, 47B, 52T, 60B, 63T, 79T, 153, 181, 183, 185M, 188, 189T, 189B, 193T, 199T, 201T, 209T

Ronald Roman 63M, 85T, 85B, 90R

Cheyenne Rouse/Photophile 87B

James P. Rowan/Photri-Microstock 111B

Rex Rystedt 8T, 18B, 24T, 26B, 28MR, 29TL, 29ML, 46T, 98, inside back cover

Devi Lynn Sanford/Photophile 28TR

Stephen J. Shaluta, Jr. 6-7, 9T

Scott Spiker/Alaska Stock Images 177T

Scott Spiker 4, 12-13, 18T, 30, 44, 50B, 51B, 115T, 116T, 127, 129T, 129M

Barry Tessman 51T, 151T

Tom Till 71T, 71M, 91, 140, 141B, 142T, 145T, 147B

Stephen Trimble 29MR, 39B, 50T

Larry Ulrich/Larry Ulrich Stock Photography 175B

Tom J. Ulrich 129B

Scott Underhill 20-21, 59T, 60T, 61, 74, 87M, back cover (top)

Tom Vezo 100T

Wiley/Wales 5T, 19, 29BL, 29BR, 54-55, 138, 142B, 147T, 148, 150, 156B, 191T, front cover

George Wuerthner 28ML, 64, 68B, 69B, 71B, 112, 119M, 137T, 137B, 159M, 180T, 180B, 206T

Maps by Equator Graphics

Design by Mary Kay Garttmeier

Layout by Mary Kay Garttmeier and Ingrid Hansen-Lynch

Index by Elizabeth Cook

T-top, B-bottom, M-middle, R-right, L-left

INDEX

Note: page numbers in italics refer to illustrations